This Dialogue of One:

The *Songs and Sonnets*

of John Donne

This Dialogue of One:
The *Songs and Sonnets*
of John Donne

PATRICIA GARLAND PINKA

The University of Alabama Press

Library of Congress Cataloging in Publication Data

Pinka, Patricia Garland, 1935–
This dialogue of one.

    Bibliography: p.
    Includes index.
    1. Donne, John, 1572–1631—Criticism and
interpretation. 2. Love poetry, English—History
and criticism. I. Title.
PR2248.P48   821'.3   81-16116
ISBN 0–8173–0104–6   AACR2

To the late Charles Crow
My teacher and friend

Contents

Preface   ix

1. Coming to Terms   1
   Genre   1
   Personae   10
   Tone   17

2. The Petrarchists   27
   The Parodists   27
   The Witty Lovers   33
   The Cavalier Petrarchists   38

3. The Extremists   50
   The Hedonists   52
   The Platonic Lovers   66
   The Negative Lover   72

4. The Dreaming Cynics   76

5. The Mutual Lovers   105

Conclusion   158

Notes   169

Bibliography   184

Index   190

Preface

A short time ago one of the panelists at a Spenser conference commented in an aside that Spenser's poetry, like Donne's, had already received too much recent scholarly attention. Everyone knew, he continued, that we did not need another book on Donne. I cringed, for I was well on my way to completing that very thing we did not need. In all fairness, the panelist's concern, and hence the starting point for his aside, was that too few people read Spenser and too many write about him. Since the first part of his statement does not apply to Donne, I believe (in good syllogistic fashion) that the second part is inapplicable as well. For much reading indeed begets much writing, as it should. My small part of that reading and writing is a synthetic study of the *Songs and Sonnets* through the personae in the poems.

There are fine general studies of Donne's poetry, which by their range must necessarily omit many of the *Songs and Sonnets*. Books on such topics as meditation, mutability, and the metaphysical mode in Renaissance poetry draw some of the *Songs and Sonnets* into their discussion, often with brilliant insights. Books on other parts of Donne's work exist: on his prose and the *Anniversaries*, for example. And many excellent articles on individual poems continue to appear. No book, however, treats the *Songs and Sonnets* exclusively and comprehensively. The few which come close to such completeness regard the poems as extensions of certain philosophic positions, as variations of Petrarchan tropes, or as examples of poetic and logical schemes. All of these approaches are very useful, and my own indebtedness to them is readily apparent.

To analyze the *Songs and Sonnets* through the personae in the poems is to reveal not only each speaker's ideas about love but also his character, particularly as that character is disclosed in action—the limits of his reasoning, his parrying with his listener for advantage in an argument, his fears, his escapes into self-delusion or fiction, his penchant for impressing his listener, his involvement with his circumstances, and his ability to transcend those circumstances in order to commemorate what he truly loves. In other words, to approach the *Songs and Sonnets* through their personae is to see both the speaker and Donne's manipulation of him, thereby arriving at a view of love, qualified by the character of the person who utters that view. This depiction of ideas about love as an extension of character not only removes the autobiographical element from the poems but also defines one aspect of the dramatic mode in Donne's poetry: the illusion of speech from one character to another, as if we were watching a play.

Like many characters in Renaissance drama, Donne's personae closely resemble stock lovers: the promiscuous jade, the cynic who dreams of ideal love, and the Platonic lover, to name just a few. These speakers avow views of love popular in the Renaissance, and they respond to their listeners in ways appropriate to their ideas about love. The cynics, for example, invariably denounce women, even insult them face to face, yet yearn for the faithful love of the very women they repudiate. Not surprisingly, a number of the poems portray personae with striking similarities to one another. Not only do the speakers espouse the same ideas about love, they also respond to their listeners in about the same way, depend upon fictions to roughly the same extent, pun with approximate frequency, and make use of homologous imagery. More surprising is the fact that similar personae appear in both comic and straightforward lyrics. For example, the witty man in "Womans Constancy" closely resembles the embittered speaker of "The Funerall" in both his cynicism about women and in his insulting treatment of the woman before him. The difference in tone depends upon Donne's manipulation of poetic and rhetorical techniques, not upon the ideas about love in a poem. Hence within the *Songs and Sonnets* Donne dismisses no viewpoint on love as a mere joke. In both "Loves Alchymie" and "Farewell to Love" his serious presentation of the jaded sensualist (whom he mocks in "Loves Diet") insists on the moral and emotional consequences implicit in any standpoint about love. And Donne spares nothing in his revelation. I have grouped the poems according to the stock character of their personae. Some of the lyrics could well be placed in other groups, but I discuss them where I see the greatest similarity.

Donne achieves the illusion of individuality in his personae through his deft manipulation of the relationship among the poet, the speaker, the listener, and the reader—that is, through his interweaving of the dramatic, lyric, and narrative modes within the poem. By giving most of his speakers a discernible listener, Donne sets them in time and sometimes in a specific place and hence distinguishes them from similar personae by their surroundings, their friends, and their response to those friends, that is, by the dramatic dimension in the poems. Donne's speakers also attain individuality by their refined feelings and ideas, by the private utterances overheard by their listeners and the readers alike.

In those poems where poet and speaker merge, the personae achieve their individuality by their witty variations of literary conventions, by the beauty or inventiveness or precision of their lyric expressions as well. The narrative differentiations, of course, depend upon the stories each persona tells.

I choose to speak of the rhetorical relationship in a poem in terms of lyric, dramatic, and narrative modes because these larger terms include the relationship between the speaker and the poet and the time plane that most interests the speaker. Not only does the term *lyric*, for example, imply that reader overhears the complexities and reverberations of a poet/speaker's solitary utterances (in some of Donne's dramatic lyrics, as the speaker draws into himself and thinks out loud, the reader and listener both briefly become eavesdroppers), but the lyric mode also insists upon a temporal emphasis far different from that of either the dramatic or narrative modes. The lyric persona expresses the timelessness of his feelings or thoughts and thus endows them with an importance beyond the fleeting moment of their occurrence. In the dramatic mode the persona is so immersed in his present circumstances that "now" for him assumes unparalleled importance. And in the narrative mode, the time period of the event related preoccupies the speaker. The emphasis on distinguishable time planes has a particular consequence in Donne's *Songs and Sonnets*, for his speakers shift among them frequently, and in some of the finest poems the personae so blend the lyric and dramatic modes that they embue a particular moment with a monumental quality. On these occasions the rhetorical relationships among speaker, reader, and listener converge, as the listener becomes at once the intended hearer of the speaker's personal utterance, an eavesdropper like the reader, and so much a part of the speaker himself that he expresses his strongest convictions as unselfconsciously as if he were alone. As one might expect, this miraculous blending occurs most frequently in the poems of mutual love. These considerations and the overriding question of tone form the major emphases of the book. A related issue arises from this approach to the poems: the possibility that the *Songs and Sonnets* presents an unstructured colloquium on earthly love.

I wish to express my gratitude to the James T. and Ella Rather Kirk Endowment Fund of Agnes Scott College for its generous support. This fund was established by the late Mary Wallace Kirk, in memory of her parents. An Agnes Scott alumna and former member of the Board of Trustees, Miss Kirk was always keenly interested in literature and the arts. Her endowment at the College continues to encourage the literary and critical endeavors she loved.

My debts to friends, colleagues, students, and family are so great I cannot name them all. A few are so large I cannot omit them. First, James D. Simmonds, under whose direction I began this study, has read and commented wisely on the manuscript in two different versions. Earl Miner and David Barton have read the manuscript and offered encouragement, challenging remarks, and tactful suggestions over the past several years. And Lillian Newman, Research Librarian at Agnes Scott College, has tirelessly secured materials for me and kept up my spirits with her constant good humor. Jane Quillman, Kathe Canby, Patricia Gannon, and Elsie Doerpinghaus all assisted in the preparation of the manuscript, which was aided by the Agnes Scott Faculty Research Fund. And finally, my husband, John, has not only read these pages in proof but has lived with John Donne and me all these years.

This Dialogue of One:

The *Songs and Sonnets*

of John Donne

1
Coming to Terms

Genre

We have been coming to terms with Donne's *Songs and Sonnets* for the better part of the twentieth century—from Eliot's discovery of their modernity through scholarly and critical analyses that link them to a meditative tradition, to Petrarchan, Ovidian, and Platonic ideas and models, to rhetorical practices, to scholasticism, a private mode, and a baroque development in European poetry during the late Renaissance. They have been discussed as semiautobiographical accounts of John Donne's developing sexual and emotional maturity, or conversely as the utterances of personae who teach the reader the thou-shalt-nots of love. Throughout these diverse studies one term recurs as a distinguishing feature of Donne's lyrics. That term is *dramatic*.[1]

Its meaning in relation to the poems is a catch-all describing the tiny encounter capped with a well-executed insult, the ranting and name-calling, the particular time and place of a poem, and, of course, those mute listeners whose shadowy beings torment the speaker into his out-cry ("For Godsake hold your tongue, and let me love"), his sarcastic question ("Now thou hast lov'd me one whole day, / To morrow when thou leav'st, what wilt thou say?"), or his sudden realization that he and his sweetheart are miraculously in love ("I wonder by my troth, what thou, and I / Did, till we lov'd?").[2] The term *dramatic*, in other words, substitutes in part for phrases like "emotional" or "forcefully effective," and it implies a confrontation. To rhetorical critics it means the dynamic rhetorical relationship among speaker, listener, and reader in a lyric poem. Because of its association with plays, some critics think of it as separating the persona of a poem from John Donne. To the biographical reader *dramatic* describes the intensity of the personal experience in the poem. Although many of the implications of Donne's setting most of his lyrics in a dramatic framework have been explored, the consequences of his engrafting need further analysis and study; for an imprecise use of *dramatic* can unhinge the poems from both their historical and their generic framework—that very scaffolding on which Donne works his most ingenious transformations of love poetry. The songs and sonnets, for all their illusion of situations, remain lyrics, most of which have a pronounced dramatic element.[3]

At the center of this consideration is the identification of the rhetorical members in a poem and their relationships to one another. At its simplest a lyric can exist between poet and reader, when the poet identifies himself with the speaker and when he addresses no discernible listener. At its most complex—a term not necessarily synonymous with the best—the poet, a speaker, a listener, and a reader all participate. In some of the songs and sonnets this complex relationship collapses when the poet reveals he has been wearing a mask (a persona) to accomplish some *literary* end, and only the tie between poet and reader remains, without which no communication exists. In other poems a different adjustment occurs. By driving a wedge between himself and the speaker (an issue I discuss in detail a bit later) the poet frees the speaker to engage his listener as if he were outside the confines of a lyric poem, that is, as if he had no literary purpose in his utterance. In this case both the poet and the reader vanish from the immediate time and place of the speaker's address. Thus they tacitly assent to the illusion of a dramatic encounter, even as they necessarily acknowledge that one is reading a poem the other has written. The distinction rests on the identification between poet and speaker.[4] When the two become one, a two- or three-party rhetorical relationship operates. When they do not, something akin to a dramatic scene takes place.

The assumed relationship between a poet and his public, Northrop Frye's "radical of presentation," provides one means for distinguishing genres and hence for gaining insight into Donne's manipulation of the lyric in the *Songs and Sonnets*. At its simplest, Frye says, the connection between the listener and the poet in a lyric is analogous to the eavesdropper garnering solitary mutterings from another room, particularly if one can imaginatively remove the speaker-listener relationship from "simultaneous presence" and "dramatic context."[5] By shifting the lyric from a strictly temporal existence and from a dramatic context (which depends on time), Frye implies that the poem conveys meaning through its spatial dimension on a page as well as through the temporal dimension of song or speech, and that neither time nor place anchors its meaning. By extension, then, the analogy of the eavesdropper breaks down, and the poet/speaker-listener relationship is complicated by the more inclusive poet-reader relationship. The poet and the reader assent to the convention of a speaker and a listener, all the while acknowledging that the matter conveyed by a lyric is internal experience, translatable only through the compressed language of poetry and understood only by an attentive reader. Sometimes the poet defines himself as the "speaker," a term necessarily in quotation marks in this case. Whatever the rhetorical adjustment, the fiction of a speaker uttering his ideas or expressing his feelings "out loud" provides a helpful image for the isolation of the lyric persona.

These considerations insist on an essential compact between the poet and the reader in any lyric, whatever else occurs in the poem. Even in the *Songs and Sonnets*, then, Donne cannot and does not alter the tacit understanding that ultimately the fullness of his poetry yields only to the reader, and the sophisticated and witty one at that, whose intelligence and persistence pierce the poem on the page.

The "radical of presentation" in a drama, on the other hand, sets the playwright at two removes from his audience: first, he disappears behind his characters; then he separates the characters from the audience by the "glass" wall at the edge of the stage.[6] He is so anonymous that the question of his own isolation or sociability never arises; hence the fiction of the solitariness of the lyric poet/speaker has no counterpart in drama. The completeness of the world of a drama requires that the audience observe that world from the outside. Thus, in one sense, the audience, like the listener/reader in a lyric poem, "overhears" the words and "oversees" the actions in a play. In a more radical sense, however, the audience's divorcement from the world of the play, intensified by the specifics of time and place in any particular drama, far exceeds the division between the lyric poet and his reader. For the audience of a play provides the third side of a rhetorical triangle—a side complicated by the pretense that neither speaker nor listener is aware of its presence.[7]

The relationship between a speaker and his listener in drama, then, expands into a series of entanglements: among speaker, listener, and an audience that the characters do not acknowledge but to which the actors direct their voices; and among playwright, speaker, listener, and audience (with the actor perhaps complicating the relationship in ways irrelevant for useful discussion here). This latter entwining provides the sharpest contrast between the lyric poem and the drama. Unlike the lyric poet with his reader, the playwright never establishes an intimate and demanding tie with his audience. Because he cannot rightly expect a second, third, or hundredth hearing (as the poet can), the playwright depends upon stage setting, costumes, and the actors themselves to carry the burden of interpretation. The writer's dialogue must be grasped and understood immediately so that it can provide and provoke action, a fact that theoretical critics underscore by labeling the words in a play "speech acts."[8] Thus, although any dramatist ultimately writes for an audience, he must define that audience in broader terms than the lyric poet does his. This distinction becomes particularly sharp when one considers that many Renaissance poets, including Donne, circulated their lyrics among only a coterie of friends from whom they could expect common assumptions, knowledge, jokes, and attitudes.

The term *dramatic*, then, has a very limited application to Donne's *Songs and Sonnets*. It does not affect the inviolable contract between the poet and the reader affirming the ultimate authority and integrity of the words on the page. It has no relevance to common assumptions, knowledge, experiences, or even jokes between the poet and his readers. It does, however, point to the split between the poet and his speaker in most of Donne's lyrics. Hence in those poems we call dramatic, Donne sets up a rhetorical triangle among the speaker, listener, and reader similar to that among the speaker, listener, and audience in a play. In both the author remains hidden and the audience/reader is removed from the world of the action. In Donne's lyrics, however, this dramatic, rhetorical triangle is subsumed by the more comprehensive tie between the reader and the poet.

Attempts to explain Donne's *Songs and Sonnets* wholly as lyrics tend to move toward a quasi-autobiographical identification between Donne and his personae.[9] The dramatic immediacy of the poem suggests the transformation of personal experience between Donne and his wife or Donne and a saucy wench, the kind of a relationship one finds in a poem by Shelley or Keats. Thus, the argument goes, the interesting aspect of a Donne poem is the speaker's particularized reaction to or perception of a rare, perhaps unique, situation rather than the beauty of his commemoration or his witty treatment of a conventional subject. Such observations overlook the many conventional elements in Donne's poetry, as well as his close attention to song. Moreover, the observations contain, as George T. Wright reminds us, inappropriate assumptions about the "I" in a seventeenth-century lyric.[10] Yet Wright's analyses of the "I" persona in the early English lyrics make it abundantly clear that many of Donne's songs and sonnets cannot be explained adequately within the traditional lyric of the Renaissance, either.

These older lyrics, Wright tells us, emphasize their close association with music by having their speaker identify himself as a man either singing or composing songs. Because he celebrates the experience of singing, whether about love or some other conventional subject, and not the passion itself, the poem reflects the poet's meticulous concern for delighting the ear and refining the lyric form, and it takes on something of a public or social quality, as if the ideas and emotions in the poem might properly be communicated to anyone, or at least to a small group of friends.[11] Wright's observations about music might well be expanded to include oratory and the manipulation of poetic conventions. In his attention to any of these, the poet reveals himself as a creator meticulously conscious of the literary convention in which he is working. Thus his claim on the reader is his invention, not his experience. He often, indeed, so shares his readers' attitudes that he gives expression to their feelings.

At first the vibrant and frequently intimate encounters in many of the songs and sonnets seem to deny that Donne's poems are lyrics of this kind. Even though the poems explore the conventional subject of love, they treat it unconventionally, sometimes even develop it through the words of iconoclastic men. And Donne's wrenched metrics and speech-like syntax have been the subject of critical observation since Ben Jonson first remarked that Donne deserved hanging for not keeping of accent. On the other hand, some lyrics within the *Songs and Sonnets*—"The Expiration" comes to mind—show Donne's ability to delight the ear. Still others, "Communitie," for example, demonstrate his skill at creating a meticulous, fallacious argument. And many of the satiric poems parody Petrarchan conceits so fully that the poems lose much of their point unless the reader knows Petrarchan poetry. Even in those poems where Donne celebrates the experience of loving rather than of singing (or orating or composing parodies), the speakers break into commemoration at least momentarily. Donne's poems, then, although not fully explainable within the older lyric tradition, nonetheless draw heavily upon it.

The more personal lyrics with which the *Songs and Sonnets* is often linked call attention to the split between the speaker of the poem (usually identified with a particular poet rather than with an unnamed singer) and the reader.[12] In them the poet creates the illusion of a man internally caught up in an emotional experience; he emphasizes his individuality by unfamiliar diction and unusual imagery. Because the speaker in these lyrics indirectly educates his reader to a highly sensitized, even inspired, understanding of his internal feelings, he stresses his superiority to the reader. He attains his identity not as a singer of songs, or an orator, or a manipulator of poetic conventions, whose claim on the reader is greater skill in composition, but as a man who has a better grasp on truth.

In spite of the similarities between some aspects of the *Songs and Sonnets* and the above description, Donne's poems really belong to the earlier tradition. The numerous critical studies that link them with well-known Renaissance love theories dispel the notion that any of the Donne personae offers a unique viewpoint or has a special grasp on truth. In fact Donne's readers in the Renaissance may well have shared their beliefs about love with any number of the men in the poems; they would have been familiar with all the ideas. Nor are the speakers themselves particularly unusual. Their wrangling and often sophistical arguments suggest that some of them step right out of the Inns of Court.[13] Others at moments seem to be reincarnations of the sonneteers. Still others manipulate all the rhetorical techniques of an accomplished classical orator. The stock situations between the lover and his mistress in some of the poems echo situations in many Renaissance sonnets and in some of Ovid's *Amores*. Even Donne's imagery is more derivative than it seems at first (the fact that Ben Jonson also uses the compass image in "An Epistle to Master John Selden" provides a case in point). Insofar as the poems are lyrics, they are closely linked with some of the most conventional aspects of the sonnet tradition.

Many of Donne's songs and sonnets differ from both these forms of the lyric because of the complex and often shifting relationships Donne establishes among the poet, the speaker, the speaker's listeners, and the reader. Once more, the basic compact between the poet and the reader regarding the ultimate authority of the words on the page never falters. Nor does the poet assume a superiority to his reader and reveal new truths to him. What does diverge, even disappear, in many of Donne's best-known lyrics is the poet's identification with his speaker.[14] As one measure of this severance, only four personae in the *Songs and Sonnets* see themselves as poets; they are singularly unsuccessful by their own admission.[15] True, in the comic poems Donne's dramatic overlay, that is, his creation of a speaker supposedly engaged in an encounter with his listener, vanishes to reveal the poet manipulating literary conventions much as he does in the *Elegies*. (Helen Gardner, incidentally, places all of these poems in her edition of *Songs and Sonnets* (I), as if they were written soon after the *Elegies*.) But in all of the straightforward lyrics, even those touched by high comedy, the speakers are lovers, not poets, not masks for John Donne. Once Donne cuts his speakers loose from himself, from even that vaguely defined self of poet or singer, he sets his personae free to establish varying and various relationships with *their* listeners similar to those that characters in a play develop with one another. They are similar, but not the same, for the lyric base of Donne's poems imposes its own restrictions.

First of all, Donne's personae exploit their listeners in ways altogether incompatible with drama. Aside from the obvious fact that because the poems are monologues only the speakers have their say, Donne artfully manipulates the rhetorical relationship among speaker, listener, and reader so that, for example, sometimes the speaker and listener become one, sometimes the listener and reader. Some of the personae seem to transform (or create) their hearers into carbon copies of themselves until the illusion of a dramatic encounter dissipates into a pretense. "The Undertaking" provides the most obvious case, where the speaker not only imposes his love of "vertue'attir'd in woman" onto his listener, but describes both the man's "heroism" and his own in identical terms, as if he had conjured up the listener as an excuse for praising himself. In other poems the speaker temporarily withdraws from his conversation with another to muse, out loud perhaps, but surely to himself, thus creating for the time the standard fiction for the isolation of the lyric persona, that he is muttering to himself. Even "The Anniversarie," that supreme celebration of enduring love, contains such a lapse in its central stanza. Indeed, this technique of having the speaker mentally drift from his listener is Donne's most prevalent means of blending the lyric and dramatic elements in the *Songs and Sonnets*. In some of the comic poems, moreover, lyrics as disparate as "The Expiration" and "The Broken Heart," the listener emerges as a patent cardboard creation used primarily to heighten the poem's and the persona's outrageousness. That is, the listener is part of a fictional rhetorical situation which the poet/speaker creates just for fun. On occasion the speaker materializes a listener out of thin air, so to speak—the undertaker in "The Funerall" or the sun in "The Sunne Rising," for example—in order to enact a fictitious drama in front of his real audience in both of these poems, his mistress. Here again Donne retains part of the standard lyric convention that the poet/speaker can pretend to be addressing an object or a fictitious creature like Cupid.[16] But the split between poet and speaker and the presence of another listener, who observes the fictitious drama created and performed solely for her, redefine the purpose of the poems in terms of the man's relationship with his lady. Conversely Donne sometimes animates the lyric muttering of a solitary man by turning his complaint into a psychodrama, as he does in "[Image and Dream]." All of these methods and a few more weave a dramatic texture in the lyric by insisting on the existence of a listener whose very presence affects the speaker, and by driving a wedge in most instances between the speaker and the poet who created him. That is, Donne's exploitation of the full three-part rhetorical situation creates the sense of a dramatic exchange, even if that rhetorical relationship dissipates later in the poem.

A second major and inseparable change resulting from Donne's blending of modes involves time and its correlative, place—the here and now that characterizes much of the *Songs and Sonnets*.[17] Poems of this sort create the semblance of an encounter, an action occurring at a particular time and/or in a specified place. Like speeches in a play these lyrics delineate the immediate responses between human beings, suggesting that these responses spring from the past and will determine the future relationship between the speaker and his listener.[18] In other words, they firmly set the poem in time. Frequently the present tense in these lyrics, therefore, is the present of immediate action—the verb tense of commands:

> Oh doe not die, for I shall hate
> All women so, when thou art gone

or of questions:

> Ends love in this, that my man,
> Can be as happy'as I can; If he can
> Endure the short scorne of a Bridegroomes play?

or of flattery so that one can obtain favors:

> Thou art so true, that thoughts of thee suffice,
> To make dreames truth; and fables histories;
> Enter these armes.[19]

The present tense of these examples, chiefly in the imperative and inter-rogative moods, creates the illusion of speech. In lyric poetry generally, however, the present tense suggests a timelessness, a sense of re-peated action, a portentousness, even a monumental quality which re-moves the subject from the fleeting moment. As Susanne Langer so aptly notes, "The lyric poet creates a sense of concrete reality from which the time element has been canceled out."[20] Donne creates his sense of concrete reality, however, in part by maintaining the time ele-ment in his lyrics, by immersing the speaker's immortal feelings into the flux of day-to-day events. But he maintains that time element only up to a point.

In the best lyrics Donne blends the eternal present of lyric com-memoration with the present of direct action, thus endowing the exact moment of a speaker's encounter with immortality, as these lines from "The Anniversarie" illustrate and explain:

> Only our love hath no decay;
> This, no tomorrow hath, nor yesterday,
>   Running it never runs from us away,
> But truly keepes his first, last, everlasting day. (ll. 7–10)

As the speaker gazes at his beloved and marks with her the first anniversary of that very moment "when thou and I first one another saw" (l. 5), that is, as he participates in a special moment in time, his response to that moment miraculously coexists both in the here and now and in that eternal present of ideas, truths, and deep feelings.[21] What differentiates Donne's treatment of time from that of most lyric poets is his insistence that the present tense of his poem applies at once to immediate action and to timeless celebration. In the passage quoted above the lover not only commemorates the permanence of his love amidst flux, he immortalizes the flux as well. Thus in some of the happiest passages in the *Songs and Sonnets* the lover, by addressing his beloved, turns their blissful moment together into a lasting commemoration. That is, unwittingly the lover sings as if he were a poet spontaneously pouring forth his feelings, giving them immortality without the necessity of paper and pen. But, of course, like the standard lyric fiction of the eavesdropper and the poet muttering out loud, this fiction of the speaker whose romantic engagement pushes him to song vanishes under the pressure of the compact between the poet and the reader affirming the ultimate authority of the words on the page.

Donne's modifications with time become knottiest in those poems where the speaker turns away from his immediate situation to narrate portions of his autobiography, to explain the origin and development of his view of love, or just to tell a story—in other words, where he moves from lyric commemoration or dramatic encounter to a shaped reconstruction of events. Susanne Langer emphasizes the implication of such a change: "When . . . narrative is treated as the central motif of a composition. . . . it tends to become the ground plan, or 'plot,' of the entire piece, affecting and dominating every other means of literary creation."[22] In those songs and sonnets where the narrative prevails, the speaker regards his encounter as subordinate to his story; his relationship with his listener modulates from the intensity of a one-to-one exchange to the more detached link between a narrator and a listener. In certain of the poems even the individuality of the hearer fades, as he or she becomes a sounding board for the speaker. Even in those poems where the narrative is subordinate, its presence marks the speaker's momentary mental withdrawal from his immediate surroundings. Of course, similar shifts of relationship occur in novels, plays, and narrative poems. In those literary creations, however, the immediate sweep of experience does not define the genre, as it does the lyric, for they create a whole action which necessarily subsumes the significance of one overpowering moment. The lyric does not. Thus Donne's modification implies either the speaker's dissatisfaction with his circumstances or his rejection of them altogether, as he ironically endows the past with an immortality through his celebration of it, or, even more paradoxically, imbues with permanence a future that may never materialize. Either way, he shapes a distant time to his own liking; and through his selective virtual memory, he creates the world anew rather than confronting and glorifying the world in which he finds himself. By superimposing something like a dramatic or a dramatic-narrative "radical of presentation" onto the lyric, then, Donne focuses on the subtle shifts in the relationship between the speaker and his listener.

Personae

All of this discussion returns us to the speaker in Donne's poems—
that character who responds to his listener and his circumstances both
inwardly and outwardly, that character who vacillates from encountering to commemorating, from acting and reacting to creating. Donne's
development of speakers who seem to be involved with their mistresses
as well as of those who mock both the language and the sentiments of
popular love lyrics perhaps grew from his reaction to the artificiality of
the sonneteers. Sidney, commenting on the subject, decries the bookishness and imitation in the love poetry of his day:

> But truely many of such writings as come vnder the banner of vnresistable
> loue, if I were a Mistres, would neuer perswade mee they were in loue; so
> coldely they apply fiery speeches, as men that had rather red Louers
> writings, and so caught vp certaine swelling phrases, which hang together
> like a man which once tolde mee the winde was at North West, and by
> South, because he would be sure to name windes enowe,—then that in
> truth they feele those passions, which easily (as I think) may be bewrayed
> by that same forciblenes, or *Energia* (as the Greekes cal it), of the writer.[23]

Perhaps Donne saw that by imposing dramatic and even narrative elements on the lyric he could infuse it with vitality and create the illusion
of sincerity, even individuality, which Sidney extols; and, conversely,
he could use a dramatic façade to expose the folly of bookish love lyrics.

Both Sidney and Donne—and I generalize from Donne's practice,
since he left no critical treatise—advocate that poetry, taking its impetus
from experience and proving its validity against experience, should be
an art so controlled that it creates the semblance of reality. Sidney makes
this point explicit:

> Vndoubtedly (at least to my opinion vndoubtedly) I haue found in
> diuers smally learned Courtiers a more sounde stile then in some profes-
> sors of learning: of which I can gesse no other cause, but that the Courtier,
> following that which by practise hee findeth fittest to nature, therein
> (though he know it not) doth according to Art, though not by Art: where
> the other, vsing Art to shew Art, and not to hide Art (as in these cases he
> should doe), flyeth from nature, and indeede abuseth Art.[24]

The specifics of Donne's method of "vsing Art . . . to hide Art" and,
contrariwise, in some of the comic poems of "vsing Art to shew Art"
provide some of the major concerns of the pages that follow.

If Donne was in some ways an innovator in mixing genres, he was
extremely traditional in the characters he created to utter those dramatic
lyrics. From the evidence of the poems, he seems to have fashioned a

core of typical lovers and rendered variations of them throughout the
Songs and Sonnets.[25] There, a number of speakers respond to their circumstances and their ladies in remarkably similar ways. First, they hold
like views of love. They react in roughly the same manner to their
listeners, keeping them equally close or distant. Their puns and imagery
approximate each other, and they depend on fictions to substantiate
their position or mollify their situation to nearly the same extent. In
other words, for all their diversity and the illusions of unique encounters, the poems refine and refurbish some stock characters in rather
comparable circumstances.

In creating kinds of lovers who become particularized by the details of
their reactions to romance, Donne reflects some basic assumptions that
also underlie Character essays, the drama, and other poetry of his day.
The first of these is the interest in individualism, in the importance of
subjective opinions, feelings, and experiences, as the popularity of portrait painting, letters and verse letters, biography, and autobiography in
the Renaissance attests.[26] But oddly this concentration on the singular
response is blended with general ideas, precepts, and suppositions for
which the individual experience provides authentication. The conception of the individual as a character type runs so deep in Renaissance
literature that it is hard to imagine a poet creating speakers who do not
originate from stock figures. Donne is no exception.

Shakespeare, for example, seems to flesh out standard characters,
who appear refashioned from one play to another. Sir Thurio in *Two
Gentlemen of Verona* and Sir Andrew Aguecheek in *Twelfth Night* derive
from a similar stock buffoon, the ugly, dim-witted fellow who foolishly
woos an unattainable and lovely lady. Both of them become the butt of
everyone's jokes because both have difficulty understanding the insults
they receive; both believe steadfastly in the power of words; and both
take a great interest in their physical attractiveness to women. Two
snatches of scenes from the plays will serve as examples. Late in *Two
Gentlemen of Verona*, Thurio inquires of Proteus whether Silvia is warm-
ing to his suit, without seeming to comprehend the derision implicit in
Proteus's reply:

THURIO.	Sir Proteus, what says Silvia to my suit?
PROTEUS.	O, sir, I find her milder than she was.
	And yet she takes exceptions at your person.
THURIO.	What? that my leg is too long?
PROTEUS.	No, that it is too little.
THURIO.	I'll wear a boot, to make it somewhat rounder. (v.ii.1–6)

Similarly Andrew Aguecheek concerns himself with his hair, all the
while remaining oblivious to the insults of Sir Toby Belch:

Sir Toby.	Then hadst thou an excellent head of hair.
Sir Andrew.	Why, would that [learning languages] have mended my hair?
Sir Toby.	Past question, for thou sees it will not [curl by] nature.
Sir Andrew.	But it becomes [me] well enough, doesn't not? (i.iii.95–98)[27]

Andrew Aguecheek is a far better drawn character than Thurio because of such individualizing details as Andrew's cowardly bravado, his sentimentality over love songs, and his almost total obliviousness to his surroundings. This observation confirms only that Shakespeare's genius grew between the writing of the two plays, not that he abandoned stock characters.

Similarly, groups of speakers in the *Songs and Sonnets* utter the same well-known views about love and share ideas about women, sexual intercourse, mind, and body. As with Shakespeare's stock characters, however, individualizing details separate one lover from another, often making one speaker lighthearted and his counterpart bitterly serious, cf. "Communitie" and "Loves Alchymie." Both lovers conclude their utterances with disparaging comparisons that reveal the men's feelings about women. In "Communitie" the licentious fellow makes a joke:

Chang'd loves are but chang'd sorts of meat,
And when hee hath the kernell eate,
  Who doth not fling away the shell? (ll. 22–24)

In "Loves Alchymie" the sated philanderer expresses his disgust:

Hope not for minde in women; at their best
Sweetnesse and wit, they'are but *Mummy*, possest. (ll. 23–24)

Both men define love as lust and pursue it. Both speak of women as fleshly objects. The difference lies in Donne's more psychological development of the man in "Loves Alchymie."

Donne's lovers also share commonalities with the figures in Character essays, a genre to which Donne contributed a few sketches. Essentially a prose Character details a single human trait, such as jealousy, although with Overbury's *Characters* the trait expands into a social type, such as the Puritan. Prose Characters flourished in England shortly after Isaac Casaubon's 1599 translation of Theophrastus's *Characters*, the finest of which fuse a generality about human nature with details so individualizing that Theophrastus might have been referring to a specific person. "Cowardice" provides a good illustration. "Cowardice, of course, would seem to be a givingway of the soul in fear; and your Coward he that if he be at sea will have it that the jutting rocks are pirate sloops, and when the sea rises asks if there be any aboard that is not initiated."[28] The item of the rocks looming like pirate ships in the coward's imagination so animates the opening definition that the essay attains an objectivity that strengthens Theophrastus's purpose in writing the *Characters*, which is to guide young men in their behavior and choice of friends.

Donne's lovers, too, come alive through individualizing details such as the gingerbread cookie in "Farewell to Love," even as that particularity emphasizes the licentious man's surfeit with sex:

> But from late faire
> His highnesse sitting in a golden Chaire,
>   Is not lesse cared for after three dayes
> By children, then the thing which lovers so
> Blindly admire, and with such worship wooe. (ll. 11–15)

And like Theophrastus, Donne offers no judgment on the lover. His speakers, however, have more breadth.

In creating his stock lovers Donne exhibits the scope and the wit of both *The Overburian Characters* (to which he may have contributed) and of Ben Jonson's Characters in his *Epigrammes*. Overbury's "An Amorist," for example, begins with a witty mockery of the commonplaces of foolish love:

> An Amorist
> Is a creature blasted or planet-stroken, and is the dog that leads blind
> *Cupid*; when hee is at the best, his fashion exceeds the worth of his weight.
> He is never without verses, and muske comfects: and sighes to the hazard
> of his buttons; his eyes are all white, either to weare the livery of his
> Mistres complexion, or to keep *Cupid* from hitting the blacke.

It ends with a splay of satire in something like an epigrammatic closure: "His imagination is a foole, and it goeth in a pied-coat of red and white; shortly hee is translated out of a man into folly; his imagination is the glasse of lust, and himselfe the trait to his own discretion."[29] The same kind of witty mockery of rampant affection occurs in "Loves Exchange," where the speaker's plea to the god of love turns into self-ridicule:

> Give mee thy weaknesse, make mee blinde,
> Both wayes, as thou and thine, in eies and minde;
>   Love, let me never know that this
> Is love, or, that love childish is. (ll. 14–17)

Both works cleverly detail the Character of a moonstruck lover, who is a social type rather than simply the embodiment of a single Theophrastian trait. Indeed, the alternate titles for some of the poems in the *Songs and Sonnets* could well be headings for Overburian Characters, "The Nothing," for example, or "Platonic Love." Ben Jonson's Characters in the *Epigrammes* also resemble poetic versions of Overburian figures and hence display scope, wit, and epigrammatic twists similar to many of the poems in the *Songs and Sonnets*. "On GVT" provides a brief example:

> GVT eats all day, and lechers all the night,
>   So all his meate he tasteth ouer, twise:
> And, striuing so to double his delight,
>   He makes himselfe a thorough-fare of vice.
> Thus, in his belly, can he change a sin,
>   Lust it comes out, that gluttony went in.[30]

Jonson's snappy turnabout in his conclusion as well as Overbury's prose equivalent brings to mind those whip ends in some of Donne's lyrics, "The Legacie," for example:

> I thought to send that heart instead of mine,
> But, oh, no man could hold it, for twas thine. (ll. 23–24)

Yet for all these similarities, Donne, like Theophrastus and unlike Jonson and Overbury, refrains from condemning his characters. Like Shakespeare, he lets them speak for themselves. Thus even the man in "Loves Exchange" moderates his self-censure by remaining in the situation. Perhaps, like Theophrastus, Donne perceived that objectivity can be more persuasive than subjective analysis. Yet with something of a witty twist Donne's lovers often hurl epigrammatic judgments and insults at their mistresses, particularly when those women are either cold and aloof or unfaithful—character types themselves. The bitter outcry at the end of "Twicknam Garden" comes to mind:

> Nor can you more judge womans thoughts by teares,
>   Then by her shadow,' what she weares.
> O perverse sexe, where none is true but shee,
> Who's therefore true, because her truth kills mee. (ll. 24–27)

In all of these ways, then, Donne incorporates some of the main features of Character writing into his portraits of lovers, who espouse and enact a number of well-known theories of love.

The fifty-four poems in the *Songs and Sonnets* have many views on love, that is, statements about love modified by the reader's understanding of the speaker. Seven of these occur in more than one poem; a number of others receive only a single utterance. The major standpoints belong to

Characters whom I call the Witty Lover, the Cavalier Petrarchist, the Parodist, the Platonic Lover, the Hedonist, the Dreaming Cynic, and the Mutual Lover. A Negative Lover speaks one poem; several wooers philosophize about the nature of love, and a woman bemoans the disparity between her affection and that of her sweetheart.

I have brought together under the name of a Character poems that resemble each other in a number of significant ways: the speakers make similar statements about love; they create the same kinds of relationships with their listeners; their imagery is homologous; and their lyric outpourings approximate one another. The individual speakers reflect the character type yet retain an identity of their own. Thus the label Witty Lover means only that the poems so classified have speakers who typify a certain kind of lover whose characteristics I shall presently describe. The speaker of any poem is at once both a highly developed individual and the representative of a type. The particular speakers in each group differ from one another as, say, country bumpkins might in several Renaissance plays by the same playwright. In certain groups where comic and straightforward versions of a similar character appear, the lyric utterances diverge from one another, although the dramatic encounters remain the same. Moreover, some of the poems I discuss under one heading have features in common with poems in another category. I note the similarities and place them where I see the strongest resemblances. The names of the character types reflect both the ideas about love that the speakers espouse and the modifications of that viewpoint that emerge from their dramatic encounters and their lyric utterances.

The Parodist mocks the Petrarchan language of the sonneteers by pretending that a conceit is literally true so that he can finally expose it as a fanciful phrase. Moreover, by drawing out its sexual puns, especially on the word *die* and its variants in such lyrical commonplaces as 'parting from one's beloved is death,' he undermines the Petrarchan lover's sincerity and cuts at the heart of Petrarchism. All this satirizing, however, occurs within the confines of a form that, like many Elizabethan lyrics, has its basis in music, so that the Parodist seems to be another lover singing to his beloved. These poems come the closest to the older lyrics in which the speaker celebrates his love—this time, however, with formal parody.

The Cavalier Petrarchist also mocks the conceits, but first the speakers use them to manipulate their relationship with their listeners. Then, bit by bit, they expose the tropes as flashy language, and finally, in what seems like an ironic reversal, they affirm the sentiment that the conceit symbolizes, this time phrasing their feelings in plain words. By caricaturing their own sentiments, the speakers create an ambiguity so that they can state their feelings without fully exposing themselves. They also, usually unwittingly, parody themselves.

A third character type, the Witty Lover, espouses both the sentiment and the language of Petrarchan love. Unlike the two characters above, he finds the conceits and hyperboles poignantly expressive of the complexities of his feelings. In rather exaggerated terms he tries to verbalize his emotions at leaving a beloved who shares his affections—a relationship similar to that of the Mutual Lovers. Finally, overcome by the realities of parting, he finds new vitality in a Petrarchan conceit; for what normally seems like hyperbolic language conveys a literal truth about his situation.

Another character type, the Hedonist declares that love is only sexual gratification, women being merely objects for men's use and enjoyment. Other speakers in the *Songs and Sonnets* who make similar claims cloud their assertions in ambiguities; the Hedonists do not. Indeed, they make every effort to present themselves as reasonable men who have thought out their position. Some state well-known philosophical tenets about the chief good of human life, leaving, of course, the terms of their assertions undefined. Others structure their utterances as syllogisms. They excuse their attitudes toward women by blaming forces beyond their control for their personal frustrations, a technique that allows them to avoid questioning their own beliefs. In addition, they form one of two groups of speakers who narrate their autobiographies rather than confront their listeners face to face, Donne's usual method in the *Songs and Sonnets*. By relating their views and experiences, the Hedonists remain aloof from their listeners. Their attention instead centers on presenting themselves and their ideas in the best possible light. Indirectly their reliance upon narration also intimates that the present for them serves only to gather support for their past.

The other character type who narrates his autobiography and philosophy of love is the Platonic Lover. These men abstain from sexual relationships with their mistresses and herald their love as superior to that which other men experience. By associating excellence primarily with the absence of sexual intimacy, however, they retain only a superficial resemblance with that form of love which Ficino and the other Renaissance Neoplatonists considered preponderant. Donne's Platonic Lovers, in fact, seem to cover up their passion with the idea of the superiority of abstinence. They see themselves as heroic in love and seek reward or recognition for their bravery in fictional prophecies about their afterlife. They are the only speakers who compose artistic autobiographies, one in song, the other in verse. Yet in spite of their own need for praise and fame, the Platonic Lovers celebrate their ladies and their love with a joy that permeates these poems as fully as it does those of the Mutual Lovers.

The Mutual Lovers declare that their love so consumes them that the world no longer matters to them; and although their women never speak, they seem to acquiesce in their lovers' feelings. Thus the poems at first seem to be celebrations of a fully satisfactory love. But, like the Platonic Lovers, these men dwell on their wishes for special consideration. They yearn for physical immortality and usually see perfect love as a means of cheating death. The particulars, of course, are never very explicit, although some speakers suggest formulae. Even when a Mutual Lover does not explicitly say that love will help him circumvent death, his overwhelming desire to free himself from the ravages of time implies his wish for immortality. He tries to argue away the fact of death and to commemorate his love with song. But ironically, only when he can lose himself momentarily in celebration can he transcend his almost stultifying preoccupation with dissolution.

The final character type presented in a number of poems is the Dreaming Cynic. He cries out that all women are unfaithful, licentious creatures; and his cynicism borders on attitudes expressed by the Hedonists. Yet with this contempt he mingles his desire for a woman he could really love, a woman true and fair. She materializes in the Dreaming Cynic's imaginary world, where he is a hero. The tension between these two aspects of his feelings resolves itself in his desire for revenge, by which he repudiates a woman (or women in general) for not living up to his ideal. He uses his imaginary world as a standard by which to measure his love relationships, and frequently he turns to that fictional world to vindicate the injustices and inequities of his life.

Tone

These general outlines sketch the similarities between poems and illustrate the basic framework on which my groupings of the songs and sonnets hang. But they do not account for that niggling problem of tone in poems that essentially "say" the same thing, follow similar patterns of development, and capture a speaker in a comparable relationship with his audience, and that yet come off, so to speak, very differently—one as a joke, the other as a straightforward, even tormented, utterance. Indeed, the somewhat larger but related question of what constitutes comic tone in the *Songs and Sonnets* arises time and again as one is reading the poems. No single generalization provides a wholly adequate explanation, perhaps, but Donne achieves his humor in several characteristic ways, all of which to some extent depend upon his speaker's consciousness of himself as a witty creator. Donne's particular methods of making his poems comic, therefore, succeed finally by destroying the illusion of a dramatic confrontation. His delicate entwining of dramatic and lyric elements requires that the reader be consistently convinced of the truth of the dramatic speaker before him, if the poem is to reach that happy state where the lover endows the immediate moment of his encounter with the timelessness of celebration. When a speaker calls attention to his own cleverness in the midst of protesting his love, his believeability as a wooer immediately vanishes. The comic speakers therefore, in Sidney's words, use "Art to shew Art."

To set some limits, then. Comic self-consciousness in the *Songs and Sonnets* borders on one side, even overlaps, the self-awareness of a speaker trying to convince his listeners of his great intelligence or his firm moral virtue. But the comic persona's overriding interest lies in his creation of a witty, well-ordered utterance rather than of a well-controlled self-portrait. The concern with wanting to seem, say, a scholar, implies a fair amount of involvement with one's listener and perhaps some need for his approval; it marks a degree of commitment to the dramatic encounter. The impulse to joy in words, on the other hand, is essentially a personal or lyric one, stemming from the delight of playing with sounds and phrases, of punning, and of joining verbal incongruities. The comic persona's pretense of an encounter provides only the backdrop against which he can deliver his creation, and the listener furnishes the excuse for the speaker to run through his performance. The opening lines of "The Legacie" furnish an example:

> When I dyed last, and Deare, I dye
>   As often as from thee I goe,
>   Though it be an houre agoe,
> And Lovers houres be full eternity,
> I can remember yet, that I
>   Something did say, and something did bestow. (ll 1–6)

With a bit of flattery the woman has been lured into becoming the butt of a preposterous joke which builds to its inevitable insult as she sits or stands there listening to it. She provides the necessary prop for his performance.

Because they are essentially lyric personae (creators and singers), the comic speakers also border on those lovers who seem spontaneously to celebrate the joy of their relationship, the passing of time, and the immortality of their mistresses. Donne's particular weaving of this lyric strand into poems other than the comic ones creates the illusion of unpremeditated commemoration, arising from, then transcending, the experience of the dramatic encounter, as opera does. For example, in "The Anniversarie," the speaker's growing awareness of the constancy of his love in a world of change, made more poignant because with his beloved he is marking the first anniversary of their meeting, generates within him the impulse to immortalize that precious timelessness:

Only our love hath no decay;
  This, no tomorrow hath, nor yesterday,
  Running it never runs from us away,
But truly keepes his first, last, everlasting day. (ll. 7–10)

The reader is left with the illusion that such beautiful poetry pours forth
impromptu, having surged up inside the speaker because of his immediate situation. Donne uses art in this utterance, again to return to Sidney's distinction, "to hide Art," in other words, to make the outpouring
seem natural. The speaker in "The Anniversarie" does not violate his
semblance of a lover by calling attention to himself as a wit.

In Donne's comic poems, however, the speaker accentuates his art
until it distracts from and finally destroys the illusion of his dramatic
encounter, in great part because his creation is too clever for the weight
of the subject he purports to be expressing. This disparity between
manner and matter in turn magnifies the growing sense of incongruity
until the whole utterance builds to a comic revelation. Or, from another
point of view, the speaker is detached enough from both his listener and
the import of his utterance to concentrate on what I shall term the game
quality of his speech—the obvious balancing of sounds (usually alliteration), an abundance of rhyme, playful metrics, an elaborately detailed
comic fiction, and puns, particularly sexual ones. Occasionally this game
quality entails the clever manipulation of rhetorical conventions as well.
Absorbed in perfecting the incongruity of his creation, the comic
speaker thus seems removed from (or unmoved by) his listener and his
immediate circumstances. Once the illusion of a dramatic exchange is
disturbed, the speaker's identity as a lover dissipates as well, sometimes
disappearing altogether; and he stands revealed as a mask that Donne
has created to heighten the amusement in the poem. The real exchange
in these lyrics occurs between the poet and the reader, and a reader
well-versed in classical rhetoric and poetic technique at that. But even
this distinction between comic and straightforward tone requires some
further qualification, for many of Donne's lyrics, "The Apparition," for
example, hover on that thin line between seriousness and humor. In
these the shift in tone often coincides with the break from narration to
dramatic encounter. In other poems, such as "The Will," the speaker's
witty game momentarily breaks down. Indeed, when a comic speaker
loosens his concentration on an impeccable performance, he often reveals an intensity of involvement in his situation of which he seemed
incapable. This particular paradox, of course, raises the question of just
how firmly the illusion of a dramatic encounter holds. In some of the
poems it vacillates so much that finally nothing really holds—neither the
creative humor nor the semblance of an engagement. These lyrics, like
"The Apparition," "Song: 'Goe, and catche a falling starre,' " "Womans
Constancy," even "The Canonization," admirably crafted as they are,

finally break apart because neither the dramatic exchange nor the poet's wit quite dominates. These borderline poems notwithstanding, Donne does provide ample evidence about the tone of any particular poem.

A brief glance at the opening stanzas of "Loves Diet" and "Farewell to Love" will provide concrete examples of some of the ways in which Donne distinguishes between comic and straightforward treatment of the same subject. In these poems both speakers are hedonistic; both, having become disillusioned with lust, offer first-person testimonies on how they have rid themselves of it; and both address unnamed listeners, perhaps a group of them, as if from a distance. As my extended discussion in Chapter 3 makes clear, in each poem Donne has the persona ultimately undercut the validity of his position. Thus in no way does a speaker's playful attitude signal Donne's automatic agreement with or even condoning of that man's viewpoint. With the comic poems, however, the question of judgment seems irrelevant; for the audacity and energy of the comic figure enable him to escape censure, to live outside of a moral context, if you will, precisely *because* he is dramatically unconvincing. The opening stanzas of the two poems follow, "Loves Diet" first:

> To what a combersome unwieldinesse
> And burdenous corpulence my love had growne,
>   But that I did, to make it lesse,
>   And keepe it in proportion,
> Give it a diet, made it feed upon
> That which love worst endures, *discretion*. (ll. 1–6)

and

>   Whilst yet to prove,
> I thought there was some Dietie in love,
>   So did I reverence, and gave
> Worship, as Atheists at their dying houre
> Call, what they cannot name, an unknowne power,
>   As ignorantly did I crave:
>   Thus when
> Things not yet knowne are coveted by men,
> Our desires give them fashion, and so
> As they waxe lesser, fall, as they sise, grow. (ll. 1–10)

In spite of its lovely, evanescent rhyme, the complex stanza of "Farewell to Love" by its variety of line lengths, its enjambment, and its heavy internal stops draws attention away from the musically pleasing techniques of lyric poetry and creates instead the semblance of a man relating his disillusionment with love and women. In other words, the

poet sacrifices lyric beauty for dramatic verisimilitude. "Loves Diet," on
the other hand, stresses its art, or more accurately, its speaker's creative
wittiness by lessening his credibility as a disillusioned lover. Indeed,
Donne seems to have reached for those selfsame artistic effects that the
Renaissance arbiters of poetic decorum reserved for comic and trifling
verse. The poem unduly emphasizes rhyme, having even *proportion*
harmonize with *discretion* and both of these with *growne* and *upon*. It
combines internal and end rhyme in "combersome unwieldinesse / And
burdenous corpulence," and later in line 21: "And that that favour made
him fat." George Puttenham, advising courtiers about writing verse,
indicates that the excessive repetition of harmonious sounds undercuts
the seriousness of the poetic matter: "Note also that rime or concorde is
not commendably vsed both in the end and middle of a verse [line],
vnlesse it be in toyes and trifling Poesies, for it sheweth a certaine
lightnesse either of the matter or of the makers head."[31] He also speci-
fies that in rhymed words the stress should fall as close to the last
syllable as possible, except in trifling poetry. The accent in both *proportion* and *discretion* occurs on the third syllable from the end of the line.
"But alwayes the cadence which falleth vpon the last sillable of a verse is
sweetest and most commendable: that vpon the *penultima* more light,
and not so pleasant: but falling vpon the *antepenultima* is most
vnpleasant of all, because they make your meeter too light and triuiall,
and are fitter for the Epigrammatist or Comicall Poet then for the Lyrick
and Elegiack, which are accompted to the sweeter Musickes."[32] These
numerous and strained harmonies all together create the tone by which
the speaker can accomplish his witty insult.

In addition to excessive rhyme, Donne uses more sound links, particularly alliteration, in the comic poems than he does elsewhere,
another means of demonstrating the speaker's artfulness. Lines 9 and 10
of "Loves Diet" provide an example:

> And if sometimes by stealth he got
> A she sigh from my mistresse heart . . .

Again Puttenham comments on alliteration, which he terms "Tautologia, or the figure of selfe saying":

> Ye haue another manner of composing your metre nothing commend-
> able, specially if it be too much vsed, and is when our maker takes too
> much delight to fill his verse with wordes beginning all with a letter, as an
> English rimer that said:
> *The deadly droppes of darke disdaine,*
> *Do daily drench my due desartes.*
> And as the Monke we spake of before, wrote a whole Poeme to the
> honor of *Carolus Caluus*, euery word in his verse beginning with C.[33]

Puttenham's warning, even about purely lyric poetry, where the speaker is already identified as a maker, focuses on the poet's inordinate delight in his skill, presumably at the expense of subject matter. In a poem where the persona assumes a dramatic role, the excessive repetition of sound even more sharply jars with the illusion of his involvement with either his listener or his circumstances. It signals his distance from the encounter, and by extension, his consciousness of himself as a witty creator.

Donne uses other means for indicating comic tone in the *Songs and Sonnets* as well. Frequently he has the speaker meticulously develop an incredible fiction, such as that of Love's being forced on an emotional regimen of only one "she sigh" and an occasional tear daily, in "Loves Diet." It might be argued that the extended analogies in many of the straightforward poems come close to being fictions or that fictions at best have a metaphorical thrust. Even in "Loves Diet" the comparison between abstaining from the sweet (or bittersweet) garnishes of love and keeping away from the cookie jar or the box of chocolates provides at its most elemental level a vehicle for illustrating similarities. In "Farewell to Love" the simile of the child tiring of the gingerbread cookie he yearned for at the fair and the man losing interest in sex, so the argument goes, serves the same function. To an extent, of course, the argument holds true. But again the speaker's conscious and particular use of his fiction or his conceit divides the comic from the straightforward lyrics. If the persona *perceives* either his fiction or his conceit as primarily an analogy, he subordinates it to the purpose (or "invention") of his utterance, as all the lovers do in the straightforward poems. If, on the other hand, the fiction becomes so interesting for its own sake that the speaker expends his energies elaborating it, as he does in "Loves Diet," the witty manipulation and amplification of the fiction become, in fact, the subject of the poem. George Gascoigne warns the serious would-be poet of just such a danger: "Your inuention being once deuised, take heede that neither pleasure of rime, nor variety of deuise, do carie you from it: for as to vse obscure and darke phrases in a pleasant Sonet, is nothing delectable, so to entermingle merie iests in a serious matter is an *Indecorum.*"[34] Again and again, then, Donne seems to write his comic love lyrics from a sheet of mistakes frequently made in composing poetry.

Another device which Puttenham repudiates and which Donne uses in the comic poems is the calculated, bawdy pun, such as on the word *die.* Such a pun is an indiscretion, at least, in a love lyric; it would insult the lady in a direct encounter, unless, of course, it occurs in a joke. Puttenham discerns just these distinctions.

Now haue ye other vicious manners of speech, but sometimes and in some cases tollerable, and chiefly to the intent to mooue laughter, and to make sport, or to giue it some prety strange grace, and is when we vse such wordes as may be drawen to a foule and vnshamefast sense, as one that would say to a young woman, *I pray you let me jape with you,* which in deed is no more but let me sport with you. Yea and though it were not altogether so directly spoken, the very sounding of the word were not commendable. . . . For it may be taken in another peruerser sense by that sorte of persons that heare it, in whose eares no such matter ought almost to be called in memory.[35]

Like the other comic devices in those poems that tread the narrow line between comic and serious poetry, the calculated, bawdy pun at once serves as a means for revenge and as a joke. The complexity arises, as I have indicated, when the speaker shifts momentarily from his role as a parodist to a man involved with the circumstances around him.

In addition to such poetic excesses as these, comic speakers sometimes manipulate oratorical conventions as well. The lover in "The Apparition," for example, by trying to frighten his girlfriend into bed with him, applies Quintilian's time-honored technique of threatening her at the end of his utterance—at his *peroratio,* if you will. The rub comes, of course, when one realizes that Quintilian advocates using this technique only with dishonorable people. Also in "The Sunne Rising," a poem structured more or less as a classical oration, part of the speaker's gamefulness arises from the fact that he makes his adversary, the sun, provide support for the lover's *argumentatio*:

> Looke, and to morrow late, tell mee,
> Whether both the 'India's of spice and Myne
> Be where thou leftst them, or lie here with mee. (ll. 16–18)

And in "The Canonization" the speaker, again an orator of sorts, blunts his listener's objections by turning them to laughter—another technique Quintilian advocates particularly when one wants to draw attention away from the facts of the case.

In poems such as these where Donne adjusts oratorical conventions with some deftness, the question of dramatic encounter or poetic games takes an additional twist. Because of their rhetorical expertise, these speakers create the illusion of a man addressing an audience. Thus even when the semblance of a serious exchange breaks down, as it certainly does in "The Canonization," a clever fellow delivering a witty and often naughty variation of a speech remains, not a poet snickering to himself as he pens his lyrics. But what matter? Not only did poetry and oratory overlap in the Renaissance (Puttenham's *The Arte of English Poesie* depends almost exclusively on Quintilian's *Institutiones oratoriae*), poets wrote and sang their lyrics, just as orators wrote and delivered their speeches. Both sorts were, first of all, creators. In all cases, the speaker's self-consciousness as a creator signals a comic tone in the *Songs and Sonnets*.

Donne seems to have fashioned some of his comic speakers, then, as literary drones or sly orators exulting in their own cleverness. We marvel at the extent of their ingenious absurdity, at the lengths to which they stretch literary and rhetorical conventions; and we delight in their jokes. But simply because Donne gives them such artful speeches, the readers are alerted not to take these men or their words too seriously, not to ponder too much their impudent prurience.

It remains yet to ask how the Renaissance with its essentially didactic poetic dealt with such toys as these. The numerous references to comic and licentious poetry in Puttenham's criticism certainly substantiate what a wide reading of Renaissance lyrics confirms, that for all the didactic poetic, many of the poets wrote risqué ditties and bawdy songs, as had Ovid, Homer, Virgil, and Catullus before them. That such writing, however, was seen to serve the very humane purposes of solace and recreation for the mind seldom receives attention in our critical appraisals. Puttenham puts just such a construction on amusing poetry, as he digresses from his discussion of anagrams to consider the larger question of the place of purely delightful verse in the lives of men:

> When I wrate of these deuices, I smiled with my selfe, thinking that the readers would do so to, and many of them say, that such trifles as these might well haue bene spared, considering the world is full inough of them, and that it is pitie mens heads should be fedde with such vanities as are to none edification nor instruction, either of morall vertue or otherwise behooffull for the common wealth, to whose seruice (say they) we are all borne, and not to fill and replenish a whole world full of idle toyes. To which sort of reprehendours, being either all holy and mortified to the world, and therefore esteeming nothing that sauoureth not of Theologie, or altogether graue and worldly, and therfore caring for nothing but matters of pollicie, and discourses of estate, or all giuen to thrift and passing for none art that is not gainefull and lucratiue, as the sciences of the Law, Physicke and marchaundise: to these I will giue none other answere then referre them to the many trifling poems of *Homer, Ouid, Virgill, Catullus,* and other notable writers of former ages, which were not of any grauitie or seriousnesse, and many of them full of impudicitie and ribaudrie, as are not these of ours, nor for any good in the world should haue bene: and yet those trifles are come from many former siecles vnto our times, vncontrolled or condemned or supprest by any Pope or Patriarch or other seuere censor of the ciuill maners of men, but haue bene in all ages permitted as the conuenient solaces and recreations of mans wit. And as I can not denie

but these conceits of mine be trifles: no lesse in very deede be all the most serious studies of man, if we shall measure grauitie and lightnesse by the wise mans ballance who after he had considered of all the profoundest artes and studies among men, in th'ende cryed out with this Epyphoneme, *Vanitas vanitatum et omnia vanitas*.[36]

His movement from viewing the poems as a form of solace and refreshment for man's wit to considering them as *memento humilitatis* obliquely raises that old paradox of Jack Donne the rake and John Donne the minister. To expend one's energies and talents on jokes and games certainly eases the mind and sharpens the wit. Indeed, one might be inclined to say that such exercise momentarily, at least, allows a man to rejoice at his own cleverness and ingenuity. That in a larger, more philosophical perspective such writing also encourages a man to consider the vanity and limitations of human endeavor, to laugh at himself for delighting in such trifles, helps to reconcile in profoundly human terms the dilemma we raise in rather limited ones between Donne the devout Christian and the comic philanderer.

Many of Donne's references in his letters to his paradoxes, problems, and poetry reflect the same philosophical position that Puttenham makes explicit in the passage above. Apparently writing to Sir Henry Wotton in 1600, Donne comments that writing his paradoxes helped him pass his time away: "Only in obedience I send you some of my paradoxes: I love you and myself and them too well to send them willingly for they carry with them a confession of their lightnes, and your trouble and my shame. But indeed they were made rather to deceave tyme than her daughter truth. . . . they are but swaggerers: quiet enough if you resist them. . . . and they have only this advantadg to scape from being caled ill things that they are nothings."[37] Almost restating Puttenham's comment that trifles of poetry are "the conuenient solaces and recreations of mans wit," Donne indicates that creating his playful paradoxes whiled the time away. Moreover, he laughs at both their bravado and, by extension, his own ("but swaggerers: quiet enough if you resist them"), thus preparing Wotton and us for his philosophical evaluation of bawdry and fallacious reasoning in the paradoxes: they "scape from being caled ill things that . . . are nothings." Only writing with a serious intention and execution can logically receive censure or, by extension, praise. The fluff relieves tedium and ultimately reminds man of his limitation. Because many of the poems repeat the same arguments and "swagger" of the paradoxes, Donne's comment applies to them as well. Some of his other references to his poetry in the letters reinforce the aptness of the application. To Sir Henry Goodyer in 1607 Donne writes of his problems: "Such light flashes as these have been my hawkings in my sorry journeys. I accompany them with another ragge of verses, worthy of that name for the smalnesse, and age."[38] When contemplating printing the poems, he adroitly remarks: "By this occasion I am made a Rhapsoder of mine own rags, and that cost me more diligence, to seek them, than it did to make them."[39] These comments evince Donne's wry self-perception and indirectly his evaluation of the vanity of his literary endeavors and his attempts to improve his lot through them.

To return from a discussion of comic tone to more general concerns, then, the speakers of the *Songs and Sonnets* are highly individualized variations of stock love characters who seem unique in part because of their dramatic vitality. By having them confront a listener rather than sing or complain as lyric speakers are wont to do, Donne uses the particulars of any one encounter to make that relationship seem singular or that individual lover seem strikingly different. In fact, however, a number of poems have speakers who markedly resemble one another, who verily seem to be versions of the same character type, differentiated from each other primarily through the enrichment of the details of their dramatic exchange.

The seeming complexity of the speakers grows mostly from Donne's modification of the lyric; for by imposing a dramatic cast on it, Donne virtually asks the reader to treat the poem both as a lyric and as a dramatic speech and to establish with the persona the relationship of the audience to the play and of the reader to a lyric. Thus the speaker must be glimpsed, as it were, both inwardly and outwardly. This double focus insists on the importance of the persona above and beyond his ideas, his conventions, or his imagery; for his particular view gains its validity primarily through his response to his listener, his present circumstances, and his past experience. Viewpoint here becomes an extension of personality, acting under the particular pressures of a specific moment in time.

Moreover, Donne handles the delicate modulation between the lyric and dramatic elements in a poem quite deftly, manipulating them to define the ever-shifting relationship between the persona and his listener, to mark a speaker's self-absorption, to indicate movement from one listener to another—in short, to signal all the complexities of relationship possible in a poem. By further adding a narrative element to some of the poems of the *Songs and Sonnets*, Donne explores the possibilities of distance between a speaker and his listener, sometimes to the point where the latter might more properly be called an audience. My own playing over these variations occupies a great portion of the pages that follow.

2
The Petrarchists

The three sets of speakers among Donne's lovers who most fully deserve the title Petrarchists all use and indirectly comment upon Petrarchan conceits as language. They also, in many of Donne's poems, examine the validity of the sincere, adoring, and uncritical love that Petrarch espouses.[1] The Parodists mock the hyperbolic language of the conceits by pretending to accept them literally. Singing complaints about the cruelty of their mistresses or the pains of leaving, these speakers turn such a commonplace as 'parting is death to lovers' into a ludicrous mockery, for the woman commits murder by bidding her sweetheart farewell. The Witty Lovers, on the other hand, find Petrarchan language appropriately rich and in an unexpected way literally accurate for expressing their complex feelings at departing from their loved ones. The Cavalier Petrarchists combine aspects of the other two characters, for they mock Petrarch's language and yet, to some degree, avow his sentiments and his constancy.

The Parodists

Although the stock conceits of the sonneteers echo through most of the *Songs and Sonnets*, they form the subject matter for only a few poems: "The Computation," "The Expiration," "Witchcraft by a Picture," and "The Paradox." This fact belies any assertion by the speakers of these lyrics that they are undergoing the pangs of parting or suffering the cruelty of rejection. Donne's Parodists, in the guise of ardent lovers commemorating their emotional unrest, undercut their own complaints by pretending that their conceits are literally true. But the conceits are so preposterous that they expose the speakers as men burlesquing the metaphors of other love complaints. Moreover, by mocking the language, these men obliquely imply criticisms of the long-suffering, adoring, unrequited lover, whose conventional pose they see as a stratagem for luring women to bed. They do not, however, offer an alternative view of love; for like the dull versifiers they mock, these witty men sing primarily of language, at once ridiculing a false convention and forming a new one.[2] In effect, then, they reveal themselves as creators, not lovers, as men terribly conscious of their own cleverness. By extension the "real" listener becomes a sophisticated reader, who, like the versifier, knows the ways of both poetry and parody. The woman, or apparent listener, is evoked only to gain and sustain the illusion of an encounter and thus to heighten the impudence of the creator's mockery.

The particular targets of the Parodists are those lyrics which repeat somewhat fatuously such commonplaces as 'the lady kills with scorn' or 'the lover dies in parting.' Petrarch himself uses these comparisons, but with a restraint seldom followed by the many lyricists who imitated him. In Sonnet 15 of his *Canzoniere*, for example, he ponders the possibility that he will die away from his Laura:

> Sometimes a doubt assails my deep distress:
> How can these limbs go on living at all,
> So far away from their soul's happiness? (ll. 9–11)

He is controlled in his comparison. He feels so distressed at leaving his beloved that he doubts his ability to get along without her; yet wryly, almost sardonically, he realizes that people do not die for love:

> But then Love answers me:—Don't you recall
> That lovers have the privilege to be
> Rid of each human trait and quality? (ll. 12–14)

Likewise his treatment of the trope 'the lady kills with scorn' retains a hint of ironic self-perception, which constrains his love lament:

> I fear much the onslaught of the eyes
> In which my death and Love lodge, live and last,
> That I fly as a child from flogging flies;
> And since I first took flight, much time has passed.
>
> From now on there is not a tiring, steep
> Place where my will is not arrived and gone
> In order to avoid who makes me weep,
> And then deserts me changed into cold stone.
>
> Therefore if to see you I have come late,
> Not to be near the one who is my death,
> My fault perhaps is not without excuse.
>
> I say more: to return to what we hate,
> And a heart free from fear and from abuse
> Were not too slight a warrant of my faith.[3]

The lover's concern for his own well-being and his delicately satiric use of litotes in the final tercet provide just enough critical appraisal of the lady to indicate that Petrarch understands even the absurdities of his passion. He does not fully commit himself to the idealized world of his metaphors.

Many of the Petrarchists, however, retain the tropes of their master but not his critical self-scrutiny. These inanities Donne burlesques in the *Songs and Sonnets*. Passages from a few Renaissance lyrics indicate the expansive and sometimes absurd treatment of the two conceits, 'the lady kills with scorn' and 'the lover dies in parting.'

> Cruel you be who can say nay,
>   Since ye delight in other's woe:
> Unwise am I, ye may well say,
>   For that I have honoured you so:
> But blameless I, who could not choose,
>   To be enchanted by your eye:
> But ye to blame, thus to refuse
>   My service, and to let me die.

Or:

> It shall be said I died for Coelia!
> Then quick, thou grisly man of Erebus,
> Transport me hence unto Proserpina,
> To be adjudged as "wilful amorous":
> To be hung up within the liquid air,
> For all the sighs which I in vain have wasted:
> To be through Lethe's waters cleansèd fair,
> For those dark clouds which have my looks o'ercasted:
> To be condemned to everlasting fire,
> Because at Cupid's fire I wilful brent me;
> And to be clad, for deadly dumps, in mire.
> Among so many plagues which shall torment me
>   One solace I shall find, when I am over:
>   It will be known I died a constant lover!

Or:

> Dreames and Imaginations
> Are all the recreations
>   Absence can gaine me,
> Dreames when I wake, confound me,
> Thoughts for her sake doth wound me
>   Lest she disdaine me,
> Then sinking let me lie,
> Or thinking let me die,
>   Since love hath slaine me. (ll. 1–9).[4]

Like these love lyricists, Donne's Parodists seem to accept their portion in life as unrequited lovers. They too complain, some of them in
what seems a face-to-face encounter with their mistresses, others in the
more traditional guise of singers pouring out their hearts. But in all the
poems, the speakers parody both the language and the sentiment expressed in the lyrics quoted above by treating the tropes as facts rather
than metaphors. In "The Computation," for example, the Petrarchan
lover sings of the death he has endured since he left his mistress a day
ago, until in his ghostly transformation he confronts her. Thus at least
until the final couplet of the poem he seems to be commemorating the
pangs of parting, which fill many, many love complaints in the Renaissance.

> For the first twenty yeares, since yesterday,
> I scarce beleev'd, thou could'st be gone away,
> For forty more, I fed on favours past,
> And forty'on hopes, that thou would'st, they might last.
> Teares drown'd one hundred, and sighes blew out two,
> A thousand, I did neither thinke, nor doe,
> Or not divide, all being one thought of you;
> Or in a thousand more, forgot that too.
> Yet call not this long life; But thinke that I
> Am, by being dead, Immortall; Can ghosts die?

For all his protests of despair, however, he retains enough detachment
to calculate the limits of his suffering so precisely as to construct his song
on the mathematical equation that every hour away from his beloved
seems like a hundred years. His hyperbolic treatment of lovers' time
("For the first twenty yeares, since yesterday,") both calls attention to
his creative wit and provides him with a vehicle for his satire. Avowing
his longing for her, the speaker says that since their parting he has lived
on love alone: he fed himself for forty years on her past favors and for
another forty on hopes of what the future might bring. That is, in reality,
he subsisted on this kind of nourishment for forty-eight minutes. He
turns the commonplace 'the lover sighs gales and cries oceans' into a
clever detail about how he made time pass: "Teares drown'd one hundred, and sighes blew out two." His strict adherence to metaphor in the
verbs parodies the language of the Petrarchists so wittily that it undermines the illusion of sincerity in his complaint. Yet all of this spoofing
occurs within a delicate lyric form of harmonious sounds, smooth metrics, and end-stopped rhymes, as if he were obeying Puttenham, who
commends the practice of "fashioning . . . our makers language and
stile to such purpose as it may delight and allure as well the mynde as
the eare of the hearers with a certaine noueltie and strange maner of

conueyance, disguising it no little from the ordinary and accustomed . . . making it . . . decenter and more agreable to any ciuill eare and vnderstanding."[5] In short, the first eight lines of the poem reveal a playful singer who toys with the conventions of love poetry.

Only in the last two lines, when the form changes abruptly and the past tense of narrative turns to the present tense of encounter, do the ambiguities multiply. The imperative verbs insist on the illusion of a dramatic exchange and hence on the lady's presence. If we assume that she is witty, the nature of that exchange splinters, for the lover offers her a personal testimony to the tribulation of dying for love and at the same time satirizes both his own role playing and the sentiment of adoring, selfless lovers. She too, then, participates in his game of love by pre-tending to be the aloof lady to whom he appeals. They both, in other words, parody Character types. If we presuppose the woman does not understand the spoof, then we must also presume a second listener (or a reader) who does. Doffing his mask as a whimsical singer of love lyrics, the speaker confronts his coy mistress. As if in response to her comment about his longevity, he says: "Yet call not this long life." By creating a spondee before a definite stop, the alliterative phrase "long life" forces attention on meaning. Suddenly the years are real, to be measured in terms of life and death. The wrenched meter and enjambment mute the rhyme, and the melodious song of the first eight lines gives way to speech rhythms. This technical alteration also initiates the speaker's shift from comic parody to a radical criticism of the Petrarchists and, insofar as the woman is a believable listener, from a complaint to a proposition.

To his wily reader (and to the lady, if she has followed him) he acknowledges that the protestations of his complaint are feigned. In reality only a day has passed: "Yet call not this long life." The indefinite *this* also refers to the pattern of life of a sentimental, distraught lover: "this," the Parodist confirms, is not "long life"; it is no life at all. The conceit that 'parting is death,' therefore, yields an unexpected criticism of the Petrarchist viewpoint, and the speaker turns this disparagement into an invitation for the lady to "live a little." With a twist on the trope of dying for love, he advises her to "thinke that I / Am, by being dead, Immortall." In other words, his experiences with "dying" for love have made something of a god of him; literature amply records how women have responded to some of those Greek and Roman deities. This sudden reversal of the man's intention throws his whole posture into an ironic perspective: perhaps his professions merely camouflage his seductive design. In his final question, "Can ghosts die?" the speaker, wasted away to a specter himself, invites the lady to test the issue by going to bed with him. At the same time to his critical reader he raises a doubt

about the virility of long-suffering adorers. Obliquely he also questions
whether the complaints of these lovers will ever cease: "Can ghosts
die?" the sexual pun on *die*, however, predominates in this final,
enigmatic retort and echoes back through the earlier portions of the
utterance to its sound links with *doe* and *divide*, both of which hold
sexual overtones. There, still in the guise of an unrequited lover, the
Parodist reminds his lady of his constancy:

> A thousand, I did neither thinke, nor doe,
> Or not divide, all being one thought of you.

Since, however, he is basing his declarations on the correspondence of
one hour to a hundred years, he professes only ten hours of faithfulness
to the woman he loves. Ironically, then, the inflated language, rather
than expressing the lover's heightened adoration, reveals his sexual
intentions and his limited capacity for faithfulness. To the witty reader
and the clever woman he has been addressing, it also supplies a cynical
and comic appraisal of the specific kind of pangs unrequited lovers
suffer.

In "The Expiration," "Witchcraft by a Picture," and "The Paradox,"
the Parodists once again use Petrarchan conceits as if they were literally
true. In "The Expiration" the farewell kiss turns each partner into a
"ghost" (l. 3), and the lover's word "Goe" (l. 7) not only kills his lady
but will probably ricochet to perform "a just office on a murderer"
(l. 10). Likewise in "Witchcraft by a Picture," the lover fears his mistress's witchlike ability to kill a person by destroying his image, as the
man watches tears which hold his reflection roll down her cheek. And in
"The Paradox" the speaker, accepting as factual the conceit of 'the lover
dies for love,' laments the fact that no one with experience can ever utter
this sentiment. He solves the problem by becoming his own "Epitaph
and Tombe" (l. 18), which reads, "Love-slaine, loe, here I lye" (l. 20).

All of this toying with Petrarchan conceits, moreover, reverberates as
a criticism of the stance of long suffering, unrequited lovers. In "The
Expiration" that reproof focuses on Petrarchan language as a cover-up
for sexual seduction, as the lover pleads, "Ease mee with death, by
bidding mee goe too" (l. 8). The sexual possibilities of being "love-
slaine" also resound through the closure of "The Paradox." And in
"Witchcraft by a Picture" the censure falls on the cruel woman of
Petrarchan poetry, who preserves her lover from death only as a means
of self-preservation:

> Though thou retaine of mee
> One picture more, yet that will bee,
> Being in thine owne heart, from all malice free. (ll. 12–14)

Even here the lover couches his appraisal of his mistress in flattering ambiguities.

In these four brief poems, then, Donne burlesques the conventions of Petrarchism by seeming to accept its conceits literally and singing of them harmoniously, by being, in other words, assiduously conventional. His subject is much more the absurdity of language than the folly of idealized love, although his sexual puns and realistic appraisals do call that into question too. Hence the sense that Donne wrote his comic poems with one hand on the thou-shalt-nots of poetry manuals confirms the literary rather than social or philosophical import of much of his parody. He seems indeed to be practicing with deft irony and meticulous care the very art that Puttenham descries:

> If the same coulours in our arte of Poesie . . . be not well tempered, or not well layd, or be vsed in excesse, or neuer so litle disordered or misplaced, they . . . do disfigure the stuffe and spill the whole workmanship . . . no lesse then if the crimson tainte, which should be laid vpon a Ladies lips, or right in the center of her cheekes, should by some ouersight or mishap be applied to her forhead or chinne, it would make . . . but a very ridiculous bewtie."[6]

Poems such as "The Expiration" and "The Computation" have about them a semblance of the clown's makeup—"a very ridiculous bewtie," indeed.

The Witty Lovers

As if in opposition to the just-named group of speakers, the Witty Lovers[7] find within the oldest Petrarchan conceits a literal validity which injects new vitality into the conventional language of love poetry. All of these men, involved in a strong emotional relationship with their ladies, seek to express themselves as they say good-bye. Under these trying circumstances, they discover that everyday language cannot convey the multiple, often contradictory strands of their responses. Only through metaphors, and very old ones at that, can they finally reveal the complexities of their situation. The process of finding the right words, of confronting and reexamining timeworn conceits, takes its impetus from the dramatic encounter. Because of the increasing pressure of the final moments of his farewell, each speaker desperately wants to convey his feelings as accurately as possible to a woman he may never see again. Both his immediate situation and his personal commitment to the truth of his feelings insist that he reassess his words, reshape or reapply his tropes, no matter how glibly he may have used them before. He must ask himself how true to his present experience is the Petrarchan expression of the lover's dying at parting from his beloved, or the courtly assumption that the lover is worthless, or the conceit that the beloved comprises his whole world. Essentially, then, the leave-taking pushes the man into a self-examination, a new awareness, and by extension a revaluation of his assumptions and his language about love. Under these stringent stipulations, the speaker's choice of a familiar Petrarchan metaphor almost automatically imbues that metaphor with fresh vitality.

In "A Valediction: of Weeping" the speaker, a fluent Petrarchist, attempts to tell his beloved how much she means to him as he prepares to leave on a journey. The fleeting quality of their last minutes together heightens his awareness of the value of their love. At the same time the ephemerality of this final meeting emotionally and intellectually overwhelms him, and he realizes that the parting he is experiencing may, in fact, mark the last time he ever sees her.

The words "whil'st I stay here" in line 2 create the dramatic framework in which the poem is enacted. In addition to reminding the speaker of time's fleeting moments, they suggest that this meeting climaxes the lovers' past experiences together and must preserve their relationship if it is to have a future. Perhaps some of the momentous significance of the occasion prompts the extreme caution and courtesy with which the speaker addresses his mistress. He asks her permission to cry, then explains his request with Petrarchan self-denigration, saying that with her image in his tears at least something about him has value:

> Let me powre forth
> My teares before thy face, whil'st I stay here,
> For thy face coines them, and thy stampe they beare,
> And by this Mintage they are something worth. (ll. 1–4)

His sense of worthlessness, captured iconically in the clear, round tear and metaphorically in the coin without denomination, is compounded through his self-definition until he projects himself into a barren future without his beloved, where his very identity vanishes because only she gives meaning to his existence. In other words, the emotional intensity of his farewell momentarily renders him incapable of concentrating solely on his mistress, and he speaks to himself as well, coming to grips with the awful realization of his insignificance without her. Quite naturally, then, he turns to defining his tears as a means of verbalizing his innermost feelings. His tears are "fruits" of his present grief and "emblemes" (l. 7) of his future sadness, that is, pictures whose full meaning depends upon the words that accompany them. These words reiterate his sense of utter devastation when he is parted from his beloved: "So thou and I are nothing then, when on a divers shore" (l. 9).

Thus far little occurs between the speaker and his lady. His courtesy, his embarrassment at crying, and his attempts at both understanding his circumstances and expressing his feelings consume him so that he stands back from his final encounter until he is able to endure it. Hence the first stanza is almost tautological, beginning with the emblem of an empty tear and ending with its explanation.

Paradoxically, the speaker's imaginative leap into a barren future awakens him to his momentous present, and he begins to search for words to express his beloved's importance to him. Grasping onto one of the oldest conceits, 'the lady comprises his entire world,' he tells her she means everything to him, indeed much more than even his metaphors can convey.[8] The movement of his analogies from globe to world to heaven reflects the growing emotional relationship between the lovers. At first only he is weeping, pouring forth those empty tears which capture his feelings of insignificance without his beloved; then he imagines that those same tears fill up with her reflections. He attempts to assimilate this image into his overwhelming sense of her importance to him by comparing the empty tear to a ball on which workmen lay a map of the world. In both cases the figures encrusted on the sphere imbue it with value, "make that, which was nothing, *All*" (l. 13). Once he has drawn his comparison, however, the speaker finds it inadequate and expands it from a "globe" to a "world" (l. 16), from the image to the thing itself. Even this intensification falls short when he notices his lady's tears, and he breaks from his analogy altogether to call her "my heaven" (l. 18). Until she begins to weep, for the first time revealing the *mutual* unhappiness his leaving brings, he grapples internally only with his own sadness and his loss of identity without her. Her tears, however, complicate his response: their dramatic demonstration of her grief elates him even as it anguishes him, and he delights in the wonder of her love even as he attempts to soothe her despair. The compressed and ambiguous syntax of his utterance captures his newly entangled reaction:

> Till thy teares mixt with mine doe overflow
> This world, by waters sent from thee, my heaven dissolved so. (ll. 17–18)

Thus the woman at once contains, creates, and destroys his heaven and earth, his very existence. Joyously he acknowledges her as his "heaven." But in the instant he avows her sublimity, he envisions her image in the deluge of tears rolling down her cheek. The picture reminds him of the imminence of his departure and the emptiness of his existence without her. At once the ephemeral revelation of his happiness is transmuted into despair: "my heaven dissolved so."

The complexities of his ever-expanding realization take one final swing as he notices his own image in his lady's tears suddenly inundated by a stream of water. The despair his imagined picture of her demise engendered grows almost unbearable at the literal sight of his own drowning, and he pleads with his beloved somehow to keep the worst of his fears from coming true:

> O more then Moone,
> Draw not up seas to drowne me in thy spheare,
> Weepe me not dead, in thine armes, but forbeare
> To teach the sea, what it may doe too soone. (ll. 19–22)

His self-concern dramatizes his departure from the Petrarchan denigration of the first stanza, as if suddenly on seeing his lady weep for him, he revalues himself upward. If this magnificent woman loves him, so his reasoning goes, he must protect and preserve himself. Thus through the acknowledgment of reciprocal love, the speaker assumes an equality with the lady which he did not recognize at the beginning of his leave-taking. Donne here exploits the implications of combining lyric and dramatic elements as much as he does anywhere in the *Songs and Sonnets*, for explicitly he uses the lady's tears, the external and dramatic expression of her love and sorrow, to correct the speaker's self-image from that of a Petrarchan lover bidding farewell to the only person who gives his existence meaning to that of a man dearly beloved by his mistress. And with his recognition of the equality of the lovers, the speaker suddenly shares the burden of his grief with the lady, in the process re-creating her in his own image as a forlorn lover almost devastated by the departure. Like himself at the beginning of his utterance, she sighs and weeps because he must go. Momentarily she too fits the definition of a being without meaning, once her lover has parted: "So thou and I are nothing then, when on a divers shore." But because she does love him, she must assume responsibility for him; she is denied the freedom for self-indulgence that either an unrequited (i.e., Petrarchan) lover or his aloof lady has, indeed that the speaker had until his beloved openly demonstrated her affection. Instead she must show her love by remaining strong both at the moment of his departure and during his absence. So must he. As Gardner aptly notes, with the open attesting of a woman's love the poem turns into "A Valediction: forbidding Mourning."[9] In this poem, however, the lover's admonition to the woman to refrain from despair holds a literal import and thus a shocking impact, which is absent in the other valediction. Having seen his picture drowning in his lady's tears, the lover begs her to stop weeping not only because he cannot bear her sadness but also because the image her running tears create ominously mirrors the fear he has left unspoken: that his boat may capsize at sea and he may drown. She must dry her eyes in order to keep his deepest apprehensions at bay. He must do the same for her. "Who e'r sighes most, is cruellest, and hasts the others death" (l. 27). Once again in this poem the dramatic interaction works back on a lyrical expression of grief—this time the Petrarchan conceit of 'the lover dies in parting'—only to refine and reshape that old comparison into a vital utterance with an awful but real signification.

Donne thus uses the dramatic situation in this poem to bring about the speaker's reappraisal not only of his stance as a conventional, Petrarchan lover, but also of his lyrical expression of that standpoint. This pattern of first trifling with familiar conceits then seeing their awful relevance recurs in "Song: 'Sweetest love, I do not goe' " and in "A Valediction: of my Name in the Window."

Both poems open with a playfulness which belies each speaker's fears about parting. In "Song" the lover tells his mistress that his leave-taking is an enactment "in jest" (l. 7) of the trope of 'the lover dies in parting' and assures her that like the sun he will return to her, his world, readily and eagerly. This offhand Petrarchism allows the man both to pledge his love and to separate himself from foolish, solemn, lovesick fellows. Likewise in "A Valediction" the man sloughs off the momentousness of his farewell with witty games about the arcane power of the signature he has engraved in his lady's window. Like the speaker the glass is "all confessing" and "through-shine" (l. 8) and presumably will serve as an example for her to be the same. He further teases her that his signature is a *memento mori*; for by reminding her of the farewell which "killed" her lover, the name will keep her faithful to the religion of their love:

> It, as a given deaths head keepe,
> Lovers mortalitie to preach. (ll. 21–22)

Both men, in other words, attempt to lighten the emotion-charged circumstances of their valedictions by submerging their fears in cavalier gaiety.

But the mere voicing of the conceits about death recoils on the lovers, until they acknowledge the physical and emotional truths in the poetic commonplaces of parting. The man in "Song" asks his lady to "thinke" (l. 37) that they are but sleeping during his absence, in other words, to expend as much mental influence as possible to make the interval of his journey just that, not the death that his sleep-death trope so ominously forebodes. In "A Valediction" the lover's realistic application of the 'lover dies in parting' conceit crosses the thin line between laughter and horror and brings an image of his mutilated body to the fore:

>Thinke this ragged bony name to bee
>My ruinous Anatomie. (ll. 23–24)

and

>Till my returne repaire
>And recompact my scatter'd body so . . . (ll. 31–32)

The graphic details shake him out of his light-hearted banter and loose him from playing the creative wit. He confronts his fears, that love needs more than a signature on a window to survive and that he faces untold dangers on his journey; and he finds that the Petrarchan commonplace of 'parting is death' expresses his feelings perfectly:

>But glasse, and lines must bee,
>No meanes our firme substantiall love to keepe;
>Neere death inflicts this lethargie,
>And this I murmure in my sleepe;
>Impute this idle talke, to that I goe,
>For dying men talke often so. (ll. 61–66)

All the witty lovers, then, confront the scene of bidding good-bye to their ladies with difficulty. To alleviate their uneasiness and to steel themselves for this painful last encounter, the men momentarily distance themselves from their situation, retreating either into contemplation or into a more casual scene of their own creation, a fictional version of a clever man's farewell to his mistress. As the moments of their final meeting pass, however, the pressure of their circumstances, both internal and external, forces them to confront their fears and anxieties about parting and to express these feelings as honestly as possible. Under this compulsion, they resort to perhaps the most common of the Petrarchan tropes, 'parting is death' and find in it new truths about themselves and their particular circumstances.

The Cavalier Petrarchists

The poems spoken by the Cavalier Petrarchists[10] combine elements of the other two sets of lyrics that explore Petrarchan language. Their flamboyant, sometimes satiric phrasing seems to disparage both the conceits and the sentiment of constancy in love. The lovers in them assume sophisticated, even cynical attitudes toward love, on occasion attributing purity to a licentious woman or mocking devoted lovers who endure unrequited affection. Yet in each poem the ridicule conceals the speaker's intense feelings and thus becomes to some extent an expression of self-contempt.

The degree of self-parody varies considerably from poem to poem and depends in great part on the speaker's ability to work out his dilemma through creating and manipulating a fiction. Each speaker tries on a role for himself at the beginning of his utterance; many of them also confirm the deception of this role by weaving into it what Erving Goffman calls "derisive collusion," those subtle signs by which a person acknowledges that his words and actions are meant for show only.[11] Through the process of the poem the speaker seems to invalidate his newly acquired posture, only to confirm its truth—sometimes its ironic truth—through a sudden reversal at the end of the poem.[12] In these poems the delicate tension between the speaker as creator and as lover undergoes some spectacular transformations. When he encounters his lady he sets his fictional role in collision with a candid appraisal of his circumstances and thus in effect addresses two different audiences: himself and, so he believes, a naïve woman. Beginning his interchange with a Petrarchan conceit, the man gradually denigrates it by avowing to see his lady for what she really is or to know himself honestly. After he has flattened every remnant of hyperbole, however, with an ironic reversal he restates in plain terms the sentiment of his original conceit. Thus, in spite of its heightened and therefore falsified language, the original posture, which each speaker undermines by the verbal equivalent of winking, is in great part an accurate one. In those lyrics that ostensibly have no listener, the speaker attributes his difficulties with love to some fictional aspect of romance and attacks that rather than the real source of his dilemma. He thus momentarily relieves his frustration through creation and at the same time removes himself from the pressure of his lovesickness. In his newly adopted role he examines both the fiction and his feelings until he reconciles the two, thus building his emotional harmony on a delicate tension.

In five of these poems the lover confronts his mistress (or her surrogate) in the guise of a long-suffering Petrarchist, and the poems become dramatic equivalents of love complaints, where the Cavalier Petrarchist proposes a remedy for his ailment. In "The Dreame" that restorative is sexual. The lover believes he can outwit his promiscuous mistress, even flatter her into going to bed with him, by treating her as if she were the aloof Laura of Petrarch's sonnets. But, as happens in many of Donne's dramatic encounters, the pressure of the confrontation pushes the speaker out of his controlled posture to the very role of the unrequited lover he so glibly mimics, until unwittingly he directs his parody back on himself.

His exaggerated compliments have just an edge of mockery and thus undercut his performance as a courtly lover, reminding us, himself, and, if she is wise, the lady that flattery is part of the game of seduction:

> Deare love, for nothing lesse then thee
> Would I have broke this happy dreame,
>   It was a theame
> For reason, much too strong for phantasie. (ll. 1–4)

Even those laudations which seem the most extreme carry an equivocation, as if the speaker calculates both the effect of his words and the limits of his own honesty. The interpretation of his whole utterance depends on how truthfully both he and the woman evaluate her character. The key word of his remarks, *thee,* he leaves undefined, thereby insisting that she construe his praise in the light of her own self-knowledge or self-delusion. The more egotistical she is, the better his chances:

> It could not chuse but bee
> Prophane, to thinke thee any thing but thee (ll. 19–20)

and

> Comming and staying show'd thee, thee. (l. 21).

To appeal to her vanity, he mixes his references to her with allusions to idealized love and perfect beings. He tells her that his dream about her was "a theame / For reason, much too strong for phantasie," thus seeming to imply that their love is perfect and true, first born of reason, then begetting desire.[13] His apology for demeaning her by mistaking her for an angel virtually equates her with God, for only He and she have the power to interpret man's thoughts. And with superlative hyperbole he leads into this most audacious claim through the parenthetical "For thou lov'st truth" (l. 14). Thus, until the woman responds to him, he has both perspicacity about his situation and control over it.[14]

But his calculations about her vanity and sophistication go awry, for she does not succumb to his flattery and follow him into bed. Rather she sees through his game, perhaps enjoying the irony of his applying such idealizing compliments to her. Thus paradoxically his plea for her self-appraisal, by which he hoped to ensnare her, turns on him, subtly suggesting his need to revaluate his situation and his judgment. His clever parody of the Petrarchan lover and his conceited mistress becomes in effect, then, self-mockery.[15] Who else is so blinded by his witty compliments to imagine that a woman would take them seriously? His assumption that he can safely speak to this woman with *double entendre* exhibits his extreme egotism (the very quality he attributes to her) and his paradoxical and foolish conclusion that a woman of the world is gullible. In other words, his absorption in his wit obstructs his ability to discern just who his listener really is. Grierson's version of the plea at line 10 clarifies the speaker's intent to play a game: "let's act the rest" in contrast with Gardner's "let's do the rest."

Having failed momentarily with his flattery, the speaker takes a different tack, intimidation, to win over the woman in the final stanza of the poem. By labeling any love which contains *"Feare, Shame,* or *Honor"* (1. 26) as weak, he hopes to trick her into proving the strength of her affection. His equation of *Honor* with either *Feare* or *Shame* raises some semantic problems, particularly in this parody of a Petrarchan lover's encomium to his beloved. More importantly, however, his change of approach from flattery, however qualified, to fear tactics exposes his desperation. His return to the role of an abject lover in the final lines of the poem thus becomes a travesty:

> Perchance as torches which must ready bee,
> Men light and put out, so thou deal'st with mee,
> Thou cam'st to kindle, goest to come; Then I
> Will dreame that hope againe, but else would die. (ll. 27–30)

Even though his similes and verbs insist through their sexual suggestions on the woman's licentiousness and thus keep the speaker's awareness of her character in the foreground, he still (perhaps in a last desperate maneuver) is driven to assume a role he finds essentially dishonest, even degrading. All the bravado of his "derisive collusion" has disappeared as he fictionalizes how his wish might be fulfilled. Ironically at this point he has lost control of his situation; like the abject Petrarchists he mocks, he complains of his lady's coldness and feeds on hopes that she might change. The fact that he knows she is a salacious woman makes his situation all the more ridiculous (or pathetic), as does his blindness to the paradoxically striking parallel between himself and the unrequited lover of his parody. He too resigns himself to dreaming—of sexual intercourse rather than a loving glance, to be sure—but the content of his imagination in no way mitigates his rejection and his solitude.

So long as the man in "The Dreame" maintains his perspicacity about both his lady and his situation, that is, so long as he remains detached enough from his surroundings to play a role, he controls the encounter. But once he gives rein to his desires for a titillating affair with his mistress, he loses all judgment and becomes the pathetic, unrequited lover he mimics. The speaker in "The Dampe" similarly reveals his need for sexual favors from a disdainful woman, confirming both his entanglement in a hopeless love affair and the aptness of his self-characterization as a Petrarchist, but with cavalier desires.

In these two poems, but especially in "The Dreame," the lover's response to his dramatic situation overpowers his creative detachment from it and he becomes the figure he jokingly sought to portray. In "The Baite" virtually the opposite happens, for the illusion of a dramatic encounter gives way to disclose the speaker as a creative wit. His stance throughout, however, parallels that of the other Cavalier Petrarchists.

Like the speaker in "The Dreame" the lover in "The Baite" pretends to be overcome by the charms and beauty of his lady, only to expose them as the sexual lures of a promiscuous woman. She is the bait that entices multitudes of poor fish to their deaths:

> When thou wilt swimme in that live bath,
> Each fish, which every channell hath,
> Will amorously to thee swimme,
> Gladder to catch thee, then thou him. (ll. 9–12)

Through a series of witty *double entendres* he affects both the hyperbole of a Petrarchist and the sarcasm of a worldly man addressing a jaded lady. Her eyes contain more warmth (heat) than the sun; he needs neither the sun nor the moon to see by, for the woman is "light" enough. His praise by comparison in this encomium celebrates her natural sexual charms over the forced sensual enticements other women offer:

> Let coarse bold hands, from slimy nest
> The bedded fish in banks out-wrest,
> Or curious traitors, sleave-silke flies
> Bewitch poor fishes wandering eyes.
>
> For thee, thou needst no such deceit,
> For thou thy selfe art thine owne bait. (ll. 21–26)

In any case sexual involvement with feminine bait brings only death, of one kind or another. Yet in the final stanza the speaker admits that for all his worldly wisdom he too has been caught. And by writing his song he celebrates the joys of being the woman's victim.

The poem contains self-parody similar to that in "The Dreame," certainly; however, such a reading unduly stresses the dramatic element. Instead the poem's ties with Marlowe's "The Passionate Shepherd to his Love" and Raleigh's "The Nymph's Reply to the Shepherd" insist on it as a bawdy burlesque of the two songs and its speaker as a ribald parodist. He directs his witty wordplay to the clever reader familiar with the other two poems and not finally to the woman he addresses, no matter how discerning we assume her to be. If we postulate that she knows the other poems and assesses "The Baite" in relation to them, she then becomes, not a second-person listener but a detached audience as removed from the exchange as any other reader. The speaker's parody of the love song, however, is strengthened through his pretense as an abject lover, his acknowledgment of his own cynical awareness, and finally his submission to his lady's power.

The dramatic situation dominates in "The Dreame" and dissipates in "The Baite." In "The Broken Heart" neither creative wit nor the encounter preponderates, and the poem splits apart. Nonetheless, it develops very much like the others in this group. The speaker, having fallen in love with a disdainful woman, tells her of his love in hope of gaining her favor. By immersing his avowals in a comic context, however, he provides himself with the means for saving face, should she reject him. He attains this duality by phrasing Petrarchan conceits in slangy language.

> He is starke mad, who ever sayes,
> That he hath beene in love an houre,
>   Yet not that love so soone decayes,
> But that it can tenne in lesse space devour. (ll. 1–4)

As every Petrarchan knows, love kills a man, and in a hurry. Likewise the speaker's analogies of love with the "plague" (l. 6) and a "flaske of *powder*" (l. 8) not only reiterate love's deadly speed but also transform the Petrarchan conventions of the hot and cold flashes of desire and bursts of passion.[16] The speaker thus uses his glittering performance as a man-about-town who flouts sentiment to arouse the woman's romantic interest in him.[17]

But as the poem proceeds, the man's preposterous fiction of a greedy god of love swallowing his victims' hearts whole ("and never chawes," l. 14) and his pose as one of those victims undercut his credibility as a lover. Instead he shows himself to be not only a witty scoffer but one who pretends to be a forlorn wooer. Thus he presents himself at two removes from any romantic encounter, as the subtle change in his subject from his love to the god of love indicates.

By generating an interest of its own, the fiction of a greedy god of love violates the *sine qua non* of Renaissance poetics (what Rosemond Tuve calls "significancy"),[18] that imagery or "ornamentation" should reinforce the subject of the poem. But, of course, that violation occurs only if we take the lover's complaint as the subject of the poem, that is, if we take the dramatic encounter seriously. The tale does support the subject of the poem if that subject is the mockery of Petrarchan idealists and the display of the creator's wit.

When at the end of the poem, however, the lover's Petrarchan avowals to his lady actually disclose something about the nature of love, they
throw the poem off balance.

My ragges of heart can like, wish and adore,
But after one such love, can love no more. (ll. 31–32)

Concisely he enumerates the guises that pass for love: friendship, desire, and awe. And although love is not composed of these feelings, it
contains them. The speaker's tale of a shattered heart thus unexpectedly
corroborates the very romantic viewpoint it was meant to destroy. With
this twist, both the man-about-town and his parody of a forlorn lover
vanish, leaving the sincere wooer beneath the two masks. The abrupt
change, however, does not finally dispel the image of the speaker as a
witty and risqué creator, and his credibility as a lover is never fully
restored. In "The Dampe" as well, but to a lesser degree, the speaker's
fiction of an imaginary battle between the woman and her giants, Disdain and Honor, detracts from the plausibility of the dramatic encounter.

Thus far, then, Donne has blended dramatic and lyric elements in
different proportions in these poems about Petrarchan language and
love, rendering some of them comic and some straightforward. As if he
were experimenting with yet another mingling of these two elements, in
"[Image and Dream]" Donne has the speaker address his mistress's
image as if it were the woman herself; that is, he has him use her image
as a mute actor in his psychodrama.[19] The fiction of a lyric poet muttering to himself thus modulates to that of a dramatic speaker staging a
solitary rehearsal of the scene in which he will break off his romance.
His original motivation fades, however, as he becomes more entangled
with his psychodrama; he projects his anger, frustration, and love onto
the surrogate until he defines his feelings. Thus this seemingly dramatic
exchange ultimately proves lyric as the illusion of even an imagined
listener dissolves into the semblance of a man thinking out loud.

As the poem opens, the lover banishes the image of his proud and
self-centered mistress, his heart, which held that image, and his reason
and supplants them with his imagination, which in turn creates a sensual rival to his lady—a dream version of her. Thus, although ostensibly
the man directs his attack and taunts at the woman's picture, in fact,
because his heart and reason hold on to her image, he is berating himself. His drama then, covers up a psychomachia, where the man's sensual imagination (and Renaissance theory gives the imagination control
over dreams) combats and momentarily defeats his reason. Yet the illusion of a dramatic confrontation with his lady's surrogate persists, as he

boasts of his sexual satisfaction with his dream mistress and vows to immortalize her in sonnets:

> After a such fruition I shall wake,
>   And, but the waking, nothing shall repent;
> And shall to love more thankfull Sonnets make,
>   Then if more honour, teares, and paines were spent. (ll. 17–20)

Abruptly he breaks from his cynicism to celebrate not only his virtuous lady but his own honorable, though frustrating, love, as if he realizes that by castigating the woman who refuses him sexual favors, he is ultimately denigrating his own idealism.

> But dearest heart, and dearer image stay;
>   Alas, true joyes at best are dreame enough;
> Though you stay here you passe too fast away;
>   For even at first lifes Taper in a snuffe. (ll. 21–24)

He moves, in other words, from a myopic vision of his circumstances to a long-range view; and his psychomachia concludes with reason defeating his sensual imagination. At the same time, having gained self-knowledge and perspective, he halts the psychodrama altogether, to pray for the strength to continue in his virtuous, maddening love.

"[Image and Dream]" contrasts with the other poems in this section primarily in the degree of honesty with which the speaker displays his feelings. That openness, of course, coincides with the fact that he is alone, pitting his sensual desires against his reason in love. That he believes himself more cynical than he is and acts on that conviction, however, perhaps throws some light on the "derisive collusion" in all of these poems. Perhaps in playing the flouter of tradition as well as the sentimental lover, each man to some extent tests the validity of each role for his particular situation.

In two other poems, "Loves Deitie" and "The Triple Foole," unrequited lovers begin by mocking Petrarchan conceits and fictions and conclude by sustaining the validity of the sentiment behind those conceits and fictions. Because these poems are not addressed to the lady in question, they contain none of the "derisive collusion" of lyrics like "The Dreame" or "The Broken Heart." Even the hint of a listener (the *wee* in "Loves Deitie" and the abrupt, colloquial opening of "The Triple Foole") evaporates, and the poems generate the illusion of a poet/speaker shaping his thoughts into song. The opposing views toward love, then, reflect the men's changing states of mind and mellowing emotions as well as their defenses for coping with loss. Among the Cavalier Petrarchists these are the most lyric singers.

In "Loves Deitie" the speaker's cry for an authority to discredit Cupid almost immediately modulates into a variation of a commonplace complaint:

> I long to talke with some old lovers ghost,
>   Who dyed before the god of Love was borne:
> ....
> But since that god produc'd a destinie,
> And that vice-nature, custome, lets it be;
> I must love her, that loves not mee. (ll. 1–2, 5–7)

Like numerous rejected lovers in thousands of lyrics, he blames Cupid's mismanagement for his plight, and the pretext of conferring with a lover who lived before that Eros-come-lately—dramatic as those present-tense opening lines sound—only initiates his clever variation on Cupid's perversity.[20] He even identifies himself as a poet, one who writes to and commends the god of love (l. 17). This man's witty rendering of Cupid lore derives from his meticulous application to it of religious terminology. Cupid exhibits his lack of charity by capriciously predestining star-crossed lovers (cf. "destinie," l. 5), even damning them, if we understand "sunke so low" (l. 4) as going to Hell (OED). In contrast, when he was truly a god of love, Cupid "indulgently" fit "actives to passives" (ll. 11–12), that is, with a relaxation of restraint—no doubt moral—he paired couples, joined men and women sexually, and all the while, in the more strictly religious sense of *indulgently*, offered them remission for their sins (OED). In addition, the lover's comic portrayal of Cupid as the child-god staging a *coup d'état* on Olympus and simultaneously subjugating men dilutes his complaint. Thus his carefully constructed fiction and smoothly melodic lines (twelve of the twenty-seven predominantly end-stopped lines rhyme) reinforce his primary identity as a poet/singer. And the interest in "Loves Deitie" arises from the speaker's witty "invention," from his new rendering of a traditional subject.

Surprisingly, then, in the final stanza the speaker not only reverses his complaint, but seems to step out of his role as poet/singer, reviewing with critical appraisal both his complicity in contributing to Cupid lore and the ultimate seriousness of his romantic rejection. In other words, he calls attention to himself as a man, not as a creator.

> Rebell and Atheist too, why murmure I,
>   As though I felt the worst that love could doe? (ll. 22–23)

By immediately defining himself as both a nonbeliever and an opponent of this fictional god of love, he obliquely questions why he is writing "Loves Deitie" in the first place, since it avers Cupid's divinity even if it does question his legitimate right to that power. More directly, *murmure*, meaning to complain or repine in low muttered tones (*OED*) and often used religiously, points to the speaker's examination of himself as one of Cupid's subjects (and, perhaps, since muttering rarely passes for good poetry, to his self-appraisal as a lyricist). He holds his rebuff in love (supposed or actual) up to close analysis and finds it less devastating than his complaint would make it seem. Rejection is not the worst experience with love a man can suffer; worse still would be to lose his interest in romance altogether or become ensnared in a tangle of duplicity. Indeed, this particular speaker's circumstances affirm both the beauty and the ideal of true love:

> Love . . . might trie
>   A deeper plague, to make her love mee too,
> Which, since she loves before, I'am loth to see;
>   Falsehood is worse then hate. (ll. 24–27)

Yet for all his abandonment of the role of singer of love songs, he continues the artistic pattern of religious language wittily applied to the god of love, the melodic lines, and the refrain in the final stanza.[21] Thus paradoxically he rejects his lyric activities in song.

In "The Triple Foole" the speaker, identifying himself as one who has tried the cure, examines the time-honored Petrarchan remedy for a broken heart, writing love complaints.

> I am two fooles, I know,
> For loving, and for saying so
>   In whining Poëtry. (ll. 1–3)

His blunt language seems to deny the human dignity in either loving or versifying, but he immediately qualifies that impression:

> But where's that wiseman, that would not be I,
>   If she would not deny? (ll. 4–5)

The abrupt colloquialism of this opening sentence hints at a listener, a scornful fellow, perhaps, whose cynicism about love the speaker has heard before and now seems to accept. But that cynical listener could as well be the speaker himself, an embodiment of his self-doubt and his haunting fears of appearing foolish, whom he addresses in graphic terms. Even if we posit a legitimate listener, however, the persona uses him as a sounding board, for the speaker backs off from the questioning that might bring answers and from the subject of love to relate his reasons for trying his hand at poetry and his consequent experiences. His subject thus becomes autobiographical and ultimately philosophical.

As he examines his reasons for writing poetry and his responses to hearing his lyrics set to music, he delves into such questions as the artist's pride in his work, the artist's willingness to have his private feelings made public, and the validity of creation as a cure for heartache. The subtle slippage from the past tense, in which he tells his original rationalization for writing ("I thought," l. 6), to the present perfect tense, in which he recounts having poems set to music by ambitious composers ("I have done so," l. 12), intimates that pride in his creation continues to dominate his decisions. He thus punishes himself emotionally for literary recognition, foolish as that may be. The listener (or the illusion of one) provides the excuse for verbalizing an internal dilemma that is underscored by the speaker's self-derision and simultaneous decision to continue writing and reliving his painful rejection. One final, tantalizing question hangs over this poem: will this lyric be set to music and sung also?

The poems of the Cavalier Petrarchists, then, confront the complex interplay between saying and feeling, between adopting an attractive pose critical of love and being sentimental. In all of the poems the man's feelings ultimately control him, no matter how much he protests. Yet to note these similarities without qualification is to misconstrue the thrust of the poems.

Like the other lyrics in this chapter, these explore the implications of speaking in the language of the Petrarchists. Hence the nature of each man's love matters less than his terminology and his posture. All of the poems, with the possible exception of "[Image and Dream]," are tinged with humor, many of them submerged in it. And for the greater part of each poem, the speaker's wit dominates, sometimes spinning preposterous fictions out of Petrarchan conceits and Cupid lore and sometimes applying the most sentimental Petrarchisms to women of questionable virtue—all with pinpoint accuracy. Yet in the turnabout closure of each poem, the speaker acknowledges his emotional bondage to a disdainful woman, acting out the archetypal Petrarchan situation. Thus many of these lyrics teeter on that thin line between comic and straightforward poetry; "The Broken Heart" even splits apart.

The vacillation in tone corresponds with the mixing of dramatic and lyric elements in the poems. Only "The Dreame" sustains the illusion of an encounter; and in that poem the speaker's parody of a Petrarchan lover turns back on him with a vengeance, virtually obliterating his lighthearted banter as he finds himself emotionally shackled to a licentious woman. In the others that create the sense of a dramatic situation, the speaker ultimately discloses himself as a witty fellow playing with Petrarchan language against the backdrop of a scene. "The Triple Foole" and "Loves Deitie" make no real dramatic claim. At the other end of the dramatic-lyric spectrum, the man in "[Image and Dream]" projects his soul-searching into a psychodrama. Unlike the man in "The Dreame," this lover adores a virtuous but aloof woman; and even though he acknowledges the emotional frustration of continuing such an attachment, he preserves his self-respect and honor in the relationship. The man in "The Dreame" does not. These two dream poems, more than any in the group, delve into the complex intertwining of sexual desire, honor, and language. And they confirm a general tenet of the *Songs and Sonnets*, that purely sexual love debases the lover.

* * *

The uses of Petrarchan language in these three sets of poems range from parody to flattery to sincere expression of complex feelings as a lover embarks on a dangerous journey. All of these applications revitalize the conceits. Many of them also question the stance of an unrequited lover who continues to adore a disdainful woman. The Parodists treat that stance as a character type fit for mockery. But since these speakers really play games with Petrarchan language, their criticisms of love are, at best, oblique. The Cavalier Petrarchists, however, manipulate courtly terminology as a ploy for seduction and in the process seem to discredit the sentiment of a forlorn lover. Yet they fulfill the very standpoint they mimic, for each in some way is emotionally chained to the posture of an unrequited lover. Only the Witty Lovers find Petrarchan conceits richly true to the complexity of their feelings at parting and literally true to the possibility of their dying on their journeys. Of the three groups of speakers, only these experience reciprocal love. Donne, then, paradoxically shows Petrarchan conceits, which derive from an unrequited romance, to be the most expressive language of mutual love.

3

The Extremists

Two groups of lovers and a single speaker create the extremes on the spectrum of love in the *Songs and Sonnets*: the Hedonists (whose views are divorced from any ethical context), the Platonic Lovers (in the vernacular sense), and a Negative Lover, if he may be called a lover at all. All of these extremists maintain a greater distance between themselves and their listeners than do the speakers in the other *Songs and Sonnets*. The relative equality of the dramatic encounter thus gives way to a superior-inferior relationship in these poems, and the vitality of face-to-face confrontation modulates to the more subdued atmosphere of a storyteller relating a yarn or a lecturer delivering an address.[1] The Negative Lover and the Hedonists approach their listeners with the formality of an orator or a professor. The Platonic Lovers, less removed from their listeners than the other extremists, nonetheless separate themselves from a direct rhetorical relationship with them because they narrate a large portion of their utterances.

All of these speakers want to justify their views about love. Hence instead of experiencing a particular moment in a relationship or celebrating the sublimity of their feelings or their mistresses, as most of the other speakers in the *Songs and Sonnets* do, these lovers try to vindicate their love lives. And some of them try to convert their listeners to a particular standpoint on love. Thus didacticism replaces intimacy in the most extreme poems; in all the teaching element dilutes the closeness of the face-to-face encounters that characterize Donne's lyrics.

One of these speakers' chief means for persuading their listeners is reference to authority. And all but one of these poems contain large segments of narration, which consists either of a pseudohistorical tale, like the fiction about the originator of monogamy in "Confined Love," or of snippits from the speaker's autobiography (or fantasized future autobiography) that support a particular view of love. "Communitie," the one poem with no narrative element, uses the terminology of Stoicism and hence supposedly the authority of that stringent philosophy to countenance sensualism.

With few exceptions only speakers with extreme views of love in the *Songs and Sonnets* rely heavily on narrative to present their philosophical positions, their experiences, their fantasies, or their beliefs about their spiritual worth.[2] Because narrative by its very nature insists that the speaker is privy to material his listeners are not, a narrator assumes a position of authority, even temporarily. An autobiographical narrator is beyond refutation. Most of the extremists to some extent are autobiographical narrators. Since as Scholes and Kellogg point out, autobiography itself contains the potential for fabrication, is indeed derived from the tradition of the traveler's tale, which has evolved into our "fish" story, the very fact that these particular speakers choose to narrate their own stories arouses suspicions about their reliability.[3] When one compounds this generic doubt with Donne's own propensity for satire, it becomes clear that in these poems Donne is manipulating the technique of a narrator for all its potentially ironic entanglements. He sets up, in other words, the speaker's coherent fiction about love and asks the reader to sift that fiction through the intellectual strainers of his own experiences and of his understanding of the narrator himself. Ironically, through his performance as orator or storyteller, however, the speaker exposes himself: his choice of imagery, the shape of his narrative, his puns, and sound or sense associations all reveal the man beneath the public speaker by showing his fears, desires, and misgivings trying to pierce the controlled and formal picture he presents.[4] These lyrical elements move on a collision course with the reporter's version of himself, with the material he consciously intends to convey. And the reader assumes the triple role of listener to the narrative itself, of spectator to a speech delivered before a different audience, and of a scrutinizing peruser of a lyric.

Another factor that distinguishes these more narrative poems from the dramatic ones involves time, particularly the speaker's relationship to his present circumstances. In the dramatic poems the speaker is so absorbed in his intense moment that the present becomes his all; he frequently draws into it his whole past and imagines his future developing from it. To the autobiographical reporter, however, the present moment of his narrative affords him an opportunity for returning to the past or for projecting a future. This subtle rejection of the present indicates the reporter's uneasiness with his situation, and he attempts to transcend it by replacing the here and now with another time, another place, or other conditions.

The fact that most of the extremists in the *Songs and Sonnets* are narrators poses some tantalizing questions about Donne's departure from his usual method of a dramatic encounter in the love lyrics. Other poems in the *Songs and Sonnets*, to be sure, contain narrative elements—"The

Apparition," for example—and the narrative elements in these poems raise many of the questions that apply to the extremists as well. With the exception of the speaker in "The Exstasie," however, only those lovers with radical views rely heavily on narration. One must ask, therefore, why Donne chooses to present the extremists as narrators. Does the fact of relating a story itself intimate an innate and perhaps necessary deception on the part of the speakers? Does the narrative-dramatic form of the poems show the speakers' need to convince themselves and others of the validity of their experiences? Does the autobiographical impulse in a lyric indicate a degree of solipsism?

The Hedonists

Forming one extreme on the spectrum of lovers in the *Songs and Sonnets*, the Hedonists define love as sexual appetite and celebrate those who can most fully satisfy their hunger.[5] When they experience the cloying of sensuality, rather than question their concept of love, they declare the emotion itself a sham. Interestingly Donne makes one of the two women speakers in the *Songs and Sonnets* a sensualist, indeed an avid enthusiast for a multiplicity of lovers.

> Good is not good, unlesse
> A thousand it possesse,

she exclaims in "Confined Love" (ll. 19–20). Perhaps this inclusion reflects the cynicism about women that appears in Donne's *Juvenilia* and many of the other lyrics, or perhaps it reflects his realization that lust consumes women as well as men.

With the exception of "Loves Usury," the poems of the Hedonists are structured as oratorical persuasions in which the speakers blame "wise nature," Cupid, "love" (an entity, almost a person separable from the lover), and the originator of monogamy for the condition of the world that necessitates a philosophy such as theirs. In other words, they create the cosmos in their own image. They try to win over their audience by acting like morally and intellectually superior men—a Stoic philosopher in "Communitie," for example, and a scientist in "Farewell to Love"— and by urging an identification between themselves and their listeners: they repeatedly use *we* for *I* and throw out rhetorical questions as if to force their audience's consent. But in the formal close of their speeches where the oratorical appeal to emotion takes place, a graphic metaphor shatters their illusion of delicacy and cautious reasonableness. In its equation of women and goods (or in "Confined Love" of men and goods), the trope puts the earlier part of the utterance in an ironic perspective and bares the persona as one who camouflages his crude views with a mask of scholarly gentility. In "Communitie," for example, the supposed Stoic advocates rampant promiscuity through a food metaphor:

> Chang'd loves are but chang'd sorts of meat,
> And when hee hath the kernell eate,
>   Who doth not fling away the shell? (ll. 22–24)

"Eating meat" is a Renaissance euphemism for having intercourse, usually with a whore.[6] And in "Farewell to Love" the man who supposedly approaches love with scientific detachment grossly equates sexual union with the anaphrodisiac wormseed:

>   If all faile,
> 'Tis but applying worme-seed to the Taile. (ll. 39–40)

After all, he reasons, a physical relationship, like wormseed, only lessens sexual desire temporarily. If by *worme-seed* the man means an anthelmintic such as swine's fennel or sulpherwort, the grotesqueness of his metaphor is intensified, although the meaning remains essentially the same.[7] By illuminating the disproportion between each man's refined language and his vulgar ideas, then, the metaphors demonstrate that for all their boasting, the Hedonists both acknowledge the baseness of sensualism and are consumed by physical desires—so consumed, in fact, that they break their tightly controlled performances to respond to it.

Although "Loves Usury," like the other poems, purports to be a speech of persuasion (this one directed at Cupid), the disparity between language and meaning is absent, as is the final revealing trope. Instead this impudent attempt to bargain with Cupid for years of philandering sets forth explicitly the details of sensual life that the other Hedonists couch in genteel and philosophical terms.

The individual sensualists differ from one another in the degree of their self-consciousness as creators, as if Donne were presenting comic and straightforward variations on hedonistic love. As we have already seen, the humorous poems within the *Songs and Sonnets* violate the rules in poetry manuals by exaggerating the tropes and rhetorical figures and by subtly shifting their subject from love to a fiction about Cupid, for example. This gamelike quality has led some commentators to read the poems as preposterous rhetorical exercises like the *Paradoxes and Problems*: delightful, complex, and insignificant.[8] Be that as it may, the most comic poems develop precisely in the same way as those whose subject matter seems more realistic, as if Donne were experimenting, consciously or not, with a given Character, with his manner of holding his audience and his means of ultimately disclosing himself—in other words, with the interplay between his need for self-definition and his pull toward self-concealment.

Like all the narrators in the *Songs and Sonnets*, most of the Hedonists reject the present for another time, past or future. They, however, disclaim not only the here and now, but reality altogether, positing instead a fictional time when life was or will be to their liking. In their narratives, therefore, they become creators of worlds as well as of words; and subtly they make a literal application of the poet acting *in imitatio dei*.

Although it opens with a direct address to Cupid, "Loves Usury" sketches the fantasies of a would-be philanderer. As the speaker details the life he would like to lead, he touches on the philosophical bases for libidinous living that all the other Hedonists illustrate. He makes a Faustian bargain by promising his body and soul to Cupid in return for a number of years of unbridled dissipation and asks for sensual pleasure without emotional entanglements, that moral limbo advocated by all of the sensualists. Indeed, for half of his utterance the persona leaps into the cosmic harem he has imagined and celebrates the joys of that world. As if to temper his licentiousness, however, the speaker pretends to be Cupid's victim. The title implies that the hard-driving moneylender, Love, will exact his due from the man; ironically the Hedonist, not Cupid, gets the best of the bargain, even though his rhetoric insists on the god's extra measure of the interest.

The colloquial opening of the poem with its impudent direct address to Cupid evokes the illusion of the one-to-one encounter of Donne's most dramatic lyrics, and with our disbelief well suspended we can almost see an astonished Eros listening to the outrageous demands of this insolent man.

> For every houre that thou wilt spare mee now,
>   I will allow,
> Usurious God of Love, twenty to thee,
> When with my browne, my gray haires equall bee. (ll. 1–4).

But the generic complexities of this poem qualify the limits of its drama, and the speaker's imaginative leap into his libidinous future, guarded as it is by his constant concern for Cupid's permission, still tends to reduce the god of love to a conventional backdrop against which this rake can act out his delightful inversion of a love complaint. By definition a complaint often appeals directly to the person or deity who can remedy the speaker's dilemma, so that the bold name-calling in the opening lines really is more traditional than it seems. Spenser uses it almost as forcefully in Sonnet 10 of the *Amoretti*:[9]

Unrighteous Lord of Love, what law is this,
That me thou makest thus tormented be. (ll. 1–2)

Numerous other sonneteers berate the naughty Cupid for his mismanagement of their affairs in rather brusque terms. "Loves Usury" in that
sense is no different, nor would a seventeenth-century reader see it as
particularly dramatic.

What does separate it from other love complaints is the specific request for unbridled sensuality and the speaker's cunning manipulation
of Cupid. Rather than lamenting his woes and pleading for solace, he
elaborates his plans for debauchery to Cupid, then asks the god to give
his assent or at least to turn his head. In other words through his
repeated "let mee's" he seems to be requesting the deity's permission to
carry on his philandering, to assist this mere mortal in his quest for
romantic bliss and the ease of his pain, very much in the manner of
straightforward complaints. In fact, however, he is duping Eros with his
guise of reverence and submission. This sensualist has written new
rules for the game of love he plays. And he, not Cupid, has stipulated
the terms of the bargain ("I will allow" is the main clause of the first
stanza). These witty variations of the lyric complaint, even more surprising than those in Spenser's sonnet above and more disrespectful to the
gods than Ovid in *Amores* 2: vii and viii, which this poem resembles,
force the reader's attention onto the poem's brilliant incongruity and
humor and ultimately onto its risqué creator.

Moreover, Donne's usual practice of making his comic poems more
artificial applies to "Loves Usury" as well. The fiction's premise of a
bargain with the god of love unfolds in meticulous legal and mathematical detail. The rate of interest will be twenty to one; and if he wants,
Eros will receive not only the lover's homage but the revengeful triumph
of having a former debauchee testify to the honor of love. Internal
rhyme frequently intensifies the obvious end rhyme of the poem, as it
does in the opening lines:

For every *houre* that *thou* will spare mee *now*,
    I will *allow* . . .

And at places the alliteration seems excessive:

From country grasse, to comfitures of Court . . . (l. 14)

Thus in one sense at least we can read this poem as a bawdy parody of
fatuous love complaints and note its speaker as a wit displaying his
brilliant sense of humor.

For all of its humor, "Loves Usury" exhibits striking resemblances with the serious hedonistic lyrics in the *Songs and Sonnets*, most notably through the speaker's treatment of his listeners, his revelation of self, and his imaginative creation of a sensual Utopia. First, for all the illusion of an encounter, this speaker really uses Cupid as an excuse to reveal the details of his life, or more precisely, of his licentious fantasy of life. The other Hedonists use their human listeners similarly. They and Cupid serve either as a backdrop against which the speaker performs or as a sounding board against which he bounces his ideas. Second, the speakers all use their listeners as support for their licentious living. In "Loves Usury" the man asks for Cupid's permission to let his "body raigne" (l. 5). Like all the sensualists, he wants to control his life yet have a scapegoat for his actions—here, of course, the best one possible, the god of love. The listener in "Loves Usury," then, like the hearers in the other hedonistic poems, provides the speaker with the excuse for his utterance, with assent (or seeming assent) for his ideas, and with the authority of one who can take the responsibility for the Hedonist's actions.

The speaker himself, on the other hand, tries to maintain the aura of reasonableness. The particular form of this mask varies from poem to poem; here is a shrewd businessman driving a hard bargain. The close attention to details of interest and reward reinforce this illusion, and his seeming devotion to Cupid makes him appear pious as well. But as he celebrates the licentious joys of his fictional future, his control breaks down and he veritably leaps at the prospect of his titillating adventures:

> let
> Mee travell, sojourne, snatch, plot, have, forget,
> Resume my last yeares relict: thinke that yet
>   We'had never met.
>
> Let mee thinke any rivalls letter mine,
>   And at next nine
> Keepe midnights promise; mistake by the way
> The maid, and tell the Lady'of that delay. (ll. 5–12)

He even uses food imagery to describe the women he will sample:[10]

> From country grasse, to comfitures of Court,
> Or cities quelque choses . . . (ll. 14–15)

These tasty dishes he claims will "transport" his "minde" (l. 16). Cupid indeed must have taken leave of his senses if he believes in that kind of traffic.

But for all its fictional framework and its carefully delineated speaker, "Loves Usury" concentrates on that man's sensual Utopia. For twelve of the poem's twenty-four lines, he details the seductive pleasures and delusions of his Don Juan existence, if Cupid will only give the nod. Thus even in this delightful burlesque, the Hedonist rejects his present for another time when life was or will be more amenable to his sexual desires. He wishes for the illusion that his paramour of last year is new to him, for the deception that any *billet doux* signals a rendezvous with him. In return for the realization of these blue dreams, he will make the most humiliating expiation he can imagine, falling in love. His comic parody of Christian redemption through love, although witty in the context of this poem, also reminds us that every Hedonist in Donne's *Songs and Sonnets* has a sense of guilt.

Both because of the comic tone in "Loves Usury" and because of the lyric convention of Cupid as a listener, neither the speaker's pose as a staunchly reasonable man nor his guilt dominates the poem. With the absence of a listener, the speaker has no need to maintain a convincingly moderate image and with a wink addresses himself instead to the sophisticated reader familiar enough with other love complaints to be amused by the shocking departures in this one.

In "Loves Diet," on the other hand, the speaker stands before human listeners. Although this poem is just as comic as "Loves Usury," the presence of an audience accounts for the speaker's intensified self-portrait as a discerning man and for his careful camouflage of his ideas and feelings until the end of his utterance. The rational, persuasive manner in which this sensualist couches his sexual philosophy immediately shows him to be well governed. He offers a testimonial on how he managed to bring love under control, thereby picturing himself at once as a fellow who rules his passions, perhaps one of the oldest and happiest images of man.[11]

> To what a combersome unwieldinesse
> And burdenous corpulence my love had growne,
>   But that I did, to make it lesse,
>   And keepe it in proportion,
> Give it a diet, made it feed upon
> That which love worst endures, *discretion*. (ll. 1–6)

With bulbous, dissonant words he describes the ugliness of untamed love's "combersome unwieldinesse" and "burdenous corpulence." Then he contrasts these heavy words with "proportion," which carries not only the sense of size but of harmony, and *"discretion,"* which alludes to rational behavior, politeness, and modesty. And from the opening stanza he pictures himself as correcting the misreadings and mistakes of love: "I did . . . / Give it a diet"; "I'allow'd him not" (l. 7); "I let him see" (l. 11); and "I let him know" (l. 15). Indeed, he exalts himself throughout his self-styled heroic utterance as the brave conqueror of that unruly fellow love, a comic inversion, perhaps, of *amor vincit omnia*.

For all the charm of the persona's autobiographical portrait, he never gets close to his listeners. His self-glorification keeps him aloof from them, suggesting a planned detachment so that he can make use of distance to generate their awe.[12] By setting himself up as an example and an expert on love and by remaining apart from his audience, he can command their respect, perhaps even their reverence, and at the same time intimidate them enough so that they will not question him (he uses *I* eleven times, frequently in places of metrical and rhetorical stress). Moreover, since he recounts his personal experience, no one can challenge his facts. He appeals to his audience less than any of the other Hedonists, only obliquely requesting their assent to the question he has already asked Love:

> Ah, what doth it availe,
> To be the fortieth name in an entaile? (ll. 23-24)

No heir could disagree with his implied "nothing at all."

The lack of intimacy between speaker and listener in this poem (and in the lyrics of all the extremists) marks a radical departure from Donne's usual practice in the *Songs and Sonnets*, a change made more significant by this persona's hearkening back to his past and reshaping the events of his love life as both his memory and his purpose in retelling them dictate. That purpose, of course, is to provide philosophical and empirical justification for his philandering. Although as a comic poem "Loves Diet" offers no serious psychological revelations about guilt-ridden sensualists, the contradictions and questionable assumptions of its speaker suggest in a light way the inner conflicts which Donne explores in "Loves Alchymie" and "Farewell to Love." The humorous tale of putting love on a diet coats the story of the speaker's romantic involvement with a woman he believed unfaithful and his consequent restructuring of his love life. The meat of the poem concerns a lover's disillusionment, the material of numerous straightforward complaints, but reshaped to minimize the man's remorse. Outrageously he boasts of his emotional indifference to her and of his intellectual cynicism toward love, both during his one notable affair and since it. But ironically his retelling of the woman's cruelty and of his successful battle against it endows these events with the permanence lyric speakers usually reserve for times of great passion. His aloofness from his audience and his restructuring of the love story also provide him with an insulation from his listeners in some ways comparable to the conventional isolation of the lyric persona. That is, the audience never knows the facts of the matter, only the

singer's interpretation of them. But unlike the lyric speaker, the autobiographical narrator reaches out to his listeners when he needs them
and fashions himself in what he considers the most acceptable image for
winning their approval.

Without distorting the comedy of "Loves Diet" and hence the ingen-
iousness of its wry speaker, one can nonetheless notice the persona's
inconsistencies and the questionable assumptions that cast doubt on
some of his basic tenets. Similar distortions occur in the serious poems
spoken by sensualists, only there they reveal the speakers' guilt and
their insatiable licentiousness. The man in "Loves Diet" builds his explanation of his mistress's behavior, and thus his rationale for controlling love, on the theory that the woman is lascivious. Although we
know nothing about her to dispel his view, his projection of his own
wantonness onto all women in the final stanza raises questions about his
competence in judging at all. The mistress becomes, in his narrative, a
version of himself, rampantly salacious. And he berates Cupid for reading her overtures to him as signs of affection. To the narrator the
woman's tears are lustful sweat, her love letters mockeries because they
were written to the "fortieth name in an entaile," a crude phrase sum-
ming up both her promiscuity and his place in her affections. Moreover,
according to the speaker, his mistress went through the same motions of
love as he does in his enlightened state:

I spring a mistresse, sweare, write, sigh and weepe:
And the game kill'd, or lost, goe talke, and sleepe. (ll. 29–30)

Ironically, by deprecating her for these gestures of love, he indicts himself as lustful: to use his own sibilant words, "eyes which rowle toward
all, weepe not, but sweat" (l. 18). Finally, in a revealing pun, he names
himself accurately: he is one of the "fawkners" (l. 28) who use the
creatures under their control. To him a mistress is like a pheasant to a
falconer: something to be killed—sexual pun intended—or lost. But,
wrenching irony out of irony, Donne has this Hedonist construe his
autobiography as a heroic tale.

As in "Loves Usury," the underlying tone of the poem is gay. The
speaker's delight in sound effects, most noticeably alliterative groupings
of words and half-rhymes, resounds throughout. He matches and contrasts sound groups in "combersome unwieldinesse" and "burdenous
corpulence" (ll. 1–2). He brines his tears with "scorne" or "shame"
(l. 14) and finds that the woman's "favor" made Love "fat" (l. 21). He
even describes his amorous activities in an alliteratively linked parataxis:
"sweare, write, sigh, and weepe" (l. 29). The hourglass shape of the
stanzas, what Northrop Frye calls the "doodle" of lyrical utterance,[13]

seems to emanate from his mental image of a shapely woman or love's trim figure, once he has gone on a diet. Moreover, the precise details of reducing love by feeding him only one "she sigh" (l. 7) a day and a few low-calorie tears undercuts the possibility of reading "Loves Diet" as a serious poem.[14] Bawdy puns fill the lyric. And some lines contain so much internal and end rhyme that even reading them aloud proves difficult, for example, "And that that favour made him fat . . ." (l. 21). Indeed, if one were to apply all Puttenham's warnings about poetic practices that lighten the tone of a poem to "Loves Diet," he would have to conclude either that Donne had been inexcusably careless or precisely correct in manipulating the tone of his poem and his reader. For behind the façade of speaker and audience in this poem lurks that witty creator and a reader as sophisticated as he.

In sharp contrast to these playful advocates of sensuality, the speakers of "Loves Alchymie" and "Farewell to Love" cry out against the despair and disillusionment they have experienced in their casual sexual encounters. They brand love a fictional trap to ensnare unsuspecting, idealistic men like themselves, and repudiate all claims of virtue or intelligence in women, denouncing the sexual act and the sexual partner as, at best, means for physical relief. Indeed they seem zealously committed to converting other men to their beliefs in order to save those men from despair; the utterances of these sensualists approach evangelical testimonials to the disillusionment of love.

In "Loves Alchymie" a disillusioned speaker attempts to discredit love (a term by which he means lust) by presenting himself to his audience as a scientific man whose experiences contradict the prevailing theories about the purifying qualities of love. He compounds his flattering self-portrait by intimating that his search for love was essentially a quest for regeneration, a first step on the Neoplatonic ladder of purification. As a scientist, the narrator says he attempted to validate through experience the philosophical theories about love's power to produce happiness. But the results do not tally. Thus in a sense he sees himself deluded by lovely words and high ideals, much as the man in "Farewell to Love" does, who "did . . . reverence, and gave / Worship" (ll. 3–4) to love. The speaker's sneering contrast between words and deeds, theory and practice, reverberates through the curt verbs *say* and *lov'd, got* and *told,* with the weight of evidence on the side of experience.

> Some that have deeper digg'd loves Myne then I,
> Say, where his centrique happinesse doth lie:
>   I have lov'd, and got, and told,
> But should I love, get, tell, till I were old,
> I should not finde that hidden mysterie;
>   Oh, 'tis imposture all. (ll. 1–6)

Thus he discredits views of love that stress its elevating qualities, jeering at them through riddling *double entendre* in which the most sacred words of Neoplatonic and Hermetic philosophy become sexual metaphors: the "centrique happinesse" "deeper digg'd" by lovers, for example, and the "hidden mysterie" of physical union.[15] His equation of lovers with the "chymique" (l. 7) who "glorifies his pregnant pot" (l. 8) culminates his reproach and at the same time propounds his self-portrait as a scientific man ready to expose the deception of both alchemy and love. He further scoffs at the "loving wretch" (l. 18) who foolishly swears to the Neoplatonic idea of a marriage of the minds, reminding his listeners that such a lamentable creature

> Would sweare as justly, that he heares,
> In that dayes rude hoarse minstralsey, the spheares. (ll. 21–22)

Old wives' tales and superstition, all of it, he seems to say. Then pressing the only logical conclusion his scientific analysis allows, he rhetorically asks:

> Our ease, our thrift, our honor, and our day,
> Shall we, for this vaine Bubles shadow pay? (ll. 13–14)

No reasonable man could answer that in the affirmative. From all practical and honorable points of view, sex (or, in the speaker's terms, love) is not worth a man's time or interest.

As in the other hedonistic poems, the persona's close attention to his image as a scientist implies his desire to impress his listeners. Yet for all his care in creating that picture, once he launches into his autobiography (even disguised as a general lesson on love as it is here), he loses control. The ugliness of his graphic metaphors, his inordinate anger, and his negation of what at first seems an invitation for a discussion about love all signify that he ultimately addresses himself, vituperating against his bitter, disillusioning, disgusting sexual encounters. Indeed they are so repulsive to him that he relates them only imagistically. He opens his speech with a challenge for those who have loved more deeply than he to reveal their mysterious discoveries. (Even if we read the opening lines as a declaration rather than an imperative, his imputation that some people, most notably the Neoplatonists, have made great claims about love seems to allow for a defense from anyone in the audience willing to take up the cause.) Yet he immediately shuts off the possibility of discussion by recounting in bare, reductive language his own amatory experiences: "I have lov'd, and got, and told." From this point on he turns inward, indulging in self-pity and spitting out his loathing for women, or, more fairly, his revulsion for himself projected

onto women. Somewhat melodramatically he recalls his earlier romantic
dreams, then juxtaposes them with his experiences.

> So, lovers dreame a rich and long delight,
> But get a winter-seeming summers night. (ll. 11–12)

Those tales about love duped him, entrapped him, as they do all men,
he declares. Yet the sexual overtones in even this lovely passage belie
his perception of himself as a once dreamy, innocent youth. His disillusionment gives way to anger, and he vents his frustration on the democ-
racy of romance.

> Ends love in this, that my man,
> Can be as happy'as I can; If he can
> Endure the short scorne of a Bridegroomes play? (ll. 15–17)

Only he can answer this rhetorical question. He alone feels the sting of
amatory equality, for he alone characterized himself as a sensitive,
idealistic youth deserving all the bliss amours could offer. The personal
nature of the rhetorical question reveals just how far the speaker has
drifted from his listeners, even though he is still ostensibly addressing
them.

In addition his crude comparisons shatter his stance of a moderate,
intelligent man, reminding us yet again that the speaker no longer
dominates his situation, perhaps that he has momentarily lost touch
with it altogether. He reviles the promises of love with reductive,
graphic metaphors for women's genitals: "pregnant pot" and "vaine
Bubles shadow"—a linkage which reveals his simultaneous obsession
with and loathing for the flesh rather than comments on Neoplatonic
idealism. Indeed he twists the language of Neoplatonic love theories
into tropes for sexual intercourse, again and again ridiculing, mocking,
and reviling his former gullibility, the illusions of love, and his present
sexual compulsion. Through his debasement of everything connected
with love (or lust) he manifests himself more intensely as a jaded sensualist. His reasonable stance and his ultimate revelation collide in
"Loves Alchymie" because the speaker has an audience, because the
dramatic illusion of the poem holds.[16] The listeners stay; the persona,
still physically in their presence, mentally and psychologically withdraws into himself, crying out at the unfairness of love, justifying his life
through his self-portrait as an innocent fooled by high-sounding words.
And everything he utters extemporaneously destroys the impression he
calculatingly tries to create.

Quite surprisingly, then, this sensualist does occasionally turn to his
listeners for a vindication of his ideas. He first very casually includes
them among the disappointed lovers of the world. As a scientific philos-

opher with a good deal of evidence he speaks *ex cathedra*: that love disillusions is a fact. No need even to ask his auditors about that. Next he identifies them with himself in the aforementioned rhetorical question about the high cost of love:

> Our ease, our thrift, our honor, and our day,
> Shall we, for this vaine Bubles shadow pay?

Here he wants agreement to more than just his basic tenet that women are fleshly objects for which men pay an exorbitant physical and emotional price. He wants assent to his feelings of loneliness after intercourse as well, to his sense that even lovemaking is illusory, a "vaine Bubles shadow." To cement his listeners' views with his, he here—and for the only time in the poem—uses the public *we*. Yet he asks too much. No audience could answer the imagistic suggestions in his rhetorical question. Moreover, when, in his second rhetorical question, he scoffs at amatory equality between him and his servant, he drifts away from his listeners altogether, even as he purports to ask for their assent.

> Ends love in this, that my man,
> Can be as happy'as I can; If he can
> Endure the short scorne of a Bridegroomes play?

Indeed the two questions treat such different matters that they create a non sequitur, as if the speaker's thoughts have raced past his words, far beyond his listeners, as he rails to himself in front of them, reexperiencing both desolation and the sting of social rebuff. His final approach to his listeners comes as an imperative and a *sententia*. Once more he assumes the authority of a scientist advising his audience and clearing up some factual misconceptions.

> Hope not for minde in women; at their best
> Sweetnesse and wit, they'are but *Mummy* possest. (ll. 23–24)

Like the speaker in "Farewell to Love," who compares intercourse to an anaphrodisiac, this man sees women (and hence the sexual act) as at best a means of physical relief, a mummy, a lump of dead flesh through which his vital powers are again restored. The man's scientific bent, apparent in his desire to discredit both alchemy and Neoplatonic ideas of love, perhaps adds an edge even to this interpretation. During the sixteenth century Dr. Ambriose Paré and other eminent physicians denounced the use of dead flesh as a restorative.[17] If Donne's narrator shares these enlightened medical views, he undercuts woman's value even more. She is merely mummy, whose supposed power to revitalize has proved ineffective after all.

Having concluded that men cannot find love in this world, the speaker zealously enlightens others on the elusiveness and deception of that emotion. His only imperative warns men about women's limitations: "Hope not for minde in women." His other present-tense statements proclaim eternal truths about the delusive nature of loving: "some . . . / Say, where his centrique happinesse doth lie"; "oh, 'tis imposture all"; "lovers dreame a rich and long delight, / But get a winter-seeming summers night"; and "they'are but *Mummy* possest." A world so constructed deserves no celebration and gets none from this bitter Hedonist. He prefers to argue for the validity of his cynicism and to commemorate his disillusionment, his guilt, and his pain in evangelical addresses to young innocents.

The hedonistic lovers in the *Songs and Sonnets* all refer to an imaginary time or realm where unbridled sport is sanctioned, a licentious version of the golden world. In the playful poems this dream land promises utter bliss; in the serious poems it becomes the object of each man's vilification, for its promise proves deceptive yet its need remains. Since all of the speakers, however, belong to our world with its moral ordering of human life, they feel guilty about their sensual desires and create fictions to justify both their yearnings and their behavior. The comic poems contain preposterous tales and delightful inversions of moral theories, both of which so capture the reader with their witty impudence that they undermine the speaker's validity. The man in "Communitie," for example, justifies salaciousness with such Stoic doctrines as determinism, "things indifferent" (l. 3), the love of virtue, and man's relationship with nature—all undefined, of course. And in "Confined Love" the woman presents herself as a historian who discredits monogamy because of the truth she has discerned about its originator. Autobiographies pervade the serious poems, shaped accounts of the supposedly true ideas which first caught each speaker's imagination and then deluded him. The man's former belief in the sacredness of love in "Farewell to Love," for example, or in the Neoplatonic "hidden mysterie" in "Loves Alchymie."

Acting on the assumption that they can vindicate their beliefs by converting others to their moral positions, the Hedonists court their listeners, even masking before them as philosophers, scientists, and deeply religious men. The man in "Farewell to Love," for example, bases his resolution to abstain from sexual intercourse on the "scientific fact" that nature made man's sexual appetite cloy as a means of self-preservation.[18] And he adopts a Puritan justification for physical union, the desire "to raise posterity" (l. 30), to cover up his yearnings.[19] Yet for all their self-conscious image making, at some point they become so consumed by their feelings that they drift away from their audience to relive their anger and revulsion, in the process exposing their irrational natures. They return to their listeners and resume their rational guises whenever they want support for their conclusions, those often out- rageous generalizations based solely on the sensualists' unexamined emotional response to lust. In "Farewell to Love," for example, the man directs to his audience the rhetorical question which contains his wish for unbridled sexual delight, free from postcoital depression, like that of the animals:

> Ah cannot wee,
> As well as Cocks and Lyons jocund be,
> After such pleasures? (ll. 21–23)

And in "Confined Love" the woman's rhetorical question about pro- miscuity cuts not only at divorce laws but at the natural law on which they are based. For such affairs she wants assent.

> Are birds divorc'd, or are they chidden
> If they leave their mate, or lie abroad at night? (ll. 10–11)

The Hedonists, in other words, fall back on the support of their listeners rather than attempt to understand and control their feelings or pursue the meaning of their revulsion to sex. For underneath their veneer of a rational person in a speaker whose basic assumptions were considered errors in much Renaissance thought. Each confuses love and lust; each equates women (or men) and the sexual act with goods, objects to be used for comfort and ease.

In the best of these poems of sensual love, Donne stretches his generic modifications of the lyric to their limits by setting each aspect of the poem in collision with every other element in it. The dramatic context, for example, the illusion of a man addressing an audience, qualifies the speaker's commemoration of his disgust with women and sensuality for no other reason than that the man asks his listeners to condone his private responses and to validate any conclusions he draws from them. In a lyric poem the illusion of isolation itself confirms the subjective truth of the speaker's feelings and ideas: these are the responses he makes when he is alone, free from the role playing and posturing he might perform in public, and free from the judgment of others. Likewise the Hedonists' revulsion against women calls into question the accuracy of their autobiographies and the depth of their self-perception, in other words the narrative element in the poems. Moreover, the distance be- tween the speaker and his listeners, a remoteness approaching that of an orator and his auditors, renders suspect any overtures the speaker makes toward an interchange with the audience. He cannot maintain both the authority of a narrator and the equality of a companion with his listeners. The limitations of any element ring through the poems *mutatis mutandis* because of Donne's generic hybridizing, but all these restrictions and qualifications ultimately reveal the complexity of the persona, Donne's central focus in his secular love lyrics.

The Platonic Lovers

At the other extreme on the spectrum of lovers in the *Songs and Sonnets* is the Platonic Lover, whose relationship with his lady excludes sexual union altogether.[20] (Those poems that celebrate physical and spiritual union, which are often termed lyrics of Platonic love, are treated in Chapter 5 under the title "The Mutual Lovers.") In one comic and one straightforward poem a Platonic Lover proclaims that love of virtue in a woman is superior to carnal love and, like the Hedonists, admits of no possible blending of the two. Each speaker reveals inner tensions that stem from a mixture of physical desire and physical loathing. Both boast of their superiority to other men because they have abstained from sexual relations, yet they yearn to be rewarded for their sacrifice. Their compensation, of their own making, comes when they turn to the past, reliving their accomplishments as they relate them, or when they project a future in which they will receive the tribute due them and due the virtuous women who have sustained them through their frustration. They shape their experiences or expectations into materials fit for commemoration. Unlike the singers of love complaints, however, these men want approval and praise from a designated listener, not for their poetry, but for their *lives*. But they protect themselves by controlling their relationship with their listener. In recounting their lives, they involve their auditors so intimately that hearer and speaker virtually become one—an identification that admits of no disapproval. Thus, paradoxically, the narrator becomes his own "ear" and attempts to hear his autobiography objectively. This shifting rhetorical relationship allows the Platonic Lover both to create his narrative and to scrutinize it as a literary work, that is, to assume the dual role of autobiographer and chronicler. At the same time if offers him the illusion of support for his ideas from someone else.

From the first word of the comic poem "The Undertaking," the persona exudes heroic bravado, impressing his listener with both the courage and holiness required to be a Platonic Lover.

> I have done one braver thing
>   Then all the *Worthies* did,
> Yet a braver thence doth spring,
>   Which is, to keepe that hid. (ll. 1–4)[21]

He stresses his mettle by proclaiming that he has dared love virtue in a woman (l. 19) and dared "forget the Hee and Shee" (l. 20). He emphasizes the sanctity of his deed by reminding the listener that it must be kept secret from "prophane men" (l. 22). In short, the narrator says he is a man worthy of canonization, someone who combines the bravery of Hector and the godliness of David, subtly underscoring his value by setting his utterance in ballad meter—the only one in the *Songs and Sonnets*. His hyperbolic claims for fortitude turn comic when we realize not only that Platonic love so defined virtually ignores Ficino's beliefs (and he coined the concept), but that by Donne's time this form of Platonic love had become "a hypocritical disguise for refined sexual passion or an empty game fashionable in good society."[22]

Having molded his autobiography into a saint's life, the speaker declares that the untutored listener can be transformed if he will follow in the footsteps of his mentor: "If, as I have, you also doe . . ." (l. 17). Then, projecting his auditor's future as a recapitulation of his own past, he sings of their individual feats in almost identical terms:

> Then you'have done a braver thing
>   Then all the *Worthies* did. (ll. 25–26)

His remaking of his listener into a carbon copy of himself virtually guarantees him immunity from criticism. And his casting of both men's "autobiographies" in almost identical terms reveals him as a creator, one who shapes facts into a preestablished pattern—a hagiography complete with converts.

This shaping and several incongruities in the poem underscore the comic tone: the man's insistence, for example, that his most heroic deed was to keep silent about his love as he relates the details of it to his listener, and his condemnation of his contemporaries for not loving virtue in women even as, through the metaphor of the specular stone, he denies the existence of such women.[23] These incongruities, then, remind us that behind the speaker sits a clever fellow poking fun at a philosophical concept that had already deteriorated into a guise for sexual enticement.[24]

In "The Relique" Donne explores more profoundly and fully than in "The Undertaking" the Platonic Lover's inordinate desire for approval, even glorification, and his wish to vindicate both his ideas and his life. The speaker in this poem formulates for his beloved the miracle of their relationship: he tells her about their future after death, or, more specifically, about the future of his bones, one of which will be encircled with a lock of her hair. Through the bone and a note that he will enclose in his grave, both he and his lady will attain renown, even sainthood, for their wondrous union. Thus, close to his mistress, and perhaps in response to

seeing an open grave, the man meditates on love and death, that primal
linkage of procreation and dissolution. Only he muses out loud, in front
of his beloved, about his own love and death:

> When my grave is broke up againe
> Some second ghest to entertaine . . . (ll. 1–2)

These Platonic Lovers have no stake in the future through children, and
a glimpse at decay and death seems to haunt the man as he resolutely
postulates just what place they will fill in the hereafter. Indeed, his
anticipation of their ultimate glorification so consumes him that he confronts his fictive future listeners, as if face to face, and yet necessarily
through a letter from the grave.

By encasing a narrative for posterity within a narrative spoken to the
woman before him, the speaker imaginatively drifts from his immediate
surroundings to a time when he and his lady will receive the reward to
which their present life entitles them. Thus, for the moment he cares
less about the image he presents to his beloved than about making a
good impression on his future audience: the fictional gravedigger who
exhumes his body, the imagined bishop to whom his remains will be
taken, and the unknown generation who will read his chronicle. Of
course the woman hears his tale and overhears the praise of her in the
note intended for posterity, and part of the tension in the poem arises
from the question of how fully the speaker manipulates his fictions to
influence her. But his inordinate need for recognition, at least until the
final lines of the poem, pushes him to create a carefully drawn picture of
himself and his lady as idyllically happy lovers.

The exact nature of their happiness, however, is open to conflicting
interpretations by the people of the future, interpretations which grow
from the ambiguity of the relic itself. For the "bracelet of bright hair
about the bone" (l. 5) creates both the figure of the theta and the image
of sexual union. As a theta, first letter in the Greek *thanatos*, the "bracelet
of bright hair" becomes an image of the speaker's mortality and his
immortality, a combination implied by the concept of relic, particularly a
saint's relic. As a symbol of sexual union, however, the "bracelet of
bright hair" conflicts with the speaker's accolades about his Platonic
friendship, all the more because the gravedigger, the bishop, and the
king all misread the relic as a sign that the two were either lovers or
Christ and Mary Magdalene in their fictional roles as lovers.[25] That is to
say, through the ambiguity of the relic the speaker creates a spectral
autobiography open for misinterpretation. Moreover, he imagines this
mistaken autobiography so vividly that he envisions himself responding
to an intruding gravedigger with a lover's wish for intimate seclusion in
the tomb:

> Will he not let'us alone
> And thinke that there a loving couple lies,
> Who thought that this device might be some way
> To make their soules, at the last busie day,
> Meet at this grave, and make a little stay? (ll. 7–11)

He imagines that the gravedigger will recognize the relic as an image of a deep and devoted affection in which the lovers' physical union symbolizes their spiritual union, the very blending that constitutes ideal love in the writings of such Neoplatonists as Leone Ebreo.[26] By conjuring up a workman with such romantic and elevated thoughts, then, the speaker brings to the fore an almost perfect mutual love, yet one that these Platonic Lovers do not share. Moreover this fictional interpretation of the lovers elevates them to saints in a land of misdevotion, and the two are canonized first on false grounds:

> then
> Thou shalt be'a Mary Magdalen, and I
>   A something else thereby;
> All women shall adore us, and some men. (ll. 16–19)

Here the complex interplay among the speaker, the fictional gravedigger, and the lady intensifies; for the gravedigger's mistake and the subsequent sainthood both confirm the validity of mutual love that includes sexual intercourse. One can only speculate on whether or how much the speaker intends this authorization to influence the lady to change her relationship with him. At the very least, the presence of this satisfying, mutual love reminds us that he acknowledges the possibility of such a union, in spite of his cynicism about women's constancy:

> (For graves have learn'd that woman-head
> To be to more than one a Bed). (ll. 4–5)

The speaker's second image of himself unfolds through his note, which clarifies the meaning of the relic and sets straight the intriguing misinterpretation it propagated. In this version he is a saint because he wondrously managed to keep his love free from sexual involvement. The audience for this version is wider, "that age" (l. 21); and the chronicle of the lovers' life together instructs people about true miracles. That is, the earlier interpretation of the lovers' romance deserves no adoration, for it was not marvelous. Platonic love in its colloquial sense *is* marvelous and does deserve adoration (twice the speaker terms his friendship a miracle, that is, an event that contradicts natural law). Moreover, by writing the chronicle of Platonic Lovers for a wide audience, the speaker implies that everyone knows the extraordinary accomplishment of abstaining from sexual intercourse and would therefore adore anyone who loved and remained continent. Thus these two people have earned their canonization. Yet the fact that this man not only writes his own hagiography but also formulates both its readers and their reaction—the fact, in other words, that he assumes the roles of autobiographer, chronicler, and predisposing psychic—does indeed create an edge to his tale. He wants recognition so desperately, his various positions seem to suggest, that he will bring it into being, if only fictively.

These various functions divert him from his immediate situation: sitting beside his beloved, reviewing their life together and postulating their tomorrows. Instead he whirls his life into a chronicle for generations yet unborn. By structuring the early stanzas of the poem on a when-then contingency and by speaking of the future in the present tense, he almost entirely obliterates the present. In the letter he even describes his current life in the past tense, molding the spontaneity and shapelessness of experience into the chiseled form of art:

> First, we lov'd well and faithfully,
> Yet knew not what wee lov'd, nor why,
> Difference of sex no more wee knew,
> Then our Guardian Angells doe. (ll. 23–26)

This transposing of time, particularly the shunting of the here and now to a period when readers can look back on it with the nostalgia and awe reserved for the past, intimates that for all its glory, the speaker's Platonic love does not quite satisfy him. He must distill it into art so that he and his mistress will receive recognition for their fortitude and virtue. In other words, full happiness depends upon some public acknowledgment and acclaim. A similar tenuousness runs through the speaker's conversation with his lady. Although he originally directs the narrative of his exhuming to her, as soon as he becomes involved with his story, he aims his thoughts and words at the people of the future until he is reciting to her a note intended for posterity. Instead of being his listener, therefore, she becomes primarily the subject of his paper—a much less intimate relationship. The only grammatical structure even close to direct address depicts the woman's future identity:

> then
> Thou shalt be'a Mary Magdalen, and I
> A something else thereby.[27]

I stretch the grammar to find this sentence so emphatic; but I can imagine the speaker gesturing to his lady here, calling her into the narration by individual mention.

This distancing between the speaker and his lady indicates that his relationship with her is more complex than simply that of lover to beloved. The direct encounter of lovers in this poem is only intimated through the situation of the two together in a conversation which elicits the speaker's musing. But all that occurs before the utterance of "The Relique," for in the poem the speaker is an autobiographer and then a chronicler, variations of the poet as singer whose task is to celebrate not encounter. Moreover, as he moves from autobiographer to chronicler, that is, as he creates an aesthetic distance between himself and his subject material, his commemoration of both his love and his lady intensifies. As autobiographer relating to his mistress their future together, perhaps looking at her as he recounts it, his needs for recognition and his ambivalence toward his sexual relationship with her jut into the narrative, complicating it with ambiguity. As chronicler, however, he is the omniscient artist, intellectually aware of both the magnificence of his friendship and of the miraculous restraint required to perpetrate it. Only when he has immersed himself in the role of chronicler, when he reads from the paper he has written, do his images of sexual union disappear. Then he can celebrate their Platonic friendship and his virtuous lady (by this time described in the third-person *shee*) with abandon, even lamenting his limited artistic skill to portray her accurately:

> but now alas,
> All measure, and all language, I should passe,
> Should I tell what a miracle shee was. (ll. 31–33)

But with Donne's usual skill for wrenching irony out of irony, it is through the speaker's artistic re-creation of his beloved that he discovers (or rediscovers) that indeed she is too good for words.

We can only speculate on the effect, even the subconsciously calculated effect, such glorification will work on the lady, for she does hear, or overhear, his praise intended for other ears and eyes, and nothing flatters like a compliment one catches by accident. Moreover, she has listened to praise of a satisfying sexual union. Perhaps the speaker's ecstatic expression of her magnificence and his seemingly unselfish love will work sea changes on their relationship, transforming the miraculous joy of their friendship into the natural bliss of a love which produces progeny against the dissolution of the grave. If so, very subtly the poem confirms the view that Platonic love in the vernacular sense masks sexual intentions. However, the tone of "The Relique" admits of no parlor-game titillation, but rather expresses man's profound physical and psychological needs both to fulfill his love and to plant a stake in the future through sexual intercourse.

Donne's Platonic Lovers in the *Songs and Sonnets*, then, torn between physical attraction and sensual repulsion, resolve their dilemma in a faithful relationship with women whom they adore and respect. In spite of their joy with these ladies, they seek recognition and reward for their abstinence, as if they need compensation for the stringent limitations they place on love. Indeed, they create their own fame through fictional autobiographies in which they receive either sainthood or the devotion due to great spiritual leaders. The comic elements in "The Undertaking" suggest that Donne pokes fun at the egotism of its speaker and obliquely at the popularized notion of Platonic love. In "The Relique," however, he explores the complex responses of a man at once happy with his friendship to a virtuous woman, cynical about women's constancy in general, and yet uneasy about the sexual restrictions of his love. The man can control and sort out the strands of his tangled affections only by assuming roles that insist upon diverse degrees of intimacy with his mistress and differing levels of self-consciousness and objectivity. The poem, then, rather than celebrating Platonic love, illuminates its limitations and conttibutes to an overall conclusion of the *Songs and Sonnets*, that in the most satisfactory relationships the lovers share both body and spirit.

The Negative Lover

The third autobiographical narrator, the Negative Lover—a name as ambiguous as his speech in "Negative Love"—arrogantly rejects everything other men call love.[28] Although the poem indicates no specific setting and no clearly delineated listener, the speaker seems to be expounding his views on love to a group of acquaintances. Yet he mocks and belittles what must be the ideas of at least some of his listeners, all the while flaunting the preeminence of his yet unrevealed version of love as "simply perfectest" (l. 10). His bravado thus discloses either an insensitivity to his auditors or such an obsession to be superior that he virtually disregards their presence, and his utterance becomes lyric self-vindication. Like all the extremists, he sees men as either Hedonists or Platonic Lovers in the colloquial sense, allowing no blending of spiritual and physical love. But to him all love is "stooping," whether it consists solely of lust or includes an appreciation of women's virtue and mind. And he seldom stoops.

> I never stoop'd so low, as they
> Which on an eye, cheeke, lip, can prey,
> Seldome to them, which soare no higher
> Then vertue or the minde to'admire. (ll. 1–4)

His witty ridicule of other lovers strikes at the core of their various conceptions of love. He makes light of the sensualists' attachment to the flesh, tagging their devotion "preying"; and he mocks the Platonic conception of love, labeling such concern for virtue and the mind as soaring up the Platonic ladder to the good. His apt verb choice not only undercuts his subject matter but demonstrates his biting humor and his adeptness at sarcasm, particularly when we recognize that his listeners may very well hold the views of love he so cavalierly discredits. Grouping together both Hedonists and so-called Platonic Lovers, he belittles these men for claiming to know what love is:

> For sense, and understanding may
> Know, what gives fuell to their fire. (ll. 5–6)

His vernacular "fuell to their fire" with its association of heat and lust intimates that in his view Platonic friendship, like sensual passion, is sparked by physical desire. The mask of virtue, he hints, is either a sublimation of sexual drives or a hypocritical disguise. And he proudly announces that he has never—well, hardly ever—fallen for such foolish ideas. Indeed he seems to rejoice at his blanket denunciation of love as other men know it: "To All, which all love, I say no" (l. 13).

The audacity with which he denies the value of any known love suggests that he protests too much. His sarcastic wit also implies a defensiveness on his part that at first seems inexplicable. Nowhere in the poem do we find a reason for his hostility toward either love or his listeners. He tells us quite plainly that he has never been in love, and his auditors are only vaguely sketched at best. Thus his description of both his plight and his own views on love is shaded with a cloud of apparently unnecessary animosity.

He describes his own affections in absolute terms:

> If that be simply perfectest
> Which can by no way be exprest
> But *Negatives*, my love is so. (ll. 10–12)

As Gardner points out, the speaker's phrasing here is reminiscent of Saint Thomas Aquinas's description of God as that most perfect being, who can be delineated only through negation.[29] The allusion in context, however, muddles the speaker's conception of love, for since he is not seeking God, he blasphemes by referring to love between people in terms applicable only to Him. His other descriptions of his amorousness also baffle us at first.

> My love, though silly, is more brave,
> For may I misse, when ere I crave,
> If I know yet, what I would have. (ll. 7–9)

By *silly* the speaker could mean that his love is simple and ignorant, as befits a man without experience. The role of innocent youth, however, conflicts with his sarcastic bravado, with the self-assurance by which he denounces everything that is known on earth as love. In the Renaissance *silly* also can mean "deserving of pity, compassion, or sympathy" as well as "weak, feeble, frail, or insignificant" (*OED*). These various definitions vibrate into an ambiguity, which can perhaps be explained by the dual audience to whom the Negative Lover speaks. To his listeners he insists on both the preeminence of his love and his unmistakable ability to recognize it when it occurs: the arrogant innocent, certainly. But insofar as his utterance is also self-vindication, he reveals that even though his love is pitiable and feeble, it is nonetheless "more brave," that is, more courageous and more showy, than the love of other men. Here, of course, *brave* takes on the brashness that we attribute to bravado; and the speaker confirms that he is making a good show, even a daring one, of what in fact is a pitiable form of love. His word choice for love, "crave," and his consolation about his limited amorous activities contain sexual overtones that throw additional light on the speaker's circumstances.

> This
> As yet my ease, and comfort is,
> Though I speed not, I cannot misse. (ll. 16–18)

To "speed" in the Renaissance frequently means to "thrive" or "prosper" and by extension "to bring to the end or condition desired" (*OED*). Thus on one level the speaker consoles himself and his listeners by saying that although he has not yet attained love, he is sure he will. A reference from Pasquine in Traunce, 1566, in the *OED* also indicates the sexual possibilities of "speed":

> For the most part she that went to bed a Virgin
> Arose from thence spedde with her errand.

Eric Partridge, citing a passage from Shakespeare's "The Passionate Pilgrim: Sonnets to Music," 3, vv. 1–4, defines *speed* as "to be sexually potent":

> My flocks feed not,
> My ewes breed not,
> My rams speed not;
> All is amiss.[30]

This sexual reading of *speed* combined with the sexual overtones in *ease* and *comfort*, which Donne uses in both "The Expiration" and his elegy "The Bracelet," turn the Negative Lover's rather innocuous assurance that he will find love into a personal revelation. Even as he laments his physical immaturity, he wryly consoles himself that he cannot miss his love, no doubt because he is still unable to aim at her. His earlier oath, "For may I misse, when ere I crave," takes on a bawdy meaning as well in this perspective, as he swears by a most embarrassing situation that he has not yet developed any sexual interests. Even his desire for self-knowledge reverberates as a question about gender:

> If any who deciphers best,
> What we know not, our selves, can know,
> Let him teach mee that nothing. (ll. 14–16)

As the alternate title of the poem, "The Nothing," suggests, the speaker seems to be pondering just who and what he is. He stays any possible questions about himself by vaunting and by attacking other men and their conceptions of love.

Here, then, as in the poems of all the extremists, the speaker's laudatory autobiography compensates for some unsatisfactory aspect of his life. The Negative Lover's biting sarcasm toward those many emotions men call love conceals his own sexual inadequacy. His bravado masks his insecurity. And his wit enables him to stage an extravagant performance for which he derives the double satisfaction of outsmarting his listener with his ambiguous words.

4

The Dreaming Cynics

Among the most vibrant of the *Songs and Sonnets* are the paradoxical poems of revenge that I have grouped under the character type of the Dreaming Cynic.[1] The speakers of these poems retaliate for women's cruelty to them by insulting, humiliating, and even terrifying their ladies. Even when the speaker addresses another man or complains in solitude of his unhappiness, he hurls sardonic, sometimes cleverly cruel, barbs at women. All of these poems end with a revengeful flourish or a smacking insult. In spite of their angry outbursts and cynical evaluations, however, these speakers seek a faithful woman or yearn to believe that somewhere ladies are "true, and faire."

They express their longings obliquely, sometimes through subtle comparisons between their unfaithful mistresses and honorable women, but more frequently through the *adynaton*, the topos of the world turned upside down. That figure becomes their metaphor for the emotional chaos and spiritual devastation of unrequited love. Seeing themselves as men dying for love, these speakers express their hapless state through the Petrarchan trope 'the lady kills with cruelty,' and, in true complaint fashion, seek help and life from their ladies and from an occasional god. Donne's lovers, however, display far more calculating and ingenious stratagems for saving their lives than despondent poetic lovers are wont to do. Many of them try to threaten their women into bed; others mock their ladies unmercifully; still others virtually order a god to execute a particular proposal of theirs. The disparity between their actions and their protestations creates a tension, and many of the poems hover between serious poetry and well-turned jokes.[2] Because most of these complaints are cast as dramatic exchanges, they have great potential for poignancy and pathos. But then in Donne's hands they also have the potential for bawdry, outrageous posturing and devastating insults. Some of them even seem to be comic versions of more serious poems in the group.

Here, as throughout the *Songs and Sonnets*, one distinguishing factor between comic and serious tone in a poem is the speaker's consciousness of himself as a creator or a wit. Thus in "The Will," for example, the speaker so exhibits his virtuosity in matching, or mismatching, heirs and legacies—pensiveness to buffoons and money to a Capucin monk, who not only must take a vow of poverty but whose pocketless habit emphasizes that vow—that he undercuts the credibility of his love complaint.[3] Moreover, by ending each stanza with a formula that explains the pairing of gifts and recipients, he calls attention to his poetic wit. And in "The Message" the speaker's manipulation of his insult to his cruel mistress through the formula of request and retraction stresses his poetic deftness rather than his broken heart. In other comic poems the seeming encounters only heighten an audacious joke. In "The Legacie," for example, the stalwart Petrarchan lover's confession to his lady that he suffers multiple demises and resurrections, one at each good-bye and hello from her, destroys any illusion of a real exchange even as it builds toward the *buffo* comic insult with which the poem ends:

> I thought to send that heart in stead of mine,
> But oh, no man could hold it, for twas thine. (ll. 23–24)

In poems like these the poet, by breaching the rules of rhetorical and poetic decorum, creates a subtle signal of recognition for his reader. But in other poems the rhetorical and poetic violations of serious lyrics occur only occasionally, and the tone vacillates between serious and comic. Moreover, in most of these the speaker, not the poet, has a dual identity as storyteller and lover, and both roles withstand the pressures of a dramatic exchange. Donne manages this complexity through ingenious generic manipulation, the discussion of which occupies much of this chapter.

All of these men style themselves as saviors, lovers who avenge their own unhappiness by enforcing retribution on women. A few have grandiose dreams such as killing off love altogether so that their ladies will not be able to find admirers, or becoming god-figures who warn men about women's falseness, or bringing down supernatural vengeance on women. Most of these lovers, however, content themselves with hurling threats and insults. Yet, aware that their listeners will not stay the term of a long harangue, most of them disguise their rebuffs as protestations of eternal love from a dying lover and create a fictional realm in which the man sets right the cruelties of love he and other men have endured. The contradictory figure of savior–dying man controls much of the ambiguity in these poems, as does the tension between the dramatic encounter and the narrative or lyric sections of each poem. For ultimately the two sides of a speaker's personality are incompatible, a disparity reflected in the break between the narrative or lyric and the dramatic elements.

"Song: 'Goe, and catche a falling starre' " begins in the middle of a strife (probably musical) about women's fickleness as the speaker reaches for hyperbole to support his contention that no beautiful, faithful women exist. Through a series of imperatives, he orders his friend to perform impossible tasks, all of which, he claims, are easier than finding a woman "true, and faire" (l. 18).

> Goe, and catche a falling starre,
>   Get with child a mandrake roote,
> Tell me, where all past yeares are,
>   Or who cleft the Divels foot. (ll. 1–4)

The frustration implicit in these adventures hints at the speaker's inordinate hostility toward his friend, at least on this particular issue. Dogmatically he enjoins his listener to impregnate the root of a mandrake, the part of the plant that was not only held to resemble a man but that was also used as a soporific.[4] In other words, the man is told to make love to a human-looking essence of sleeping medicine. The mandrake's additional association with the gallows, where it supposedly generates from the sperm of a hanged man, reinforces the speaker's contempt.[5] He further orders his listener to reexperience the child's disappointment of vainly chasing a falling star and the adult's sad and somehow incredulous realization that he is growing old, both of which leave one with a sense of helplessness. Then he insists that his listener verify the legendary notion that the devil has a cleft foot. Thus through a strident version of the *adynaton*, he stresses the lamentable condition of love in the world and consequently the absolute rightness of his position that all attractive women are fickle.

By the fifth line of the poem, however, the speaker's concern about winning his contest lessens as he is transported through his list of impossibilities to an imaginative realization of the world as it ought to be—an inversion of the ancient topos of the world turned upside down.[6] Simultaneously he modulates his relationship with his listener from commander and servant to learner and teacher. Instead of ordering him to accomplish perverse and frustrating feats, the speaker asks for guidance in searching out the secrets of an imaginatively beautiful world, one where men can hear the song of mermaids, where honesty is rewarded, and where envy does not sting. He wants, in other words, a world where men can realize their dreams.

> Teach me to heare Mermaides singing,
>   Or to keep off envies stinging,
>   And finde
>   What winde
> Serves to'advance an honest minde. (ll. 5–9)

Even though these tasks are as impossible as the earlier ones, they indicate the speaker's yearning for a place where life conforms to ideals—a world set right side up, if you will, where one just might meet a beautiful and faithful woman. Thus the speaker's perverse game of listing impossibilities unexpectedly generates a disclosure of his dreams, and the Cynic stands vulnerable before his listener. The lyric texture of his imaginings is interwoven with the flowing *s* sound, a marked contrast to the grating *c*'s and *g*'s of the opening lines.

As the speaker continues, he undergoes a sympathetic identification with his listener. Instead of commanding the man, he suggests trips on which his hearer might like to embark: "If thou beest borne to strange sights, . . . ride" (ll. 10, 12). His subtle shift of pronoun for the listener from the modern and formal *you* to the archaic and intimate *thou* underscores the newly established closeness between the two.[7] And because the speaker sends his friend in lieu of himself, a vicarious identification develops between them:

> Thou, when thou retorn'st, wilt tell mee
> All strange wonders that befell thee. (ll. 14–15)

Thus the listener's feats become the Dreaming Cynic's as well: in his fancy he will "Ride ten thousand daies and nights" (l. 12), encounter "strange wonders," and try to find a woman "true, and faire." His quest imagery calls up the world of romance, "marked by its extraordinarily persistent nostalgia, its search for some kind of imaginative golden age in time or space,"[8] and the speaker becomes a knight looking for a golden world. Thus momentarily he drops the stance of the Cynic and posits an ideal realm, but only tenuously: he sends the listener in his place, as if he will not risk exposing his hopes to the test of the journey.

His romantic reverie falters at that very point where the speaker's experience with women clashes with his hopes to find one "true, and faire." Still maintaining his courtesy toward his listener and thus by extension still detached from his earlier bitterness at women's fickleness, the Cynic nevertheless refuses to admit the possibility of a beautiful, faithful woman. Instead he puts his own suspicions into his listener's mouth: "Thou . . . wilt . . . sweare / No where / Lives a woman true, and faire" (ll. 14, 16–18). But unsure that even these conclusions hold, he vacillates a bit, terming the journey to meet such a woman a "pilgrimage . . . sweet" (l. 20) and implying that he would embark on such a quest. Thus he almost professes that he still has a romantic dream.

Then abruptly he returns to his strife with his listener, dogmatically insisting on feminine fickleness and swearing that he "would not goe" (l. 21) next door to meet a supposedly faithful woman. Without evidence he repudiates the listener's findings as inaccurate: the woman may have remained constant for a few minutes, but she will not continue so. The Cynic once again dissociates himself from his friend with the formal pronoun *you*, and his hyperbolic claim that the woman will sport with two or three other men by the time the speaker can venture next door underscores his wish to win his argument at any price, even by making a fool of his listener.

The Cynic's relationship with his friend and by extension his inordinate resolve to win his point provides a touchstone to this man's internal complexities. Argument by hyperbole creates the possibility that the exaggerated claims may recoil on the speaker and wreck his defense. That this man expresses both his original claim and his mocking proof in hyperboles necessarily exposes him to the possibility of laughter and raises serious questions about the validity of his case.[9] Yet he risks such derision and even forces consent to his viewpoint by the comic hyperbole intended to make his listener seem foolish:

> Though shee were true, when you met her,
> And last, till you write your letter,
>   Yet shee
>   Will bee
> False, ere I come, to two, or three. (ll. 24–28)

Simultaneously, then, he plays one-upmanship with his listener and mocks him—a swift cut of rancor unexpected from the man who seconds earlier had imagined his listener an alter ego. The mocking suggests that the contest itself is enacted before an audience whom the speaker can win over with laughter and in front of whom he can ridicule his sentimental friend. Yet nothing else in the poem points to a third party. Both this odd rhetorical intimation and the speaker's excessive hostility make sense, however, if one considers the implications of the listener as the Cynic's alter ego. During that portion of the poem where the speaker agrees with his listener, he displays an openness to imaginative beauty, to dreams, to ideals, and to love, which makes him, like his listener, vulnerable to women. In defeating and mocking his listener, then, the speaker in effect symbolically quells that part of his own personality that responds to love, wishes, dreams. That self must be soundly trounced if the speaker is to maintain his worldly figure, and more importantly, his self-image as a Cynic. Thus the objective argument mirrors the speaker's psychomachia between his idealistic and his cynical selves. The hint of an audience that must be persuaded reinforces what the speaker's own divided personality suggests: that the denunciations of women are too sweeping and too hyperbolic to be convincing.

This dazzling performance, from one point of view, creates an ingenious insult to fickle women in which the hyperboles of the fictional world merely magnify the ridicule. Through his witty paradox the Cynic seems to get the last laugh on his listener and on women as well. Indeed, the last stanza of the poem could almost stand alone as a salty, misogynistic epigram addressed to a sentimental reader. But with the underlying suggestions of the imagery, the modulating sound pattern, and the complexities of the relationship between the speaker and the listener, the paradox on which the poem is built—that it is harder to find an attractive, faithful woman than to uncover incredible wonders—gives way to another paradox, that the Cynic who denounces women secretly yearns for one both "true, and faire."

Two of the most scoffing Cynics utter "Womans Constancy" and "The Indifferent." Both men seem to advocate sexual promiscuity, as do the Hedonists; yet they berate women for their inconstancy even as they paradoxically deny any interest in a continuing relationship with their ladies or any value in faithfulness. The poems create the semblance of verbal battles in which the men fight for dominance over women until the outcome hangs in the balance. Then with an impeccably timed insult, which implies that the engagement was not worth the speaker's time, these men withdraw from the confrontation altogether. Although contradictions in their utterances suggest that these Cynics yearn for honest women, the flawless timing and the precision of their affronts detract from the more subtle implications of their interchanges, and the poems often seem like meticulously planned and executed insults.[10] Hence the poems tread that fine line between the poet's calculated games of one-upmanship with his readers and confrontations for which the speaker has rehearsed his lines.

As "Womans Constancy" opens, the Cynic and his mistress are sitting or perhaps lying in bed together. Something—very possibly the end of their sexual tryst and its consequent association with love and death—reminds him of time, and he sarcastically praises the woman for remaining faithful to him "one whole day." Immediately he conjectures, then rehearses, the excuses she will make for leaving him on the morrow.

> Now thou hast lov'd me one whole day,
> To morrow when thou leav'st, what wilt thou say? (ll. 1–2)

What follows is a list of ingenious explanations, heightened by the speaker's re-creation of the nuances in the voice of a woman wriggling out of a difficult situation: for example,

> Or say that now
> We are not *just* those persons, which we were? (ll. 4–6)[11]

As the excuses become more preposterous (they range from the rationalization that oaths made under fear are invalid to the sententious
logical niggling that the woman can be true to herself only by being false
to her lover) they accrue about them an interest for their own sake and
hence sever the illusion of a dramatic confrontation that the opening
lines establish, much as the formula and refrain do in "The Will." And,
as he does in "The Will," the poet pierces his cardboard persona by
displaying his contentious virtuosity.

Paradoxically Donne executes his poetic, epigrammatic wit best
through the illusion of a tense dramatic encounter.

> Vaine lunatique, against these scapes I could
>   Dispute, and conquer, if I would,
>   Which I abstaine to doe,
> For by to morrow I may thinke so too. (ll. 14–17)

The speaker's *volte face*, his reneging from argument with the woman at
just the moment he should shatter all her "scapes," shocks the reader
with surprise, just as the turn in some of Ben Jonson's and Martial's
salty epigrams does and as epigrammatic theory in the Renaissance
prescribes.[12] Thus the poem, building slowly through those ingenious
excuses, explodes into a meticulously executed *macho* joke—the kind of
sardonic performance a jilted lover might dream about but never carry
off with aplomb under the emotional pressure of a confrontation.

Yet the opening intrusion into the middle of an intimate scene remains, for with a mere shift of metrical emphasis the poem reads like a
demanding personal inquiry about the behavior of this particular
woman at the end of this particular assignation: "To morrow when *thou*
leav'st, what wilt *thou* say?" From this perspective the speaker's precise
imitation of flimsy excuses indicates that he has heard those words
many times before and that he wants to know what pretext this woman
will offer. The more ingenious the the explanations become, however,
the more they lose the rhythm of conversation and pick up the scholastic
bookishness of mock disputation:

> Or, as true deaths, true maryages untie,
> So lovers contracts, images of those,
> Binde but till sleep, deaths image, them unloose? (ll. 8–10)

Hence the pretexts seem to be the speaker's fabrications rather than the
excuses he has heard from a number of women.[13] The question of why
he invents these then arises, perhaps teasing us out of the poem. Will
his hairsplitting actually shame the woman into constancy and thus
subtly provide the very disputation he claims to decline? Does his inge-

nuity itself deflate any argument he thinks the woman could offer and at the same time chauvinistically demonstrate his rhetorical prowess? Or do his insulting rationalizations create a personal buffer against any verbal onslaught the woman might advance?[14] The Wife of Bath, after all, advocates attack as the best protection from accusation. Perhaps all three motives apply. Moreover, when the speaker derides his paramour's inconstancy by comparisons with faithful love (hence making her fickleness more despicable), he obliquely supports lasting oaths and vows, in spite of his ebullient *volte face* at the end of the poem. And even there, just as he is ready to admit his own promiscuity, he indicts the woman for her changeableness, calling her "vaine lunatique," a proud woman whose romantic behavior is influenced by the fluctuations of the moon, as well as a foolish and mindless creature. He then compounds this accusation by labeling her excuses "scapes," or outrageous sins, often, according to the *OED*, breaches of chastity. That is, he blasphemes her and then immediately boasts that they share the same fickle nature. In addition, precisely because the speaker's performance sounds rehearsed, his renunciation of this mistress seems to be a standard retaliation against all women for the faithlessness he has encountered in one or two. In other words, he is crying sour grapes.[15]

Other problems arise when we consider the poem as a dramatic confrontation. The speaker's bravado rebuff should figuratively smack the lady in the face, not pat her cheek with a bit more than usual force, if he is really affronting her. But it does not. At the very point where he should be most outrageous in his insult, he admits only the possibility of boredom with this mistress: "By to morrow, I *may* thinke so too." Thus the retaliation sounds more like a threat than a denunciation. Perhaps it is the speaker's ploy to keep her, his psychological stratagem to make her want what she cannot have—a reversal of sour grapes. Donne uses a similar psychological maneuver in "The Apparition."

The fine line between joke and dramatic monologue in "Womans Constancy" is too blurred to insist on either reading, although the poem's inversion of Donne's paradox "A Defence of Womens Constancy" suggests a trifling playfulness. The precision with which "Womans Constancy" builds to an epigrammatic point, or *argutia*, further contributes to a comic tone and reveals the skill of a craftsman, especially since that point works best as a surprise on first reading. Yet the idea that in jokes we sometimes express our deepest feelings applies to the poem too. Donne's persona recoils from the woman as he tries to allure her, denounces her infidelity as he boasts of his own. He so wants to win this round in the battle of the sexes that he has rehearsed his lines. Ironically the lines contain ambiguous words which set his argument askew. In the *Songs and Sonnets* revenge in love always has these

edges. Donne explores their sharpness and their devastating wounds in
other, more straightforward utterances of these Dreaming Cynics.

To move from "Womans Constancy" to "The Indifferent" is to turn
from rhetorical bravado to something like operatic tour de force, with its
attendant modulations in tone and metrics. The analogy gains some
credence from the speaker's admission that he sighed this song (l. 19), or
love complaint, to Venus about the devilish constancy of women.[16] But
that comment appears in the final stanza, in the past tense, as evidence
of supernatural sanction for other songs the persona has been addressing to a far different audience.

As the poem opens, the speaker is boasting to a group of women of
his sexual prowess, his ability to make love indiscriminately and inex-
haustibly: "I can love" (l. 1). He might be standing, legs astride, as
Leporello does in act 1 of Mozart's *Don Giovanni*, when he enumerates
the don's universal conquests and catholic tastes to Donna Elvira. Both
men exude the same prurient bravado. The comparison with Leporello,
whose catalogue of Giovanni's amours closely parallels the list in "The
Indifferent," provides one clear means for distinguishing the listeners
and audience in the poem. Both of these works diverge greatly from
Ovid's tongue-in-cheek lyric confession in *Amores* 2.4, with which "The
Indifferent" is frequently compared.

First of all, both "The Indifferent" and Leporello's aria "Madamina, il
catalogo è questo" have a dramatic context. Leporello pulls out his
tabulation of the don's paramours and shows it to one of the statistics on
the roster, much to the lady's displeasure. Leporello hopes by his revelation to discourage Donna Elvira in her pursuit of his employer. The man
in "The Indifferent" boasts about his own virility—presumably authen-
ticated by experience—to a group of women who at first seem to have no
personal relationship with him. Then he points his finger at them and
addresses them as "you and you" (l. 8), thereby virtually picking out his
next conquests; his boasting seems calculated to arouse their desires. Yet
both men misread their listeners. Leporello's revelations only confirm
Donna Elvira's determination to wreak revenge on Giovanni, and the
Cynic's indifference to the particular charms of the individual ladies no
doubt finally insults the very women he would seduce. But Donne's
poem does not develop this dramatic possibility, does not make the
vaunting of stanza 1 precipitate an exchange betwen the women and the
speaker—the very technique that Donne displays so brilliantly in "A
Valediction: of Weeping" and "The Dreame," to name only two. The
wrangling of stanza 2, although ostensibly directed at the group of
women, seems to generate from within the speaker, as if he were wrestling out loud with the morality of his philandering and with that niggling question of constancy, for the intensity of his choler is dispro-
portionate to his circumstances at the moment of the poem. In spite of its

dramatic gloss, stanza 2, like Browning's dramatic monologues two hundred years later, remains essentially a lyric expression.

Both Donne's cynical persona and Leporello have other audiences, however, to whom the catalogue of sexual exploits is far more entertaining. The operagoer delights not only in Leporello's boundless energy (the ebullient music expresses his prurient glee in retelling the don's amours) but also in the geographic details of Giovanni's successes, especially since they reinforce some stereotypes about passionate Latin lovers.

> In Italia seicento e quaranta,
> in Almagna duecento e trentuna,
> cento in Francia, in Turchia novantuna,
> ma in Ispagna son gia mille a tre!

("In Italy six hundred and forty, in Germany two hundred and thirty-one, a hundred in France, in Turkey ninety-one, but in Spain there are already one thousand and three!")[17] Donna Elvira is not amused. A similar delight springs from the speaker's quick and sometimes witty pairing of opposite women, all of whom he can love in "The Indifferent": "faire and browne" (l. 1) or "whom the country form'd, and whom the town" (l. 4), antitheses often equalized by their identical metrics. (In lines 2, 3, and 5, both the comma that separates the items and the caesura fall in the exact center of the line.) Moreover, after the Cynic runs through the most obvious counterparts, he performs something of a tour de force in compiling rhymed contraries—a feat seeming all the more difficult because it appears to be spontaneous.

> Her who still weeps with spungie eyes,
> And her who is dry corke, and never cries . . . (ll. 6–7)

The reader, like the operagoer, delights in the creator's skill and in the comic listing of such an eclectic sexual appetite, partly because the eclecticism itself mocks the stereotyped, ideal lady of so many sonnets.[18] The focus is on poetic wit, not on the drama of the poem. Indeed the illusion of a confrontation does not fully emerge until the pairing of opposites is over and the speaker points to specific women in his audience:

> I can love her, and her, and you and you,
> I can love any, so she be not true. (ll. 8–9)

Then, the supposed encounter here and in many of the other poems in this chapter strengthens the poetic (and specifically the epigrammatic) wit of the creator by making all the previous lines appear extemporaneous.

With the intensified illusion of a confrontation in stanza 2 the distinction between dramatic and lyric becomes blurred. The constant direct addresses, the wrangling questions, and the imperative, present-tense verbs all make the stanza appear to be the speaker's insistent argument with a group of women who have upbraided him. To read the stanza without the playful opening of the poem is to experience the illusion of walking in on the middle of a rather nasty quarrel in which the man has been deluged with accusations and marriage threats from all his former mistresses (something akin to the situation Don Giovanni might find himself in if all his conquests became Donna Elviras). But the speaker in "The Indifferent" does not know his listeners even by name, let alone by the far more intimate relationship of his plea "Let mee . . . twenty know" (l. 15). Hence *dramatically* (and here for emphasis I redefine the term as an act that springs from the past but is directed toward a future) the stanza is out of context and virtually meaningless—for these listeners. But because they are women to whom the speaker has flaunted his virility, they resemble those other women whom he has known intimately; momentarily they become surrogates for his ex-paramours. Perhaps he has waged this argument many times before, either face to face or in a solitary reenactment of what he might have said. His labeling his argument a "song," or love complaint, lends weight to the latter possibility. And here, perhaps for the first time, he upbraids women—even the wrong ones—directly:

> Will no other vice content you?
> Will it not serve your turn to do, as did your mothers?
> Have you old vices spent, and now would finde out others?
> Or doth a feare, that men are true, torment you? (ll. 10–13)

His ranting, his taunting questions, his unilateral denunciation of women in every generation (*mothers* can refer to all female ancestors), and his cynical conclusion that by both constancy and promiscuity women in general manipulate, control, and even emasculate men—all these ejaculations (pun included) suggest that the speaker has projected his internal conflicts onto a literal but inappropriate scene.[19] In other words, *because* of the relative anonymity between the man and his listeners, stanza 2 is essentially a psychodrama whose curative effects, if they occur, grow merely from this man's enactment of his inner turmoil. His earlier interest in impressing these women listeners with his virility—the dramatic potential of the poem—has vanished.

Except for a brief respite, the speaker continues to air his private amorous conflicts in public throughout stanza 2. For a moment he seems about to rekindle his seductive line with his listeners by attributing inconstancy to all men and advocating it for all women. "Oh we are not [faithful], be not you so" (l. 14). But instead of baiting his lure with the ensnaring possibilities promised by his opening posture, the man lapses again into intimate wrangling intelligible only as a quarrel between one man and one woman.

> Let mee and doe you, twenty know.
> Rob mee, but binde me not, and let me goe.
> Must I, who came to travaile thorow you,
> Grow your fixt subject, because you are true? (ll. 15–18)

That is, out loud and in front of a group of women, he reenacts a former squabble with a possessive woman, or at least his version of that tiff, and in the process discloses his own fears of dominance with the rather grotesque image of sexual impaling. (Both "travaile thorow you" and "fixt subject" describe control of the amorous relationship in explicitly physical terms.) Once again, he is in the midst of his psychodrama, this time both begging for and commanding promiscuity, as if it alone can relieve his dilemma over power and control in a romantic entanglement, or indeed keep him from the vulnerability of such an entanglement.[20]

The switch in both verb tense and tone with which stanza 3 begins signals the speaker's return to his listeners, the women before whom he paraded his virility. He is telling them a narrative for which stanza 2, uttered, in the dramatic present tense, provides specific details. Oddly, almost incredibly, the Cynic classifies his wrangling as a song which he sighed to Venus and which she, benevolent protectress of philanderers, answered with her own inimitable, sententious damnation: "You [constant women] shall be true to them, who'are false to you" (l. 27). Thus obliquely he admits the autobiographical nature of the argument he reenacted, although his transformation of a tiff into a love complaint suggests that he reshaped the original confrontations. And he restructures the material in his current performance as well. Through the Venus fiction he provides supernatural evidence of the damning afflictions faithful women shall suffer and thus rationally leads his listeners to the brink of a seduction (if, indeed, women can be argued into bed). He even has Venus label them "poore Heretiques" (l. 24). Their only salvation, therefore, lies in frequent and various bedding, presumably some of it with the speaker himself. Hence in a sense he fulfills the lure that his cocky strutting anticipated. Through Venus he also strikes out at those other women whose possessiveness frightened him in the first place.

But the relationship between speaker and listener in stanza 3 is not the main focus. For that illusion of an encounter only heightens the parody and fiction, as it did in the poem's opening. The audacity of this Cynic's treating his plea for licentiousness as a love complaint provides much of the amusement of the stanza, as it echoes the emotional fears and amorous requests of numerous other lovers in literature. For example, Venus, unlike poor Juliet, who panics when Romeo swears by anything so inconstant as the moon, takes her vow by "Love's sweetest Part, Variety" (l. 20). Here, much to the dismay of many a forlorn knight, "constancie," not aloofness, is "dangerous" (l. 25), that is offish, niggardly, and sparing. Moreover, the impeccably outrageous application of the religious metaphors to the cult of Venus Natura demonstrates Donne's ingenuity even more, so that the relationship between speaker and listener here ultimately buckles, as it does in stanza 1.

But what of the middle stanza, caught as it is between two comic tours de force? One can see its intense tone and its calculated illusion of angry speech as a ploy so that stanza 3 becomes even more ludicrous in relief.[21] But if the foray into psychodrama in context serves as the ruse for a surprise, out of context it shows the germ of the complex psychological struggle Donne's disappointed Cynics experience in the less playful lyrics. The love-hate ambivalence toward women crops up here; so does the speaker's fear of sexual vulnerability. His assessment of promiscuity as the way of the world thus both salves his conscience and frees him from the possibility of romantic anguish. Moreover, his joke, his sardonic fiction that Venus curses and damns faithful women, lets him retaliate for past difficulties in love without assuming the responsibility for his revenge. But in context, in the middle of sparking wit and amusing parody, the wrenching questions of stanza 2 are muted by more ebullient melodies.

The line between comic and serious tone, which wavers in stanza 2 of "The Indifferent," almost disappears in "The Apparition," where in reenactment of "Womans Constancy" a Dreaming Cynic confronts his mistress face to face. The poem contains such an imaginative and dominant creation that it sometimes seems no more than an elaborate affront or a skillfully plotted scheme for embarrassing a woman. Yet the dramatic framework establishes enough credibility so that the poem vacillates between being a joke and an insult. In this ironic love complaint, the man details his ghostly revenge to the lady who has scorned him and in the process visits some punishment on her. He vents his frustrations in a bitter practical joke whose narrative creates a scene of ghostly terror made all the worse because its outcome is left hanging. And in that narrative he transforms the woman into a rejected paramour, "neglected" (l. 11) by a "worse" (l. 5) lover, who is exhausted from his sexual tryst with her—poetic justice indeed. The hissing s's and trailing k's that orchestrate this horrifying tale reach their climax in the image of the mistress as a "poore Aspen wretch" (l. 11), "bath'd in a cold quicksilver sweat" (l. 12).[22]

The impeccable narrative of lines 4 through 13 so demonstrates the speaker's creative skill that momentarily it puts his identity as a cynical revenger in jeopardy. From one point of view he, like so many other forlorn lovers, has tried to ease his pains through creation, as Donne says in "The Triple Foole," by drawing them "through Rimes vexation" (l. 9). And although the lover does not lament his pangs here, he does find satisfaction in poetic wishful thinking, a technique of the satirical love complaint as evidenced, for example, in Wyatt's epigram, Poem 42:

> Who hath heard of such cruelty before?
> That when may plaint remembered her my woe
> That caused it she, cruel more and more
> Wished each stitch as she did sit and sew
> Had prickt mine heart, for to increase my sore.
> And, as I think, she thought it had been so:
> For as she thought 'This is his heart indeed'
> She pricked hard, and made herself to bleed.[23]

The identification of Wyatt's speaker as both a satirist (as *epigram* implies) and as a forlorn lover prepares the reader, to whom the poem is addressed, for a salty turn at the end of the poem. The fact that the narrative need not withstand the test of truth that only the lady's eyes can give it hints that this delicious revenge is poetic indeed. Donne's lover neither claims satirical intent nor addresses a reader, both actions that would establish his identity as a poet/creator. Indeed, his avenging himself through intimidating the woman rather than appealing for help at first glance seems to remove him from the poetic posture of an abject lover and the poem from the genre of a complaint.[24] He sets his menacing narrative in a dramatic exchange so that the threat will alter his relationship with his mistress in life, not in daydreams or on paper. And he wants quite an alteration. He seeks not only a vent for his rancor through name-calling ("murdresse," l. 1; "fain'd vestall," l. 5; and "poore Aspen wretch") and through innuendoes about the woman's venereal disease and declining sexual charms, seeks not only the satisfaction of terrifying her, but also hopes that he can frighten the woman into going to bed with him.[25] Hence his narrative, his careful *poetic* creation, serves the dramatic purpose of arousing the woman's romantic inclinations. In this respect "The Apparition" turns inside out a poem like "The Indifferent," where the seeming dramatic exchange between the man and his audience of women in fact affords him the opportunity to project his own amorous difficulties in a psychodrama.

The man's contradictory self-images in the dramatic framework of "The Apparition" reinforce the complex of reasons for his utterance. Although he addresses his mistress in blunt, vernacular terms, he nevertheless at first presents himself to her as a lover dying from her scorn, a posture at least as denigrating as that any Petrarchist ever assumed:[26] "When, by thy scorne, O murdresse, I am dead . . ." (l. 1). His vengeful threat of supernatural haunting, then, by his own admission is a cry of despair, albeit a very neatly executed one and therefore perhaps a more successful one than pure invective would be. The man's second self-image is that of a vindictive rather than a sad but still hopeful lover. After his tale is finished, he castigates the woman and his foolish attachment to her, saying:

> Since my love is spent,
> I'had rather thou shouldst painfully repent,
> Then by my threatnings rest still innocent. (ll. 15–17)

He is so embittered by her cruelty that he has lost all compassion for her, he says. These final lines provide the man with his last chance to seduce the lady, and his resorting to a threat rather than to cajoling or pleading marks the extent of his desperation. He has tried all the other postures for winning her before, from acknowledging her control over him to promising supernatural retaliation, apparently without success. The only resources he has left are terrors of the unknown and a renunciation of her in plain English: "my love is spent." Yet because he has not invalidated his tale of supernatural haunting, he tacitly still assents that she holds the power of life or death over him. His posture of a Cynic is thus purely strategic. He employs the age-old gimmick of telling her she cannot have him, no doubt to arouse her interest in the unattainable. At the same time he reminds her that supernatural threats like his have converted sinners like her in the past, in effect dangling before her the means to "rest still innocent," very likely in his bed. However, because he words all of this last desperate stratagem in the negative ("I will not tell thee," l. 14), he still preserves the possibility of saving face, should she refuse him altogether.

Both satiric epigrams and persuasive orations offer numerous examples of strategic endings very similar to the one in "The Apparition." And since the poem's closure demonstrates both finely chiseled, epigrammatic wit and an emotional appeal to the listener characteristic of the conclusion of an oration, perhaps those forms will illuminate the artifice in the speaker's tactics.

Rosalie Colie likens the straightforward language in the couplets of many of Shakespeare's sonnets to epigrams, which develop and make their point with blunt force and simple language. The epigrammatic point or *argutia*, moreover, according to the Renaissance theorist Julius Caesar Scaliger, must be felt, even experienced, in the paradoxical, clever, or unexpected ending of the poem.[27] Donne's "The Apparition" is a sonnet too, although certainly not a quatorzain; and his structuring of its final three lines as a tercet, a form often used as a variation on the couplet, suggests that he was giving the poem's ending an epigrammatic force as paradoxical and unexpected as Scaliger recommends. The speaker's abrupt change in identity is marked, as I noted earlier, by blunt language: "my love is spent," a phrase which forms the first of three rhymes in the tercet. That is, for the first time the man pretends to doff his posture as a forlorn lover and repudiates the woman without any of the tact or courtesy that his earlier self-portrait implies. In the remaining two lines he culminates his denunciation and releases his anger full force.

> I'had rather thou shouldst painfully repent,
> Then by my threatnings rest still innocent. (ll. 16–17)

This latter action illustrates the psychological explanation for epigrams according to Puttenham:

> Bvt all the world could not keepe, nor any ciuill ordinance to the contrary so preuaile, but that men would and must needs vtter their splenes in all ordinarie matters also: or else it seemed their bowels would burst, therefore the poet deuised a pretty fashioned poeme short and sweete (as we are wont to say) and called in *Epigramma* in which euery mery conceited man might without any long studie or tedious ambage, make his frend sport, and anger his foe, and giue a prettie nip, or shew a sharpe conceit in few verses.[28]

Donne's speaker, by uttering his epigrammatic barb directly, perhaps emits his frustration and anger with more vehemence than if he had sublimated it into the vigor of creation. No doubt the lady also experiences more shock by hearing the reproach than by reading it. And Donne enriches the possibilities of the lyric by transfusing it with drama.

This consideration of the poem's closure as a direct, face-to-face appeal to a listener also relates "The Apparition" to the classical oration, particularly to the emotional entreaty in the *peroratio*. To arouse the feelings, Quintilian advocates that the orator create verbal "visions, whereby things absent are present to our imagination with such extreme vividness that they actually seem to be before our very eyes." The effect, he says, "makes us seem not so much to narrate as to exhibit the actual scene, while our emotions will be no less actively stirred than if we were present at the actual occurrence."[29] This discussion sounds like a summary of the speaker's technique in "The Apparition" and of the response his verbal visions create not only in the woman but in the lover as well. Quintilian also advises that fear can be used honorably to stir unprincipled men:

> The minds of such an audience are . . . moved . . . by demonstration of
> the advantage that will accrue from such a policy, or more effectively
> perhaps by pointing out the appalling consequences that will follow the
> opposite policy. For quite apart from the fact that the minds of unprinci-
> pled men are easily swayed by terror, I am not sure that most men's minds
> are not more easily influenced by fear of evil than by hope of good.[30]

Donne's lover seems sardonically to understand, with Quintilian, that
appeals to his lady's sentiment and sympathy will have little effect. For
Donne's readers really familiar with Quintilian's writings the association
between that rhetorician and this poem of seduction would prove comic
indeed. As they contemplated, for example, this speaker's dishonorable
intentions, they might wryly reflect that Quintilian, like Cicero, believed
a good orator must first of all be a good man. That Donne so skillfully
has this cynical man manipulate a crass woman by using Quintilian's
elaborate rules is in itself preposterous.

We confront again the questions of tone and audience, both of which
return us to speaker and creator, the place of the poet in the poem.
Insofar as the persona narrates a tale in order to persuade his cold lady
to relent, he, of course, is the speaker, she the listener; and the poem
lives as a dramatic unfolding. Donne's couching a narrative within a
dramatic framework gives the speaker (not the poet) a creative dimension not usually discernable in a dramatic lyric: he is a very persuasive
orator and a very skilled storyteller as well as a frustrated lover. Thus the
narrative does not dispel the illusion of an encounter in this poem.
Moreover, the sibilance and dissonance in the tale of haunting convey
the speaker's anger as he details the horrors of his revenge; they also
provide poetic orchestration. The fact that the poem is structured as a
single sentence with pauses in the midst of lines further reinforces the
illusion of a confrontation. "The Apparition," then, is very convincing
as an encounter. If and when we read it as such, the man's love-hate
ambivalence toward his mistress emerges, as does his awareness that in
loving or lusting for an unprincipled woman he becomes unscrupulous
himself.

Yet strong and deep as these resonances of "The Apparition" are, bits
of the poem reverberate to another tune. Donne's putting Quintilian's
techniques to work in the mouth of this unscrupulous speaker offers one
example of the comic irony in the poem. Perhaps because the narrative
dominates the poem in actual lines (eleven of seventeen) as well as in its
magnificent execution, the dramatic framework (as the word implies)
sets off the tale in order to accent it even more. And in itself the story is
delightfully preposterous, the insults magnificently nasty, the poetic
justice wrathful indeed. The epigrammatic about-face thus clinches the
delicious affronts with an even blunter one. From this point of view, the

poet behind the speaker—the one who shapes the whole lyric, not just the narrative—displays his masterful skill and wry, intelligent humor. The reader, then, sophisticated enough not to analyze it at all, experiences the comic surprise of the ending first. On a second and third and hundredth reading his laughter may ring hollow, however, for the serious tones of "The Apparition" compete strenuously with its declamatory jocularity.

Both the comic poems and those that vacillate in tone, then, offer similar characterizations of the Dreaming Cynics, characterizations which deepen in "The Funerall" and "Twicknam Garden." Frustrated because of their involvement with an aloof woman or disappointed by a former love affair, these men seek retaliation, usually in the form of an epigrammatic insult to their mistresses or to women in general. Their revenge, however, does not satisfy them, for they want their ladies, yet fear emotional attachment. Thus a love-hate ambivalence toward woman fills their poems: the journey to find "a woman true, and faire" in "Song," for example, is both a "pilgrimage . . . sweet" and a waste of time; in "The Will" the speaker, dying of unrequited love, nonetheless happily sees that with his demise his mistress's "beauties will be no more worth / Then gold in Mines, where none doth draw it forth" (ll. 48–49). All of the poems of the Dreaming Cynics agree on these points. To varying extents they sketch some other characteristics.

Most of the speakers disguise their revenge as a beneficial act for mankind, a first step in turning around the world that is upside down. For to these men the topsy-turvy earth reflects the emotional chaos of their unrequited love. Thus the man in "The Will" cries, "I'll undoe / The world by dying; because love dies too" (ll. 46–47). In "Song" the lover yearns to "keepe off envies stinging" (l. 6) as much as to find "a woman true, and faire." Both, it seems, are absent from the world turned upside down. And in "The Indifferent," by punishing constant "poore Heretiques" (l. 24), Venus sets the world of love aright, that is, sets lovers free from dangerous emotional involvement.

Disguising revenge as an act of salvation suggests either that the lovers are blind to their motivation or willfully choose to ignore it; for even in those poems where momentarily the men acknowledge their complicity in the emotional chaos of the world, they nonetheless see themselves as saviors. The man in "The Blossome," for example, calls his heart "thou which lov'st to bee / Subtile to plague thy selfe" (ll. 17–18), as he berates it for wanting to remain with an unfaithful mistress. The jet ring that symbolizes the lady's heart in "A Jeat Ring Sent" is a figure for the man's heart too; it is black not only in its constancy but in its bitter degradation of the woman as well. In "The Message" the speaker can provide justice in the world only by becoming as corrupt as the woman he condemns:

> Yet send me back my heart and eyes,
> That I may know, and see thy lyes,
> And may laugh and joy, when thou
>   Art in anguish
>   And dost languish. (ll. 17–21)

And in "The Will" the man contributes to the chaos and grim injustice of a world under the domination of Cupid by willing his medical books "to him for whom the passing bell next tolls," (l. 37) and his bronze medals "unto them which live / In want of bread" (ll. 40–41). Yet all these men praise themselves.

In the two bitter utterances of the Dreaming Cynics Donne pursues even further the strands of heroic bravado, self-deception, a love-hate ambivalence, and complicity in one's emotional chaos. Because these poems do not end with a flourishing affront, the vengeance of the unrequited lover recoils back on himself; the men remain locked in their unhappiness at the end of the poems.

Almost a bitter version of "The Apparition" or "The Will," "The Funerall" develops from the Petrarchan conceit 'the lady kills with scorn.' Unlike the other two poems, where the speakers project their deaths into the future, "The Funerall" seems to be the lover's post-mortem instructions to his burial attendant, echoing through his death chamber; his startling "who ever comes to shroud me" (l. 1) is a direct response to the approaching footsteps. The poem almost sustains this illusion until the final quatrain, when the speaker at last addresses his mistress and thus indicates that she has been present all along, as he does in "The Will." His uncertainty about time and the changes death brings, however, disturbs the impression that the poem is a spectral command. Ordering the attendant to leave the lock of hair untouched, the lover explains its significance in terms of the future, not the present, as if he had not yet experienced the ecstasy of his soul:

> 'Tis my outward Soule,
> Viceroy to that, which then to heaven being gone,
>   Will leave this to controule. (ll. 5–7)

This small confusion signals a deeper uncertainty on the speaker's part. Not only has he been enacting an imaginary encounter in front of his mistress, as the final lines of the poem reveal, he has, in direct opposition to his assumed Petrarchan role of a man who graciously dies of unrequited love, also fashioned that imaginary exchange as an instrument of revenge on the woman whose "subtile wreath of haire" (l. 3) he ponders. The more convincingly he plays the role, the more surely he can prime his lady for his affront. Even though his occasional bursts of anger and frustration disturb the illusion of sincerity in his little drama and hence mollify its shock effect, the lover wreaks ruinous revenge on his aloof mistress.

Donne here modifies the technique of encasing a narration within a dramatic encounter (c.f. "The Apparition" or "The Legacie") to that of enclosing a miniature dramatic monologue within a larger one—a variation, surely, of the play within a play. The results are devastating. As numerous other critics have noted, the lover's refusal to acknowledge his lady's presence and his references to her in the third person rebuff her more subtly and more completely than any insult could do. But there is a rub. Simply because the speaker has contrived this elaborate show as a retaliation for her disdain, he demonstrates how consummately engrossed in her he is.

The particular nature of his anger and love emerges during his imaginary monologue. At first he seems to indicate the preciousness of his love by instructing the attendant to be both careful with and uninquisitive about the lock of his lady's hair. Then, anticipating at least some query from the undertaker, he explains "that subtile wreath" in mystical terms: "The mystery, the signe . . . / 'tis my outward Soule" (ll. 4–5). Such a holy arcanum should put off any further inquiry. But, almost contradictorily, the lover continues his explanation, saying that the woman's hair will "keepe these limbes, her Provinces, from dissolution" (l. 8). That is, he disregards his own instructions by elucidating the private significance of the tress, thus violating whatever secrets the pair might have had. Yet his rhetorical posture of seeming to discourage prying questions lets him pretend to protect the sanctity of his love. Strategically his stance as a devoted lover at once flatters the woman, his real listener, and creates the framework through which he can insult her. His explication of the meaning of her lock of hair continues his love-hate ambivalence toward her. His religious imagery seems to indicate that he and his mistress are joined in a sacred union, perfect and ethereal, almost unknowable to the common man. The attendant should question no further. Yet as the lover elucidates the capabilities of his lady's hair, he subtly denigrates his love. Hyperbolically he attributes to the lock the power to keep his body from decay, just as many Petrarchan poets ascribe miracles to their ladies' eyes, gifts, or even clothes.[31] But there is a catch. Her hair as his "outward Soule" will keep only his physical being intact. For only his body, perhaps just his arms ("these limbes"), are "her Provinces," her spheres of action. Disguised by religious language, the arcanum of the lock turns out to be the promise of a spectral assignation; the lover unmasks himself as a cynic, mocking in the image of a ghostly tryst his mistress's well-preserved virginity.

Donne's sophisticated use of hyperbole here demonstrates its ironic potential for a speaker who addresses a dual audience. Donne's lover, indeed, manages both to elevate and disparage his lady in one burst of exaggeration—the two ends of hyperbole that Puttenham describes: "This maner of speach is vsed, when either we would greatly aduaunce or greatly abase the reputation of any thing or person, and must be vsed very discreetly, or els it will seeme odious."[32] Donne's lover, seeming to flatter the woman by ascribing great power to her hair, in fact insults her. First he intimates to the attendant that his unresponsive lady so desires his flesh that she is exerting her powers to keep his body intact— ultimately a greater compliment to himself than to her. But because his mistress, his real listener, knows that his hints are false, she hears herself sarcastically praised for the passion she lacks.

Almost immediately the illusion of a post-mortem exchange fades, and the lover seems to be musing out loud about the meaning of his mistress's hair. Under the pretense of sincere inquiry, he sarcastically drives home to his lady the import of her gift. His hyperbolic comparison of the lock's power to preserve him physically with the brain's power to coordinate his body by transmitting nerve impulses throughout takes an acid edge as he defers to her superiority.

> These haires which upward grew, and strength and art
>   Have from a better braine,
> Can better do'it. (ll. 12–14)

His ambiguous "can better do'it" seems to refer to "make mee one of all" (l. 11), the brain's coordinating power. Hence her lock will keep his body intact. But that her hair can preserve him better in death than his brain could in life suggests a witchlike power and perversity in the woman and raises the question of her motivation for sustaining the body. It is this question he ponders.

> Except she meant that I
>   By this should know my pain,
> As prisoners then are manacled, when they'are condemn'd to die.
>   (ll. 14–16)

He slips into this denunciation as if it were an afterthought, thus preserving his mask of the dejected lover who accepts his fate. But in the comparison he sees himself cruelly reminded of his impending death by being forced to wear its symbol. The wreath becomes a shackle, the love-token an image of bondage. The intertwining of love and death illuminates the perversity of his mistress, and the speaker destroys all pretense that he is a forlorn lover. Yet he clings to the language and trappings of the Petrarchan figure.

Describing himself as "Loves martyr" (l. 19) and his lady's strands of hair as "reliques" (l. 20), he enjoins the attendant to preserve the sanctity of his love by burying the lock with him. He even imagines the tress falling into others' hands and becoming the impetus for a new religion of love, but one insufficiently based on true knowledge of the lady to be orthodox, therefore "idolatrie" (l. 19). Yet after his comparison of the ringlet to a manacle, these hyperbolic glorifications ring with bitter taunts, and his role as a devout lover cannot withstand the critical pressure he brings to it. He seems to indict his own blind devotion to this woman as "idolatrie" and with severity to appraise her as an "idol." In the sixteenth and seventeenth centuries that word not only meant "false god," but had taken on the sense of insubstantiality from its Greek import as image. Hence the lover denies his mistress's humanity; he means she is an imitation or false woman, even perhaps an inactive person who has the form without the proper activity or energy of a woman (*OED*). She has attracted him, but cannot or perversely will not fulfill the promise of her seductive form. Ironically he has become "Loves martyr" for such an idol. His sardonic awareness of his complicity in his own destruction finally shatters his miniature drama and with it any pretense of decorum toward the lady. He addresses her directly for the first time with a satiric onslaught.

> As 'twas humility
> To'afford to it all that a Soule can doe,
>   So, 'tis some bravery,
> That since you would save none of mee, I bury some of you. (ll. 21–24)

With crackling irony he terms his hyperboles "humility." By also calling his gesture of burying her ringlet "bravery," he unleashes the most resonant of his denunciations. The submerged sexual puns of his quasi-religious image and of the poem's shaping Petrarchan conceit come to the surface. The erotic associations of "bury" and "Loves martyr" as variants of "die" ring their ironic undercurrents through his angry condemnation. In burying her hair—itself a token of physical love—he symbolically wreaks sexual revenge on her, "kills" her for love as she has "killed" him by denying her love.[33] He makes a show, "some bravery," an act of bravado, of burying her curl. But with the critical eye of self-appraisal, he sees the limited effect of his actions. It is bravery indeed to wreak revenge symbolically, bravery indeed to repudiate a disdainful woman for his unrequited love by assuming the mask of a lover who faces his destruction without cynicism!

　　This lover, more than the other Dreaming Cynics, realizes the limits of the heroic role in which he and they cast themselves. His sarcastic labeling of his insult as "bravery" obliquely applies to the actions of these other heroes of rebuke as well. One cannot retaliate for a broken heart; one can merely make a show of saving face.

"The Funerall," unlike the comic or even semicomic poems in this chapter, ends with no chiseled flourish. It finishes more with a gesture than with a flinty verbal slap, as if, somehow, the lover's anger were too deep, too pervasive, to be clinched by a witty, epigrammatic *argutia*, and as if the target of that anger were too ambiguous to be shot with a straight insulting joke. Moreover, the man develops his fictional role as a lover killed by his lady's disdain grotesquely, not comically, as most of the other Dreaming Cynics do. His "who ever comes to shroud me" sets up an intimate and yet morbid relationship that, *mutatis mutandis,* mirrors the relationship between him and his mistress. The dressing and undressing in bed, the lock of hair, the preservation of his body—all contain sexual possibilities, frustrated, indeed turned into funerary details, by the unresponsive, perhaps perverse woman he in fact addresses through his speech to his funeral attendant. The tenor of the Petrarchan conceit he enacts includes no comic humiliation or reformation for the woman. He does not threaten her, even obliquely; for a threat implies hope, and he has none. His one attempt at saving face, burying the ringlet, affords little satisfaction to him, little ridicule or mockery of her.

Even more cynical and despairing in tone than "The Funerall," "Twicknam Garden" depicts an abject lover lamenting his loss and seeking vindication in the fecund pastoral world of an Edenic garden (the only pastoral setting in the poems uttered by Dreaming Cynics). Even the garden's vernal balms, however, cannot cure his lovesickness, and the man ends the poem where he begins it, deep in the emotional wilderness of self-pity.[34] Like Milton's Satan in Eden, he cannot sufficiently extricate himself from his mental anguish to see and feel the possibilities of renewal all around him.

The form of the poem—a pastoral complaint with an imaginative, dramatic projection in it—frees this speaker from the restraint an audience imposes on many of the other Dreaming Cynics and lets him unleash his vindictiveness and mawkish self-pity. In spite of his direct address to Love and later to some imaginative lovers, the speaker concentrates on defining himself, wrestling internally with his despair, and conjuring up retribution for his lady, so that none of his listeners materializes in the poem.[35] The lyric thrust of his complaint (as opposed to, say, the narrative dimension in pastoral complaints from Theocritus's Idyll 11 onward) surfaces through his self-definition. He never recounts the details of his dilemma. Even his allusion to his lady's perverse truthfulness in the final line reveals nothing specific. Since he is addressing himself, however, he has no need to repeat what he already knows.

He begins by seeing himself as a victim, even to the point of describing his own sighs and tears in oddly passive participles:

Blasted with sighs, and surrounded with teares,
   Hither I come to seeke the spring. (ll. 1–2)

That he recognizes his deterioration and abuse, attributes some of it to sighs and tears, and yet refuses to acknowledge his own part in the destruction marks just how deluded, self-absorbed, and maudlin he is. The military inner facing of both "blasted" and "surrounded" (here carrying the conflated sense of the late Latin *superundare*, "to rise in waves," and the more modern meaning, "hemmed in on all sides") suggests that he is at war with himself, an idea which rises to his consciousness a few lines later in that ambiguous vocative "O, selfe traytor" (l. 5). But at first, as he enters the place of renewal, he puts the blame for his decline totally on external factors. And conversely, he at first expects that external factors alone will save him, until his experience refines his theory and he learns the internal impetus of happiness.

   And at mine eyes, and at mine eares,
   Receive such balmes, as else cure every thing;
      But O, selfe traytor, I do bring
   The spider love, which transubstantiates all,
      And can convert Manna to gall,
   And that this place may thoroughly be thought
   True Paradise, I have the serpent brought. (ll. 3–9)

With that curious "O, selfe traytor," at once an appositive and a vocative,[36] he seems momentarily to achieve the objectivity and distance that direct address implies. And in that second he knows his own concurrence with self-destruction. Yet refusing to accept identity with his own "spider love," he sees himself, in some measure at least, as a latter-day Adam duped by love for a woman, this time in full knowledge of good and evil.

   He analyzes the nature of his love and blames that for his unhappiness. His sarcastic appraisal of it in the end, however, amounts to sardonic self-criticism. His first name for his love, "spider love," at once raises the image of a love so entangling, limiting, and possessive that it destroys its object. Perhaps the man has stifled his beloved and hence killed her love with his jealousy, his need to control her. With its mythological allusion to the proud Arachne, moreover, "spider love" also associates his affections with pride, even arrogance. In the Renaissance Ovid's tale of Arachne's challenging Athena to a handiwork contest and consequent metamorphosis into a spider was generally treated as an allegory of pride; Edward Topsell understands it that way in his bestiary.[37] The spider image in "Twicknam Garden" thus suggests that strands of jealousy and pride are so entwined with this man's love that they spoil everything for him, transubstantiate "all." And in images of the Eucharist reversed, he delineates the exact nature of that transformation: "convert Manna to gall" (l. 7). The reversed transubstantiation of the sign of God's love during the Exodus and the substance offered Jesus on the Cross captures the wracking pain, despair, and helplessness the lover feels in his abandonment as well as the nurture his love once offered him. His torture is all the worse because he has betrayed himself to such pain. And through a series of associations between the serpent as traitor, the serpent as a symbol of pride and jealousy, and the serpent as Satan, the speaker momentarily assumes a demonic link with death, chaos, and destruction. He compresses all of these complex feelings and realizations into the sarcastic comment that his retreat to Twicknam Garden has turned that paradise into a true Eden, snake and all.

Having acknowledged his alliance with death and destruction, the speaker next seeks a form more fitting for him than that of a man— another version, surely, of self-definition. He wants the outward resemblance of a man, but not the emotions. But he also wants to express in some ostentatious way, either by groaning or weeping, the sadness he will no longer feel.[38] He also insists that he remain in the garden: only such a well-delineated transformation will do.

> Love let mee
> Some senslesse peece of this place bee;
> Make me a mandrake; so I may groane here,
> Or a stone fountaine weeping out my yeare. (ll. 15–18)

The speaker's plea implies a wish for recognition of his despair. But he prefaces his request to Cupid with a proviso for cutting off social contact inside and outside the garden:

> But that I may not this disgrace
> Indure, nor leave this garden . . . (ll. 14–15)[39]

The "disgrace" ambiguously refers to the public tittering about his loss and to the mockery which he believes the vernal trees guilty of, simply because they appear so new and vital. He seems to want to escape from everything. Through the particulars of his transformation, however, his retreat to Twicknam Garden includes some communication with the larger social world. The speaker thus does not denounce the values of that world by his withdrawal; he repudiates only his failure in that world and the woman who caused his humiliation. The particular meta-

morphoses he seeks, moreover, imply either his innocence or his victim-
ization: the mandrake was held to germinate from the sperm of a
hanged man,[40] and every weeping statue of a person is cognate with a
Pietà. The speaker's prayer to Cupid is a request for a new identity as
the epiphany of the lover's subjective self-evaluation: he is blameless
and guiltless.

Having assuaged himself of any responsibility for his own unhappiness, this Dreaming Cynic is ready to confront at least part of the larger
social world in his new identity as a fountain. He sees his transformation
as an apotheosis and immediately envisions himself summoning lovers
to receive salvation from him. In fact, his imaginative projection is so
intense that he addresses those hypothetical lovers and at the end of his
speech offers them Communion:

> Hither with christall vyals, lovers come,
>   And take my teares, which are loves wine,
>   And try your mistresse Teares at home,
> For all are false, that tast not just like mine. (ll. 19–22)

The latter-day Adam has become a savior in the religion of love; his tears
of grief and despair have been transubstantiated into Communion for
his followers. "My teares . . . are loves wine," he says, "come," "take."
In his daydream, his tears and the wine of love they produce provide
what neither Adam, Saint Paul, nor any number of church fathers
could—an acid test for faithfulness. The transubstantiation of his sacrifice repairs the havoc and chaos which the "spider love," the "serpent,"
wreaked on him: it upends the topsy-turvy world his mistress created.

The possibility that in his new form as a fountain and in his new
occupation as a savior this lover might be a false god, an idol, never
occurs to him. But then for him, as for the other Dreaming Cynics, a
dramatic exchange always coincides with a retreat from self-knowledge.
One measure of this man's self-delusion is that he ignores the irony of
his godlike posture even during an imaginary encounter.

Once he has initiated his fictitious listeners into his religion of love,
this cynical "god" teaches them its doctrine. The great revealed truths
turn out to be truisms about the discrepancy between appearance and
reality, dressed up in aphoristic garb.

> Alas, hearts do not in eyes shine,
> Nor can you more judge womans thoughts by teares,
>   Then by her shadow, what she weares. (ll. 23–25)

These maxims drive home the single great "verity" that women are
deceitful. The phrasing alone saves them from being ludicrous. In

accordance with his new public role as a savior, the speaker fashions his judgments as aphorisms, a word whose meaning in both Latin and Greek is derived from the fact that such utterances resemble the decrees or resolutions of public bodies. He thus subtly confirms his new public identity as a figure whose opinions and judgments, whose *sententiae*, are beyond question.[41] Yet the "alas" with which he introduces his aphorisms reminds us that his wisdom comes from personal experience.

The imaginary dramatic scene, then, is overlaid with a lyric complaint in which "you" means "I." Generalization softens the man's sense of isolation and special mistreatment; the fictional encounter confirms his *sententiae*, but beneath all of these rhetorical palliations he is bemoaning his lost love. No wonder, then, that in the final couplet he repudiates women:

> O perverse sexe, where none is true but shee,
> Who's therefore true, because her truth kills mee. (ll. 26–27)

Immediately he cuts from general name-calling to "shee"—at once a designation for any woman or for a specific woman, perhaps the speaker's mistress. This ambiguity suggests that the generalization that follows might derive from the speaker's recent misfortunes in love. His lady, like all women, speaks truthfully only to injure her lover. For a moment a phrase from "Womans Constancy" resonates:

> Or, your owne end to Justifie,
> For having purpos'd change, and falsehood; you
> Can have no way but falsehood to be true? (ll. 11–13)

Yet immediately the intensity of "Twicknam Garden" separates the two.[42] There is no verbal playfulness with truth and falsehood here, only the speaker's ironic awareness that he wishes his lady had lied to him and his deep cynicism about love. Perhaps the final couplet contains the Cynic's conclusions about women, which he will pass on to the lovers who come to him in the garden. Its epigrammatic form makes it particularly mnemonic. Yet culminating the strangely personal details of man's inability to read a woman's thoughts in her eyes, the couplet seems to sum up the lover's chain of feelings rather than his studied conclusions; he relives his disappointment rather than teaching others about love and duplicity.

In "Twicknam Garden," then, the lover imagines that he rights the wrongs of love by warning men about fickle women and offering them a test for their ladies' truthfulness. That his heroism occurs within a lyric complaint, however, reveals the lover's hopelessness, even his wish to continue pitying himself. He daydreams rather than acts. Moreover, instead of retreating to the garden for regeneration and renewal, he escapes into it. There, alone and out of place with the verdant plants, he cries out in despair for a metamorphosis by which he can regain his identity as an innocent duped.

In these poems Donne performs some of his deftest generic modifications. The figure of a forlorn lover turned cynical revenger suggests a complexity too entangled for either a lyric complaint or a straightforward confrontation anywhere but in a soap opera. "Song: 'Goe, and catche a falling starre' " and "Womans Constancy," generically the simplest of these poems, spill over their lines. Their speakers impose their past experiences with love onto their present moments until their listeners become not only the people the speaker originally addressed but an aggregate of people and feelings in each man's past life. In other poems Donne compresses the richness of feelings and experiences into encounters that veer into narrative, slip back into lyric reverie, or give way to a remembered or imagined confrontation far more vivid to the lover than his present engagement. Some poems have all of these elements. In "Twicknam Garden," for example, a lyric complaint suddenly materializes into a fictional Eucharist, which in turn fades into an imaginary address to a group of women, among whom is the man's former sweetheart. This shifting of listener quite naturally implies a modification of the speaker as well. As the listeners change, so does the speaker's relationship with them; each man assumes a role suited to his audience as he perceives it at any given moment. In "The Indifferent," for example, the speaker is a virile boaster, an angry and fearful lover, a supplicant to Venus, and a revengeful man—different facets of his being that emerge in his various encounters, real and imagined. In those poems where the reader is the real audience, where the persona and his cardboard listeners are both blatantly fictitious, the same kind of shifting occurs. In "The Legacie," for example, the speaker makes it quite clear that his tale of an autopsy is pure hokum: he lets the reader in on his game. Then he proceeds to engage his cardboard lady with that narrative as if she believed him.

The idea of a speaker's changing his personality to suit his listener touches the larger but related issue of the speaker's honesty and straightforwardness. As a rule (which proverbially proves itself by exceptions) these lovers withhold the complexity of their feelings in a dramatic exchange. Since most of the encounters resemble battles, quite naturally the speaker presses his arguments as strongly as possible and ignores those related issues and those ambiguities about his love that detract from his main point—that women treat men cruelly. But none of these poems stands up as just an exchange. Even in "Womans Constancy" the improbable rationalizing exceeds the dramatic situation and obliquely suggests the speaker's experience beyond the poem. All of the speakers lapse sufficiently from their immediate circumstances to indicate another dimension of their beings. In those poems that sustain the illusion of an encounter, the additional revelations about the man's complicity in his romantic difficulties and about the improbability of his revenge conflict with the impression he tries to make on his listener, and he usually dismisses those revelations because he cannot or will not cope with them. Hence all of the poems end with a satiric flourish, a return to the confrontation that the speaker concludes with a stinging rebuke. Simply because Donne creates the illusion that his speakers exist beyond the limits of their utterances, however, he insists that the success of their rebukes be measured in terms of the man's life. And on this scale these cynical men are far less successful. They become the emotional equivalent of the metaphor by which they describe themselves—men killed by their mistresses. They no longer respond to love or have the resiliency to renew themselves spiritually. Instead they insult, rebuke, and revile women, a pattern of life ultimately self-destructive. The personae who mask as lovers stand up to the same measurement. Their lives beyond the poem, however, are vital: they create and wink and laugh.

5

The Mutual Lovers

The most frequently quoted and praised of Donne's *Songs and Sonnets* celebrate the joys of fulfilled love.[1] As numerous critics have pointed out, they "record the poignant delight of mutual love-making," depict "the rapture of fulfillment and the bliss of union in love," and sound "the finest note in Donne's love-poetry . . . the note of . . . the joy of mutual and contented passion."[2] Confronting the natural miracle of mutual love, these lovers respond with an almost formal celebration, as have sonneteers from Dante and Petrarch to Sidney, Spenser, and Shakespeare.[3] Yet even as these speakers commemorate the joy of mutual love, they feel the mortal coil tightening around them, its pressure made stronger because of the very bliss they experience. Donne's Mutual Lovers react by denying their mortal bonds and wrangling with any suggestion of their dissolution. They try to argue death away and celebrate instead the immutability of their love and hence their lives. They vacillate, to use Earl Miner's phrase, between "lyric affirmation and satiric denial."[4]

Ironically the object of their satire, of their abhorrence and hence denial, lies within themselves, indeed is the very condition of life. Their mortality at once defines the enormous possibilities of their love and sets its limitations. Within time, these speakers know, their love grows, ripens—and decays. Hence they wrestle with time, affirming it, denying it, using it up. They are all haunted by the "houres, dayes, months" which turn into "yeares and yeares" and ultimately lead to "absence, darknesse, death."[5] Even those lovers just embarking on romance bring mortality into their utterances, albeit sometimes playfully. Time and death obsess those men who have fully tasted a rich and heady love; those two subjects nearly madden the men whose mistresses are dying. Happy lovers in and out of Donne's poetry, of course, feel that their love will endure forever. Part, indeed, of the wonder of love consists in its power to erase the sense of time. Donne's Mutual Lovers share this general exuberance and freedom. But they also insist on exploring the truth of their feelings about immortality. If one can posit the lovers' intellectual positions from omissions in their utterances, these men deny such conventional palliatives as immortality through poetry. With equal vigor they retreat from the Christian, Neoplatonic consolation of heavenly immortality, although they do not deny that their love might continue in some form after death. (Only the speakers of "The Canonization" and "The Exstasie" affirm the spiritual nature of their love.) Instead Donne's Mutual Lovers insist on wanting physical immortality, on having life continue as it is forever. Nothing less consoles them; hence nothing consoles them.

These men intellectually pursue their apprehensions about dissolution sometimes to the point where their fears threaten even their happiness. In "The Anniversarie," for example, that most joyous of Donne's love poems, the speaker moves away from both his lady and his commemoration of their first year together to stare with his mind's eye into the "two graves" (l. 11) which will "divorce" (l. 12) them after death and to glance imaginatively at the blandness of eternal love. That is, his apprehensions about their mortality threaten to spoil the couple's celebration, to keep them from loving "nobly" (l. 28) and living deeply. And in "A Fever" the lover so consumes himself with arguing away his lady's approaching death, so absorbs himself with alleviating his fears of dissolution, that he virtually ignores her lying on the sickbed. Argument in these poems is always directed inward, always removes the speaker from his dramatic situation and hence from his beloved. Ultimately, moreover, it magnifies man's inability to modify universal law with even his cleverest syllogism. Conversely, the necessarily frustrating limits of argument project the speaker back into his dramatic situation, back into time and place and contact with his beloved, where he can truly loosen his psychological shackles to mutability by living fully and nobly and commemorating his love. Donne's Mutual Lovers finally commit themselves to the nobility of living deeply in spite of their mortality, that nobility Sir Thomas Browne comments on in *Hydriotaphia*: "But man is a Noble Animal . . . solemnizing Nativities and Deaths with equal lustre, nor omitting Ceremonies of bravery."[6] Browne might have added love to his list of brave commemorations.

The miracle of each of these poems is that the lover can slough off his preoccupation with mortality to celebrate his lady and his love, thereby affirming the idea that deep human feelings can for a moment make time irrelevant. Donne himself writes of this idea in a letter to the Countess of Bedford, appropriately undated:

> It makes no difference that this [letter] came not the same day or bears the same date as his [her brother's]; for though in inheritances and worldly possessions we consider the dates of Evidences, yet in Letters, by which

we deliver over our affections, and assurances of friendship, and the best faculties of our souls, times and daies cannot have interest, nor be considerable, because that which passes by them, is eternall, and out of the measure of time.[7]

"Times and days" are not "considerable," nor worth reckoning, in matters of affection, friendship, and religion, Donne says, for these matters are "out of the measure of time." Donne's Mutual Lovers affirm the same paradox. With full and painful acknowledgment that their lives are tending toward the grave, each man commemorates his love, paradoxically thereby freeing himself from his psychological and spiritual, mortal shackles. Immortality inheres, as it always has, in celebration.

The women who initiate such glorious commemoration are incarnations of physical and metaphysical union with their lovers. They embody perfect and true love, born of reason and consummated by sexual intercourse.[8] As such they have become their lovers' whole world, as have the ladies of sonnets since Petrarch's time. Through the metaphor 'the lovers are the world to each other, 'each lover creates a reasonable and orderly, sometimes even a magnificent, cosmos as an extension of himself and his mistress.[9] These earthly objective correlatives of the relationship (or more precisely, of the speaker's perception of that relationship) insist that the love contain sexual consummation as well as a blending of the couple's minds and spirits. Beyond this, each man's imaginative world of love corresponds to his psychological needs at the moment of his utterance: the perpetually new and warm hemispheres "without sharpe North, without declining West" (l. 18) of the man in "The Good-morrow" first experiencing true love; the "spheares" (l. 11) or spiritual perfection of the man in "A Valediction: forbidding Mourning" who is about to leave his lady behind as he sets off on a long journey; the whole world turned back to "the first nothing, the Elixer" (l. 29) after the man in "A Nocturnall upon S. Lucies Day" experiences his beloved's death. The attributes each man assigns to his microcosm provide paths for understanding the speaker and his state of mind.

Like all of Donne's love poetry, even these lyrics commemorating the joys of mutual love really delineate little of the reciprocity between the couple, focusing instead on the speaker's shifting thoughts, feelings, and responses. Part of that exclusion, of course, inheres in the form of the dramatic monologue. Yet for all the absence of mutual cherishing, the woman's presence and responses remain just beyond the words of these poems. Without her the words could not come into being, for the speaker would not be the same man. To phrase the matter somewhat differently, the woman stands behind each of these Mutual Lovers in the best sense of the proverb, "Behind every great man there is a woman." In a particular lyric she might also stand before him or lie beside him, but her being has in some miraculous way become subsumed into his and changed his. The trope 'the lovers are the world to each other' is a figure of this unity. The mutuality of these lovers, then, is almost a unity, for the woman comprises the man's world. He sees her less as a separate entity than as an extension of himself and as both the source and the object of his love. Hence without a second thought the man in "The Good-morrow" uses the pronoun *we* to summarize both his and his mistress's feelings about love and their past experiences with it. Another measure of this conjunction is the ease with which a Mutual Lover slips from encountering his lady to thinking out loud in front of her. That is, he not only readily makes her privy to his inmost thoughts and feelings but he treats her as an extension of himself, an ear which hears him muttering to himself. From one point of view such a joining is miraculous; from another the woman loses her individuality in the process of being her lover's world. Donne's lyrics of mutual love imply the former. In any case, this closeness not only initiates the great joy of these poems, it also initiates the man's fears. For to lose his lady would be to lose himself.

As their titles indicate, both "The Good-morrow" and "The Sunne Rising" commemorate a first, joyous realization of mutual love, and, like many of Petrarch's sonnets, link that awareness to nature's most prevalent symbol of rebirth, the dawn.[10] Both are variations of the *aubade*, or dawn song, in which the lover serenades his lady, and of the related *aube*, in which the lovers express regret that the day has come so soon to separate them. "The Good-morrow" celebrates the dawn of a new love through phrasing and imagery appropriate for the dawn of the new day, thus paradoxically setting the time and place for the lovers' initiation into an immutable world of love. As the two awaken from their first night together, the speaker suddenly finds himself incredibly happy and overwhelmed with the feeling of rebirth.

> I wonder by my troth, what thou, and I
> Did, till we lov'd? were we not wean'd till then?
> But suck'd on countrey pleasures, childishly?
>   Or snorted we i'the seaven sleepers den? (ll. 1–4)

His former experiences seem more like illusions than reality; everything runs together as in a dream. Although he includes his lady in the inquiry about their previous love, he does not seek the details of her past romances. He wants only the assurance that she is real and that she shares his dazzling joy. Her wonder confirms his; her sense of a happy estrangement from all other amorous involvements corroborates his.

With the certitude of her love, he symbolically closes the door on his past life. " 'Twas so" (l. 5), he says, fixing all of his previous experiences in a nebulous former time.

His pronoun of oneness, *we*, substantiates the transformation of these two lovers by delineating their complex unity. Because the man seems to derive his metaphors from his past experiences with love, in one sense his *we* is presumptuous. Yet because it is true emotionally for them both, true in a manner that obliterates factual details, his *we* is right. His " 'twas so" thus also closes the past for both of them, the different particulars of their experiences notwithstanding.

He compresses the details of their past into images of infancy and of a 187-year sleep, both of which imply a continuance into the present.[11] His reference to the "seaven sleepers" in particular not only impinges on their present life but defines it. These youths, under persecution from Decius, hid themselves in a cave, were walled up by their pursuers, and left to die. Miraculously a long sleep fell over the youths, and they woke up to a new world.[12] Like the seven sleepers, these lovers rouse themselves to a new world of love. They too have escaped; they too have experienced a Rip Van Winkle–like separation from time and events. Yet guidelines for their new life derive from their past experiences, including the sexual "countrey pleasures."

Having affirmed the miracle of their mutual love in his single voice of two, the man turns to his beloved and professes his personal wonder at their love.

> But this, all pleasures fancies bee.
> If ever any beauty I did see,
> Which I desir'd, and got, 'twas but a dreame of thee. (ll. 5–7)

She not only makes all his dreams come true; she makes all former truths as shadowy as dreams. He even seems to see his earlier mistresses dimming from his memory as he speaks about them. His "beauty I did see" becomes a "dreame" of the flesh-and-blood wonder before him. His former paramours even lose their sexual appeal as he thinks about them, for he refers to "any beauty" whom he "desir'd" and "got" quite suddenly with a neuter pronoun, *'twas,* as if the particular women faded into a generalized concept of beauty which in turn manifested itself in his beloved. Thus like both of their past lives, his former loves dissolve into a nebulous realm of his preexistence.

With something akin to ritual, the man solemnizes the lovers' passage from their former half-existence to the full life of their love by welcoming their souls, their spiritual dimensions which have lain dormant until this momentous morning of awakening.

> And now good morrow to our waking soules,
>   Which watch not one another out of feare;
> For love, all love of other sights controules,
>   And makes one little roome, an every where. (ll. 8–11)

The salutation "good morrow" in the Renaissance still retains its original blessing, "God send you a good day"; sometimes the phrase is even written "god morrow" (OED). This religious tenor fills the lovers' greeting to their souls, and the hallowness of the welcome suggests that for this couple the awakening of true love resembles the great reawakening of the souls on Judgment Day. And at the dawning of his new love, the man, overcome with the sublimity of his experience, seeks to define it. Gazing in his lady's eyes and seeing her soul shine through her loving look,[13] he explains the constancy of their glances first by negation. Unlike other lovers, these two "watch not one another out of feare." He again measures their love by earlier experiences and marks the difference. Speaking for both of them and for the first time from a position of authority, the lover explains the most fundamental element of mutual constancy: the lovers restrict their gazes because in each other they find everything, heaven and earth. He expresses love's magical paradox of contraction and expansion in an aphorism, that particular kind of *sententia* best suited to speakers whose authority and character are beyond question.[14]

> For love, all love of other sights controules,
>   And makes one little roome, an every where.

The singular voice of two corroborates the verity of the conclusion.

To say that the lover here speaks only in the single voice of two, however, is to diminish the importance of the scene: their bedroom in the quiet early morning after a first night of love. As the man looks deeply into the eyes of his beloved, his words, however general and aphoristic, convey his own great happiness, his own willing submission to remain fixed in this chamber of love. His lady thus becomes his listener, the subject and object of his praise, as well as the mute speaker (to use an oxymoron) in their mutual conclusions about love. And the impersonal dignity of the *sententia* expands to include personal endearment as well.

Overcome with the perfection of his love, the man breaks the formality of this intimate scene with rhapsodic imperatives for his new life. He banishes the most exciting discoveries of his time—events as engaging as the space explorations in our day—with virtually the back of his hand, exalting instead his love.

> Let sea-discoverers to new worlds have gone,
>   Let Maps to others, worlds on worlds have showne,
> Let us possesse our world, each hath one, and is one. (ll. 12–14)

The perfect tense of "have gone" and "have showne" suggests the attraction these discoveries and tales of discoveries generate. Others will follow, but not these lovers. Inside the universe of their "one little roome" their conquests will yield all that the territorial and astronomical explorations can offer, maybe more. The imperatives in this rhapsodic renunciation once again focus attention on the complex speaking voice. Here, as earlier, the man represents the two of them. But as he voices the imperatives to which both assent, he also directs both himself and his lady to follow those imperatives. His rapture thus fulfills a didactic purpose: his ebullient commemoration teaches the two of them how to live and love well. Thus he is speaker and listener, extoller and learner. She occupies these dual roles less fully.

By stanza 3 the man applies his skills of rhetoric to his teaching, "proving" to his beloved by homey *sententiae*, rhetorical questions, and axioms drawn from natural philosophy the supremacy, even immortality, of their love. Some of his earlier exuberance is gone; so is the assurance implied in his earlier dialogue of one. In this stanza he raises the question of individual responsibility in love and with it gives a fleeting sign of apprehension about the permanence of their love and their lives. Looking into his lady's eyes, he first assures her of the truth before her.

> My face in thine eye, thine in mine appeares,
>   And true plaine hearts doe in the faces rest. (ll. 15–16)

He follows this certitude with a rhetorical question to which she should tacitly reply "no where":

> Where can we finde two better hemispheares
> Without sharpe North, without declining West? (ll. 18–19)

If he stopped his argument here, the lover would have confirmed through rhetoric the assurance and happiness of their love, which he has already commemorated. But somehow amidst all his joy and celebration, the lover has momentarily retreated into himself, there to confront a complex of feelings: the sense that his love is too perfect to die; the strong desire to immortalize this moment, not in verse as poets do, but in fact; and the doubt, however fleeting, that his mistress does not love quite so strongly as he.[15] He therefore appeals to her to immortalize the two of them by loving him as much as he loves her. From a practical standpoint, he is asking for an impossibility, upending the natural course of things. And as if to combat just that sort of practical reaction, he draws his syllogism about the possibility of their immortality from an axiom out of scholastic philosophy:[16]

> What ever dyes, was not mixt equally;
> If our two loves be one, or, thou and I
> Love so alike, that none doe slacken, none can die. (ll. 19–21)

His analogy, at first applied to the stability of an equally mixed love, suddenly takes in the lovers as well. And the man both apprises and assures his lady of the possibility of their continuance through time in a physical state that miraculously escapes the ravages of time. He thus lends scientific truth to his wishes, putting the responsibility for their immortality within their own power. His qualifying "if" states openly the slight doubt that argument implies.[17]

Yet the lover's affirmation controls the poem. The man's gestures of persuading his beloved by argument and of drawing proof for their immortality from scholastic philosophy, while revealing his uncertainty, temper ever so slightly his assertion of their perfect world of love. Through his *sententiae*, his rhetorical questions, and his glorification of his lady, he verbally creates an immutable microcosm "without sharpe North, without declining West"—without sorrow, heartbreak, and death. His balanced phrasing underscores his belief in the mutuality of their love: "My face in thine eye, thine in mine appears," for example, with its caesura after the fifth syllable, beats out their reciprocal affection. And his speaking in the single voice of two conjures up a realm of perfect oneness, where the two lovers think and feel and speak in unison. Like the delightful coincidence when lovers or friends suddenly utter the same words at the same time, this speaker knows and feels his mistress's thoughts and thus can speak for her.

From the fabric of his feelings, then, this Mutual Lover creates an imaginative world of love. By assertion he banishes from it all danger and destruction; by assertion he makes it and all its hemispheres adhere to the simplest and thus most profound concept of honesty ("true plaine hearts doe in the faces rest"); and by assertion he endows it with the possibility for permanence. From the moment the speaker comes to the emotional apprehension of himself and his beloved as a microcosm, however, he imaginatively leaves the time and place of his original *aubade*. Instead of lying next to his mistress in a little room the morning after their first night of love, he finds himself emotionally in another world that he and his lady have created by their love. Their awakening at once symbolizes waking up in a new realm, and, with another bridge from emotional truth to physical truth, waking up in a realm free from mortal shackles. The man's *aubade*, which by definition commemorates a specific time and sometimes a specific place, thus ultimately glorifies the eternity of a world without a fixed place and to which the term *place* itself is incongruous. Likewise his lady accrues an identity infinitely more powerful than the one in the opening lines, as she becomes the lover's whole world, metaphorically and emotionally, and then his literal means of immortality.

Donne modulates the sober joy of "The Good-morrow" to high comedy in his other *aubade* commemorating mutual love, "The Sunne Rising." There the presence of a third "person" opens up the comic possibilities for the genre and mutes the speaker's celebration of his mistress and his love. Unlike the lover in "The Good-morrow," who ignores the sun altogether, the speaker in "The Sunne Rising" directs his bombastic oration to the personified sun and thus seems to shatter the quiet intimacy of lovers alone in a curtained bed. Yet because he enacts his oratorical performance just for his lady, he in fact builds a close relationship with her by fabricating a speech, jokes, and compliments, generating through his witty scenario the deepest kind of private joy.

The oration is a masterfully comic application of rhetorical rules to a fictitious declamation, a witty exercise no educated Renaissance man would miss. Unlike the speakers in many of Donne's poems who manipulate poetic or oratorical conventions solely for the benefit of their readers, the lover in "The Sunne Rising" entertains and delights his mistress with his forensic skill. Thus the dramatic situation of the poem holds. The larger scene of lovers in their bedroom at dawn encloses a miniature mock drama between the man and the sun.

From his opening words the speaker insults his listener, the sun, whom he is trying to persuade.

> Busie old foole, unruly Sunne,
>   Why dost thou thus,
> Through windowes, and through curtaines call on us?
> Must to thy motions lovers seasons run?
>   Sawcy pedantique wretch, goe chide
>   Late schoole boyes, and sowre prentices. (ll. 1–6)

He upbraids the sun for intruding on the lovers' domain. Then he disputes its authority, attacking the great ruler of time as unruly; questioning its age, intelligence, and voyeuristic tendencies ("busie old foole"); and insinuating that the sun is out of its realm, rather small of size, and somewhat niggardly in dispensing its powers—all of which are implied by *wretch*.

This ranting speaker thus turns the *exordium* of his oration, the opening remarks designed to dispose his listener favorably, into bombast; the sun is unlikely to prove tractable after such an attack. But, of course, that touches the essential point. No matter what anyone says or does, the sun will not conform to man's wishes. Ovid's elegy from which Donne apparently derived "The Sunne Rising" ends with just that realization. And Donne's lover, knowing all too well the futility of his yearning to make time stand still, burlesques a speech of persuasion to entertain his mistress. In the process he also defies his mortality, if comic bombast qualifies as defiance, and mocks himself by treating humorously his deepest wish and bitterest frustration: "must to thy motions lovers seasons run?" But on the surface he entertains.

Indeed the lover follows rather closely the standard rhetorical means for creating humor. His apostrophes to the sun not only express his indignation, but generate laughter by pointing up the keen resemblances between the actions of the majestic sun and those of officious and petty men: the sun is a Peeping Tom leering at the couple in bed and a sanctimonious scold certain of the holiness of punctuality.[18] Their abrasiveness reminds us of Quintilian's conception that "laughter is never far removed from derision. . . . when we point to such a blemish in others, the result is known as wit, it is called folly when the same jest is turned against ourselves."[19] On the surface Donne's lover displays wit, even gaiety. In spite of the fictional nature of the speech and hence its humor, its purpose, to persuade the sun to "shine here" for the couple, is a restatement of lovers' age-old yearning for permanence fitted out in witty dialectic. But the wit ultimately shows the speaker making jokes at his own expense—the other side of Quintilian's reveries about laughter and derision. In a metaphorical way the sun presents the insurmountable obstacle to the lovers' complete happiness, which the speaker counters with insults because he cannot attack it any other way. The presence of a real struggle underneath the banter accounts for the intensity of his antagonism toward the sun: his brusque assertions, biting questions, and the placement of the adversarial pronouns *thou*, *us*, and *thy*.[20]

It is with the realization of life's shortness, then, that this man celebrates the permanence of his love so passionately:

> Love, all alike, no season knowes, nor clyme,
> Nor houres, dayes, months, which are the rags of time. (ll. 9–10)

Although these lines present the compressed statement of facts, the *narratio* in the speaker's argument, to a greater degree they commemorate the lovers' sense of living in an eternal present: the happiness the two share as the man clowns before his lady and the sun filters through the tissued curtains of their bed. Recognizing fully his immediate situation, he modulates his comic harshness to song. His *sententia* immortalizes his happiness, his security, and his oblivion to all else but love. "Love, all alike, no season knowes, nor clyme." The double possibilities of *knowes* as "perceives" and "is subjected to" give the word single importance to both his song and his argument. For even as he realistically extols the lovers' blissful distraction, he boasts to the sun that time has no effect upon the two of them, that they live outside the limits of death, chance, and mutability. The intensity of his celebratory language, moreover, strengthens the impact of his *narratio*.[21]

Having touched the emotional center of his speech, the lover rebounds with outrageous banter in his performance before his lady. Belittling the sun's strength, he brags that he can "eclipse and cloud" the sun's beams "with a winke" (l. 13), never mentioning who will be left in the dark.[22] He inverts our experience with the blinding rays of the sun by impudently and hyperbolically praising the greater glory of his mistress. "If her eyes have not blinded thine, / Looke," he directs the sun, (ll. 15–16), and stuffs his audacity into a subordinate clause as if it were too commonplace for particular notice. Moreover, because this section of his speech comprises the *argumentatio*, or proof, he displays unprecedented arrogance by commanding the sun to verify for itself that the lovers' microcosm far excels the macrocosm. His actions at this zenith of his comic performance insist on his superiority to the sun and on the supremacy of the lovers' world to the earth. With something like defiant gesture he derides and mimics the symbol of time whose presence and power he cannot ignore.

As he moves through proof for the magnificence of the lovers' world, he describes the microcosm in terms of the distilled excellences of the macrocosm: the Indies rich with spices and gems, kings, kingdoms—the best the world has to offer. The description itself helps to reconcile the lovers' world with the larger realm the speaker dismisses in the *exordium* and intimates that his earlier hostilities are more rhetorical than real. His manner toward the sun remains somewhat abrasive, but even that bends under his impulse to extol his lady. His song mollifies the sarcasm of his disputation and in turn tempers his adversarial relationship with the sun.

> Aske for those Kings whom thou saw'st yesterday,
> And thou shalt heare, All here in one bed lay. (ll. 19–20)

To put all of this another way, even speaking about his beloved is enough to shake the lover loose from his obsession with time and death and mutability—all symbolized by the sun. Her magnificence also pulls him away from his self-conscious humor so that he concentrates on her for once. Until this point his witty disputation has put him in the spot—I mean sunlight; it has made him the center of interest. His praise of his lady shifts that center onto her. Insofar as the man's quarrel with the sun is a projection of his revolt against mortality, his ability to immortalize his love under the shadow of death bespeaks her greatness and his affection more eloquently than his most elevated comparison.

By the *refutatio* virtually all signs of argumentation disappear, and in the manner of a man confident about the truth of his feelings, he glorifies his love by avowing its grandeur and quintessence.

> She'is all States, and all Princes, I,
>   Nothing else is. (ll. 21–22)

The eloquent simplicity of his language, the assertive mastery of his tone, the sparseness and density of his words transport this *refutatio* far from wrangling and haggling over proof. The wonder of our love shines so clearly, the man seems to say, that commemoration alone is fitting for it. No argument remains; nothing but our love exists, "is." That tiny word hangs heavy with meaning.

When the speaker returns to the sun in the *peroratio*, he continues his mellow tone. The modulation itself registers an inner accommodation to the world and to time. Instead of fighting the inevitable mutability which the sun symbolizes, he accepts it and welcomes the sun with a proper *aubade*, greeting it at its rising. In other words, after the speaker fully experiences the wonder of his love and the freedom with which the truth of his feelings imbues him, he can extend generosity to his old adversary.

> Thou sunne art halfe as happy'as wee,
>   In that the world's contracted thus;
> Thine age askes ease, and since thy duties bee
> To warme the world, that's done in warming us. (ll. 25–28)

The morning has become sufficient unto itself; the sphere that brings that morning, the sun, may participate in the lovers' joy. And because the speaker accepts the inevitability of his own age, change, and decay, he treats the aged sun gently and sympathetically at this point.

Delightfully, but not comically, the speaker's change of heart occurs at just that point in his oration where he should make the strongest emotional appeal to the listener. And he does, but with a twist. The orator's emotional appeal generally tries to guarantee that the judge will decide in favor of the orator's case. The speaker in "The Sunne Rising," however, has not really made a case. He has argued that the lovers' world excels the earth; he has boasted about his superiority to the sun, as if the two were rival powers operating in different spheres. But he has asked nothing directly. He now makes that request, in the *peroratio*:

Shine here to us, and thou art every where;
This bed thy center is, these walls, thy spheare. (ll. 29–30)

Under the guise of shortening the sun's daily itinerary, the speaker entreats it literally to make the lovers' room its sphere. By implication he also asks it to abandon the rest of the world, let it freeze and die. These latter realities, however, never enter his words nor his consciousness, as reality has never touched the oration from its start. The lover merely makes a witty application of the rhetorical appeal to emotion for this fictitious encounter with old Sol. His specific references to bed and walls further suggest that the speaker gestures as he delivers his final words, pointing out vividly to the sun the smallness of its task if it changes orbits. With the greatest gentility he asks the all-seeing sun to share his viewpoint for a moment, to look down on the bed and see everything worth noticing. This pleasant and clever mixing of metaphor and fact, of course, continues to entertain the lady, as her lover demonstrates that his wit can gleam as well as sparkle. And yet there is ever so slight an edge to his jubilation. For all his wit, for all his charm, for all his deep love for his lady, the lover still asks for the one thing he cannot have— physical immortality. Here and now are all, he seems to say, but, oh, if only they could last!

This urge to assert the immutability of the lovers' world modulates in some of the poems to an avowal that mutual affection will not decay, even though the lovers are mortal. The speakers declare that in a world of change only reciprocal devotion endures. "Song: 'Sweetest love, I do not goe,' " "Loves Growth," "Loves Infiniteness," and "The Anniversarie" commemorate the immortality of human love and resolve the contraditions through metaphor.

In "Song"—a poem of parting that can as feasibly be discussed in Chapter 2, with the valedictions of the Witty Lover—the speaker attempts to assure his lady of the permanence of this affection as he leaves her. He also tries to convince her and himself that he will fare well on his journey and that the Petrarchan conceit 'the lover dies in parting,' will not prove literally true. To do so he comically rationalizes his departure as a feigned death, but his jest evaporates into a bit of ghastly self-mockery.

But since that I
Must dye at last, 'tis best,
To use my selfe in jest
    Thus by fain'd deaths to dye. (ll. 5–8)

That is, much as he tries he cannot laugh away the fear the two of them share about his survival. Similarly his argument that, like the sun, he will depart and return lacks conviction, and he asks his lady to "be-leeve" (l. 14), that is, have faith, in both his constancy and his security.

Indeed, faith and trust in the power of mind over matter seem to be all that are left to him. He breaks from his teasing to ponder how fully man is a slave to fortune, unable to prolong his good luck or to stop the fears and memories of bad luck; he pleads with his lady to keep from presaging his end. Their solace, he insists, rests in her optimism and in the fictitious mental construction she gives to his departure.

> But thinke that wee
> Are but turn'd aside to sleepe;
> They who one another keepe
>   Alive, ne'r parted bee. (ll. 37–40)

Even in this emotion-laden valediction, the lover keeps his hopes and consolations within the realm of possibility. All his lady can do to save him, he says, is to think positively and to remember him always. Although he colors these simple acts with metaphors that impart super-natural power to them, both people are aware of the limitations of his tropes: his self-parting metaphor, a palliation of the sleep-death anal-ogy, intimates his forebodings about the journey; and the final two lines present a bit of homey wishful thinking: that out of sight will not be out of mind. Yet the lovers accept these metaphors as verbal comfort in a time when no other comfort is available.

In sharp contrast to "Song: 'Sweetest love, I do not goe' " and the two *aubades*, where time and place control the lovers' utterances, "Loves Growth" lacks the nubby specificity of setting. Although the speaker breaks from his musing and turns to his lady in the final lines of the poem, thus acknowledging that she has been present all along, his mental grappling and hence the subtlety and honesty of his mind fill the lyric.

The man in "Loves Growth" begins by denying all of the poetic claims for love he has heard: its purity, its infinity, its immutability. Instead he hard-headedly bases his definition and understanding of love squarely on his own experience, careful to weigh his preconceptions against the empirical evidence.

> I scarce beleeve my love to be so pure
>   As I had thought it was,
>   Because it doth endure
> Vicissitude, and season, as the grasse;
> Me thinkes I lyed all winter, when I swore,
> My love was infinite, if spring make'it more.
> But if this medicine, love, which cures all sorrow

With more, not onely bee no quintessence,
  But mixt of all stuffes, paining soule, or sense,
And of the Sunne his working vigour borrow,
Love's not so pure, and abstract, as they use
To say, which have no Mistresse but their Muse,
But as all else, being elemented too,
Love sometimes would contemplate, sometimes do. (ll. 1–14)

He discredits the purity of a love that endures through its own changes; he rejects the completeness of a love that grows; and his physical desires tell him that love "bee no quintessence." By negative definition, then, he frees love from poetic illusions.

For all his insistence on proper definition, the speaker's denial of romantic grandeur in no way diminishes his love. Indeed his appraisal of love's toughness and goodness, for all its impurity, more fully confirms the strength of their relationship than poetic distortion would. This man's hard-headed praise finds its proper form in the stanza, a quatorzain similar to the sonnets in which other poets have celebrated their "erroneous" versions of love.[23] Yet most of the lines in "Loves Growth" pause, then push on with the movement of dialectic, for the man's concentration on correct definition momentarily keeps him from commemoration.

He continues his analysis in the opening sections of stanza 2, reaching paradoxically for those very comparisons by which poets have long idealized love—the sun, the stars, and the rebirth of spring. He, of course, applies them as analogies to understand the dilemma of a love which seemed infinite and yet increases, in part through the resurgence of his sexual desires.

And yet not greater, but more eminent,
  Love by the spring is growne;
  As, in the firmament,
Starres by the Sunne are not inlarg'd, but showne.
Gentle love deeds, as blossomes on a bough,
From loves awaken'd root do bud out now. (ll. 15–20)

The speaker is trying to cope with the newly revived facet of his affection that would "sometimes do," as the phallic "loves awaken'd root" confirms.[24] Yet in the process he, like poets before him, immortalizes the sense of rebirth and renewal that love creates. The elucidation of his sexual yearning thus unexpectedly yields to an expression of his tender feelings, which he can explain only with one of the oldest similes in love poetry—the reawakening of spring.

Nowhere does analogy burst into metaphor more magnificently than at the emotional peak of the poem, when the lover turns to his lady for the first time and sees the rightness of the conventional comparisons he has been disparaging.

> If, as in water stir'd more circles bee
>   Produc'd by one, love such additions take,
>   Those like to many spheares, but one heaven make,
> For, they are all concentrique unto thee. (ll. 21–24)

From his analogies of unity in diversity, the concentric circles in water and the spheres in heaven, he accounts for the unexpected increase in his desire. He experiences emanations from the same deep love he has always felt, not somehow from a new and greater one, as he suspected. Then, as if in a sudden manifestation of his love, his lady catches his eye. And as he applies all of his comparisons to her, they change from analogies to metaphors for feelings he realizes at that moment. To him she is perfection incarnate. Her comparison with the fixed center of a circle implies her permanence as well as her idealization; her association with heaven hints at her spiritual purity as well as her physical loveliness. She is, moreover, the man's little world, the earth around which the spheres of love revolve (if Donne had a Ptolemaic universe in mind) or the sun around which the planets turn (if he were thinking of a Copernican one).

Then he outlines for her their future together, specifically his projection of the continuing ardor of their love. This time he finds no difficulty accommodating a miraculous element into his definition of a love whose passion steadily increases through the years. Like the level-headed analyst in the opening stanza, he compares the growth of his love to the rise of taxes. Yet he embeds this analogy in a poetic cyclical metaphor by which love surpasses nature. The speaker's love will endure the literal seasons, indeed will imitate spring with its increased "heate" (l. 25). Miraculously improving upon nature, however, it will never suffer the death and coldness that winter symbolizes.[25] In other words, he sees the growth of his love in terms of the expected return of warm weather in spring and of the predictable spiral of taxes in time of war. To express the continuance of his love at such a high level, however, he introduces marvelous elements into his analogies. Like the irrational maintenance of high taxes in peacetime, the constant intensity of the speaker's love defies logic. He can account for it only as something beyond the predictable course of nature.

In "Loves Infiniteness," too, the speaker uses metaphor to reconcile his desire for all his mistress's love with his realization that "all," a fixed and static concept, cannot possibly apply to living affection. Like the other Mutual Lovers he wrestles with the human frustration of a finite being yearning for something of infinity. He concentrates on love rather than life, juggling his words to accommodate boundless affection to a limited and human capacity.[26] The specific term by which he confronts the frustration of human limitations matters little. Up against the reality of man's confinements like the other Mutual Lovers, he resolves his quandary with "loves riddles" (l. 29) and "a way more liberall" (l. 31), which as a comment on his treatment of a logical dilemma means a way less literal. He and his sweetheart will "joyne" hearts (l. 32) and "be one, and one anothers All" (l. 33), an organic metaphor, which nonetheless contains a determination to live fully and deeply together.

In spite of the similarity between "Loves Infiniteness" and the other poems of mutual love, its speaker is far more preoccupied with rhetoric and argument than the other lovers, as even this cursory outline of the poem indicates. His deft dialectics indeed detract from the illusion that he is seriously worried about having all of his lady's love or that he is really wrestling with human limitations. With Procrustean wit he devises a scheme for garnering her affection: since her stock of love may grow in the future and since he has already depleted his resources for securing it, he will merge with her. The marketplace metaphor enables the speaker to manipulate his argumentation so that he arrives at a satisfactory conclusion, but through the fallacy of speech respective. That same metaphor illuminates his wit: having purchased his mistress (l. 5) with all his Petrarchan currency of "sighs, teares, and oathes, and letters" (l. 6), he worries that in the future he may lose her to a more voluminous lover who can "outbid" him (l. 17). His solution is to offer "a way more liberall" (l. 31), more generous, than the usual exchange of the courtiers' marketplace—a witty demonstration indeed.

"Loves Infiniteness" thus seems more a game or a clever parody of scholastic argumentation than a serious exploration of love. The speaker preoccupies himself with his invention rather than with his life's circumstances: he shows off his creativity, not his emotion. Unlike the man in "Loves Growth," this lover reaches the resolution to his logical dilemma purely through the manipulation of words. Indeed, his puzzlement emanates from the logic or illogic of having all his mistress's love, realizing that her love might grow, and pondering his claim to that future love. In "Loves Growth" the dilemma springs from the increased passion the man feels in the *presence* of his mistress, that is, from the dramatic situation in the poem. Significantly, the man in "Loves Growth" examines his own feelings; the man in "Loves Infiniteness" speculates on his lady's.

In "The Anniversarie," as in the three previous poems, the speaker leaps in the face of logic to associate his love with immortality. He, like most of the Mutual Lovers commemorating a definite occasion, is haunted by mutability. The occasion itself happens in time and must be marked in time. Yet his steady and consuming love simply by its constancy eradicates his sense of fluctuation and change. The tension in this poem is particularly poignant, for an anniversary to people in the Renaissance marked a person's death as well as his marriage or the beginning of his love. And the mortal associations of an anniversary seem to mingle with this speaker's happiness as he proclaims to his beloved the perpetuity of their deep affection.[27]

The man and his mistress, alone together, are radiantly happy after a year of love. He turns to her and somewhat playfully announces the permanence of their affections in contrast to the mutability of the strongest and most powerful forces on earth.

> All Kings, and all their favorites,
>   All glory'of honors, beauties, wits,
> The Sun it selfe, which makes times, as they passe,
> Is elder by a yeare, now, then it was
> When thou and I first one another saw:
> All other things, to their destruction draw,
>   Only our love hath no decay. (ll. 1–7)

His public tone, the sense that he, the king of love, declares the age and change of all save him and his beloved, conveys his gaiety, his ability to play in his joy. For a second he smiles at his own imperiousness, but only for a second. His lighthearted proclamation develops poignant overtones: even as the sun makes times, they pass away. Everything flows quickly by. This second vanishes almost as soon as it arrives. He halts before "as they passe" and pauses long on "now," as if he were measuring the length of the moment, holding it, then feeling it go. The passage of this year has signal importance for them because it marks how long ago that first deep glance sparked loving recognition between them. He implies but cannot or does not say that as that gaze "is elder by a yeare, now," so are the gazers. Instead he dismisses such considerations by telling his lady that their love transcends "all other things," and by commemorating its constancy.

The cloud of mutability drifts through the man's thoughts, then, even as he extols his love and plays king for his mistress. His particularly graphic words reveal how vividly he imagines death: all things "draw" to "destruction," everything must "decay." His many references to time (at least eighteen in the first stanza alone) disclose his preoccupation with it. And when in the process of affirming the permanence of his love he repeats the Christian paradigm of "first, last, everlasting day" (l. 10), he imaginatively leaps from his room of love to the grave. That devastating non sequitur with which stanza 2 begins signifies his abrupt distrac-

tion; and even though he continues to address his mistress, his rhetorical relationship to her changes radically. Instead of entertaining her and
praising her, he ponders aloud so that she overhears him rather than
hears him.

He conceives of death purely as physical separation from his lady (a
wryly literal test of the Petrarchan conceit 'the lover dies in parting'),
almost playfully fancying that their union would continue if they could
be buried in the same grave. As he ponders the separation, he projects
himself to the moment of his death and reviews his love from that
vantage point. And from that perspective, even their sorrows are felici-
tous. He and his beloved

> Must leave at last in death, these eyes, and eares,
> Oft fed with true oathes, and with sweet salt teares. (ll. 15–16)

He experiences something akin to double vision, as if the lady standing
before him suddenly turned stony cold and he remembered her as she
had been in life. He virtually (and perhaps actually) touches "these eyes,
and eares," and immediately envisions them blind and deaf in death,
unable any longer to be "fed" by his "true oathes" and "sweet salt
teares." This shocking mental overlay, rendered as if before his very
eyes, pounds home the definition of death as separation from the
woman he loves; he counters it by dwelling on his happiness "here
upon earth" (l. 23).

He further consoles himself and to some extent his mistress by returning to the assurance that their love will keep its "first, last, everlasting
day."

> But soules where nothing dwells but love
> . . . then shall prove
> This, or a love increased there above. (ll. 17–19)

His reverberating word *prove*, however, conveys his own skepticism
about a heavenly love that could surpass such an eminently satisfying
earthly one. Even as *prove* indicates that their souls will show their love
to be immortal, magnificent, and more, it also signifies that their souls
will put their love to the test, will find out the genuineness, the validity,
of their earthly affection. Thus implicit in the test is the possibility that
love as they know it may not continue. But choosing momentarily the
possibility that love in heaven will excel all earthly experience, he
claims, "And then wee shall be throughly blest" (l. 21). But again a
certain uneasiness on the part of the speaker intrudes. *Throughly* here
means perfectly and completely, in keeping with the purified, immate-
rial nature of their being after death. But *throughly* has a physicality

about it also, when it means the whole thickness, substance, or extent. And the speaker momentarily imposes a materiality on their afterlife by seeing their love as better because its blessings will penetrate them more completely than on earth. Immediately the inappropriateness of that application hits him, perhaps because it conflicts with the idea of the soul as being without form. And he visualizes an equality in heaven sharply at odds with the supreme individuality he feels on earth.

> And then wee shall be throughly blest,
>   But wee no more, then all the rest.
> Here upon earth, we'are Kings, and none but wee
> Can be such Kings, nor of such subjects bee. (ll. 21–24)

The uniqueness of their earthly love pulls him away from further speculation, and he rejects heavenly bliss in favor of a love he knows.

Having chosen earthly felicity, the speaker turns his full attention once again to his lady, this time instructing her on how they can live all the moments of their years together as fully as possible.

> Who is so safe as wee? where none can doe
> Treason to us, except one of us two.
>   True and false feares let us refraine,
> Let us love nobly, 'and live, and adde againe
> Yeares and yeares unto yeares, till we attaine
> To write threescore: this is the second of our raigne. (ll. 25–30)

Through his rhetorical question and advice for the future he banishes all diversions that keep them from their love, and in his celebration of life he advocates absorbing themselves in the ever-running present by refraining from fears about the continuation of their relationship. Neither desertion nor death should concern them, he says, for only by attending totally to life as it happens can they psychologically create the illusion of permanence.

The toughness of his advice almost disappears in his triumphal tone, and yet only the assumption behind his majesty accounts for that toughness. He has internalized the nobility that alone can make him king of love, ruler over accidents, time, and chance. And he urges his mistress to do the same. He insists upon loving magnanimously, without self-pity or self-indulgence: "Let us love nobly." Consequently, since life and love are virtually synonyms to him, he demands they live the same way. The bareness of his entreaty reveals its profundity. Such discipline, such vulnerability, such generosity of self, differentiate them from other lovers, elevate them so that in spirit they really become love's nobility, kings. That role which the speaker donned lightly in the opening of his address assumes a dimension of truth in his resolution.

His fully realized royal *we* and his commands that dissolve into entreaties provide appropriate accouterments for a king of mutual love whose partner is equally designated a monarch. The nobility of his commitment to live one minute at a time as long and as deeply as he can makes him truly worthy of his title. He marks this anniversary of his ascension to the throne of love as other kings do, publicly, with a formal, perhaps even written proclamation. The bold tone with which the poem opens and closes resembles the majestic flourish of such royal decrees: public commemorations of a king's anniversary, birthday, or coronation. Unlike truly public proclamations, however, this one reaches the ears of only two people. But then these kings hold a public position only in the realm of love. Since each has but one subject, all the realm hears the decree. Apart from the delicately witty extension of the royal metaphor, however, the triumphal closure enacts a ritual marking of this extremely private anniversary. The lovers, even in their solitary domain, commemorate the continuation of their union in writing, verify the truth that they have lived together as kings of love for one whole year. Perhaps they sign their names and affix the date on a parchment bearing a poem or on a line in a family Bible. In any case—and the particulars of the paper are irrelevant to the ritual—an air of solemnity surrounds their writing as the two usher in the second year of their life together:

> Let us love nobly, 'and live, and adde againe
> Yeares and yeares unto yeares, till we attaine
> To write threescore: this is the second of our raigne.

The lover looks into the future, perhaps glances at the blank page beneath their signatures, and envisions lines of signatures and dates under the first one, until in his imagination the two of them "attaine to write threescore."[28] Their reign, just in its beginning, will surpass the expected tenure of kings, even the lengthy rule of Elizabeth's forty-five years. The speaker's lines with their fully realized royal *we* could be a ritual toast uttered by the two of them to mark their anniversary. They are not, but the man alone rightfully can give voice to their mutual commitment.

By the end of "The Anniversarie," then, the speaker has resolved the tension arising from his sense of permanence in his love and his simultaneous awareness of mutability—or resolved it as well as man can. He has projected the length of his love as almost the expected years of a man's life, and from the vantage point of their first anniversary, sixty years stretches far indeed: "yeares and yeares unto yeares." He has rejected the consolation of a Neoplatonic love "increased there above" in favor of love as he knows it, even with the inevitability of time and change and death. But the cost of such a choice demands that the lovers spend their years well, free from distracting fears, true or false. The ritual ending of the poem seals their vows as they usher in the second year of their reign together.

In all of the poems of mutual love discussed thus far, the speaker directs his utterance to his mistress, although in the course of it he sometimes drifts into reverie. Even in "The Sunne Rising," where the lover upbraids a sun he himself has personified, he in fact entertains his lady with a comic oration to a fictitious intruder. This is as much as to say, then, that the poems of mutual love discussed thus far create a sense of intimacy by having only the lovers share an understanding of their love and the commemoration of it. The privacy of the couple's knowledge of their love as well as the intimacy of their shared experience helps create for them (and incidentally for us, the readers) the sense that they are a world apart—a microcosm, to use their most prevalent metaphor. The presence of a listener other than the woman by extension disrupts their insularity. For once an outsider participates at all in their love, even if he merely overhears a discussion of its nature or oversees the couple embracing, that intruder breaks up the integrity of the lovers' world. Conversely, the speaker's willingness to let his lady overhear his thoughts indicates his intimacy, even oneness, with her.

The breakdown of exclusiveness occurs in only three poems I include in this chapter: "The Canonization," "The Extasie," and "A Nocturnall upon S. Lucies Day, being the shortest day." In the last of these the death of his mistress has already destroyed the speaker's little world before he approaches the young lovers and uses them as a sounding board for examining the validity of his love. In "The Canonization" and "The Extasie," to differing degrees, certainly, the speakers ask sanction for their love from outsiders and thereby raise the possibility that they do not quite believe all they say about their romantic relationship. The men in these poems also employ persuasive rhetorical tactics similar to those used by the Hedonists. And both of these speakers insist a bit too much on the religious nature of their love. None of the other Mutual Lovers does. That is, they seem somewhat defensive about their love.

The speaker in "The Canonization," caught in the midst of an attack upon his love affair, impudently defends himself by telling his listener to mind his own business, then proceeds to elaborate to his outsider some intimate details of his patently sexual relationship. That is, for all his protesting, he makes his love his listener's business. And that peculiar tension caused by berating a listener whose sanction one seeks creates some of the difficulties with the poem.[29] For the first third of the poem, the speaker concerns himself with little else than establishing a superior stance toward this outsider, much as the lover in "The Sunne

Rising" does in jest. In both cases the tactic corresponds with the orator's emotional appeal to his listener in the *exordium* of the speech—an appeal which presumably will make the hearer tractable. The man in "The Canonization" maneuvers to get just the right tone of carelessness into his speech, even to the point of feigning lack of interest in his own age, health, wealth, and all worldly affairs around him. For only with such superiority (or the illusion thereof), born of a calculated disregard for life, can the lover so intimidate his friend, who humanly cares about the things of this world, that the friend will assent to the "canonization" of such an "unworldly" pair.

What occurs in the opening lines, therefore, is a hyperbolically mocking self-portrait by a man who says he has little interest in his physical well-being. The picture he paints so far exceeds anything his opponent might say of him that it puts the opponent on the defensive.

> For Godsake hold your tongue, and let me love,
>   Or chide my palsie, or my gout,
> My five gray haires, or ruin'd fortune flout,
> . . . .
>   So you will let me love. (ll. 1–3, 9)

The lover is a self-described paralytic, plagued by arthritic attacks and swollen legs, and broke. Oh yes, he also has five gray hairs, which, as others have duly noted, he vainly counts. Yet his love can transport him from any concern with these maladies and misfortunes. His hyperbole suggests that he directs some of his mockery outward, and a hint of flippancy comes through his tone—a practiced carelessness, a delight in caricaturing himself in order to elicit pity. Once he has done that, he begins to intimidate his listener by showing contempt for all of that man's interests:

> With wealth your state, your minde with Arts improve,
>   Take you a course, get you a place,
>   Observe his honour, or his grace,
> And the Kings reall, or his stamped face
>   Contemplate. (ll. 4–8)

With impudent disdain he checks off the trivialities with which his acquaintance might amuse himself, his very manner revealing his studied air of reproach.

One particularly telling aspect of that manner is the speaker's careful attention to the artifices of rhetorical style that create the impression of natural charm. He inverts his syntax in the two clauses of line 4 by demonstrating his skill at pleasing the ear. Then he links disparate concepts together by grammatical parallelism (ll. 6, 7) and thus exhibits his own fineness of thought and precision of distinction. In each of the four lines immediately above he uses at least one grammatical, auricular figure: chiasmus (l. 4), homoeoteleuton (l. 5), zeugma (ll. 6, 7), and antithesis (l. 7). Some of the figures overlap, and an extended rhetorical analysis here is not the point. Nonetheless it is relevant to note the particular weight and use both classical and Renaissance theoreticians assign to these figures. Puttenham regards them as delightful trivialities: "So also may your whole and entire clauses be in such sort contriued by the order of their construction as the eare may receiue a certaine recreation, although the mind for any noueltie of sense be little or nothing affected. And therefore al your figures of *grammaticall* construction, I accompt them but merely *auricular* in that they reach no furder then the eare."[30] Quintilian says much the same thing, adding that when used properly these figures give the impression of natural charm. However, following Cicero, he insists that unless they emphasize vigorous thought, they are mere trivialities.[31] Donne's lover seems bent more on conveying natural charm than on emphasizing the fine points of a vigorous argument: his opprobrium, paraphrased, says merely, "Attend to any political, intellectual, or prestigiously social matter you want; just let me love." Similarly the grammatical figures he uses highlight his glib dismissal of the world rather than his sharp analysis of its evils or limits.

The second stanza also illustrates little but the speaker's wit. In effect, he says, my love hurts no one or nothing, and draws the listener into agreement with him by casting his defense of love in rhetorical questions.

> What merchants ships have my sighs drown'd?
> Who saies my teares have overflow'd his ground?
> When did my colds a forward spring remove?
> When did the heats which my veines fill
> Adde one man to the plaguie Bill? (ll. 11–15)

In spite of the argument of these lines, that the speaker's love is an innocent occupation, wit dominates. The man's deft treatment makes Petrarchan commonplaces about effusive and unrequited lovers sparkle anew.[32] With just a tinge of ridicule, he characterizes himself as a woebegone lover—crying, sighing, burning, and freezing at the whim of his mistress. But with a surprising comical twist, he admits that for all his emotions, he cannot quite match those much-sung lovers whose heartaches devastate the earth.

> What merchants ships have my sighs drown'd?
> Who saies my teares have overflow'd his ground?

This "modest" self-appraisal, possible only because he accepts the hyperbolic Petrarchan conceits literally, undercuts any of the listener's serious objections by turning them into laughter.[33] For by conceding and enlarging upon the core of his friend's opposition—that love is ruining the speaker, even transforming him into a romantic fool—the speaker blunts the attack altogether, a tactic that Quintilian advocates, particularly when one is trying to distract the audience from the facts of the case.[34] With the adroitness of a skilled orator he also diverts his friend's argument to his own advantage. The listener has, no doubt, elaborated upon the folly and dangers of abandoning all for love, and the speaker at first seems to be refuting this position. In "who's injured by my love?" (l. 10) he virtually begs the question of his own decline, then deflects it onto other people, a social consideration altogether irrelevant to the argument. But it is the social dimension he pursues— through his references to lawyers and soldiers, whose occupations injure others—while innocently he and his mistress "do love" (l. 18). By changing the import of the listener's objections, then, from personal harm to social harm, he distracts his friend, but only at the expense of logic, through the fallacy of speech respective. Donne's contemporary readers would pick up the inconsistency immediately.

This witty self-defense turns to titillating descriptions in stanza 3, as the speaker hints at, then sanctifies, the intimate details of his sex life. This man who seemed to shield his love from both gossip and criticism with the imperative, "Hold your tongue," now invites such comment ("call us what you will") and justifies his actions in the name of love ("wee'are made such by love," l. 19). Hurling epithets at himself before his listener can join the fray, he compares himself and his mistress to those salacious insects, flies (l. 20), or butterflies, and to "tapers," which at their "owne cost die" (l. 21).[35] The sexual pun on *die*, the incapacitating lust suggested by the popular emblem of candles consuming themselves, the comparison with lascivious insects—all confirm the sexual nature of the speaker's love and corroborate, perhaps surpass, his friends' worst imaginings. Yet the man courses through his comparisons: the strong, masculine eagle; the gentle, feminine dove; and finally that fiery, androgynous bird, the phoenix, which throughout Renaissance lore symbolizes Christ.[36]

> The Phoenix ridle hath more wit
> By us, we two being one, are it,
> So, to one neutrall thing both sexes fit.
>   Wee dye and rise the same, and prove
>   Mysterious by this love. (ll. 23–27)

His blasphemous audacity resounds through such phrases as "to one neutrall thing both sexes fit" and "wee dye and the rise the same," where he not only puns on *dye* but uses *fit* to mean sexual joining.

Through all this teasing, the speaker seems to withdraw a bit from his

listener to play with words. His wittier riddle of the phoenixlike lovers
implies a more conventional version of the puzzle, presumably, from
the allusion to the Resurrection, Christ's own mysterious death and
rebirth. And the speaker congratulates himself in part for finding a
cleverer solution to the riddle than writers and emblemists before him:
"The Phoenix ridle hath more wit by us." He launches into his explanation with great relish. Under thinly disguised sexual allusions, he details
his indefatigable virility, his mistress's constant readiness, and their
insatiable desire for one another, pretending all the while that these are
fitting applications of the phoenix's miraculous and mysterious recreation. His audaciously comic comparisons hint that he is bent on
shocking his listener and delighting himself. With the phoenix riddle,
then, the speaker begins to back away from his argument and to play
with words. As he does, his relationship to his listener gradually
changes. Instead of rebuffing his friend and defending his own romance, the man structures the story of his love life to fit the detailed
procedure for canonization in the Roman Catholic church.[37] In the process he becomes a witty narrator, even autobiographer and autohagiog-
rapher, whose tale generates an interest for its own sake and only
obliquely furthers the ongoing argument.

By stanza 4 the speaker tries on the complex role of a lover whose
legend lives in poetry, perhaps his own. He speaks in the voices of a
lover and a critic, maybe even of a writer, and eventually of a metamor-
phosized saint. The conflation of roles reflects his ambivalent relationship to his listener, born of the sport of the moment. Once again a
sexual pun launches his comparison of the lovers as saints:

> Wee can dye by it, if not live by love,
>   And if unfit for tombes or hearse
> Our legend bee, it will be fit for verse. (ll. 28–30)

With that slight aspersion about poetry and the consequent acknowl-
edgement of the impropriety of his love affair, he boldly applies two
combined steps in the process of canonization—the investigation of the
subject's personal sanctity and a detailed scrutiny of his writings (if we
assume that the lover is a poet as well) to himself and his mistress—
finally calling the details of their life together "hymnes" (l. 35). And in
the last lines of the stanza, as his metaphors congeal into a full-blown
fiction of the saints' legend, he finds just the right bravado:

> And by these hymnes, all shall approve
> Us *Canoniz'd* for Love. (ll. 35–36)

Never mind that the hymns precede the sainthood or that this man
fashions his hagiography while he and his mistress are still alive and

hence before a proper examination of the burial place can occur. This fiction emerges from the repartée of the moment, where chronological details (and hence the validity of the speaker's tale) have little relevance.

The complex relationship between the lover and his friend at this point comes into focus through his designation of the worshippers as "all." Insofar as the word applies to the people of the future, the speaker merely informs his friend how widespread his following will be. But because he makes the universality of his future disciples a detail in an argument, *all* may well include the friend too. You will live to pray to me, the lover implies, but does not quite say. He thus maintains something like a one-to-one engagement with his listener, even as he complicates his rhetorical posture by reshaping his autohagiography in front of that listener.

By the final stanza the lover slips almost completely into his role as a patron saint, repeating the invocations of his worshippers to his friend, who has challenged the wisdom of giving up all for love. The situation itself is absurd: the speaker transports himself through time and space, cannonizes and metamorphosizes himself, then creates and repeats the prayers of his faithful followers, and all to convince his friend that he has not made a mistake in love. He even makes his disciples' address delineate the perfect and sacred union he shares with his mistress. And his performance is a comic masterpiece capped with a mock-serious supplication.

> You whom reverend love
> Made one anothers hermitage;
> You, to whom love was peace, that now is rage;
> Who did the whole worlds soule extract, and drove
> Into the glasses of your eyes,
> So made such mirrors, and such spies,
> That they did all to you epitomize,
> Countries, Townes, Courts . . . (ll. 37–44)

The "proof" overwhelms the issue, as the fiction of the saints' legend overshadows the dramatic encounter. In the final words of the poem, this role-playing lover pulls the *coup de grâce* when, as a saint of love, he orders his friend to make supplications to him:

> Beg from above
> A patterne of your love! (ll. 44–45)

With these words the speaker resumes his initial argument with a vengeance, winning by supernatural intervention (as does the man in "The Indifferent") but with the added fillip that this fellow provides his own aid.

"The Canonization," then, develops into a witty extravaganza, where the speaker's kaleidoscopic role playing heightens the fun. The listener, unlike those fabricated straight-men in "The Legacie" and "The Expiration," never quite vanishes, but he never quite retains his initial identity as a prudent man either. For he too is engaged in the game of witty repartée. No doubt both men exaggerate their positions and heighten their defenses with hyperbole.[38] Yet within this rhetorical strife, the lover does both define and defend his relationship with his mistress in rather profound terms. Like the other Mutual Lovers, these two see each other as microcosms, for they "did the whole worlds soule extract," each epitomizing "Countries, Townes, Courts" to the other. The incantation, comic in its context as part of a mock saints' legend, unexpectedly details the perfect sufficiency of these Mutual Lovers, who are "one anothers hermitage" (1. 38) and whose love is "peace" (1. 39), It is as if the speaker finally can offer a serious defense of his love only within a playful context, for to a cynical or even a practical man—anyone not immersed in love—such devotion seems ridiculous. And one can best defend folly with folly, with excessive, impossible, wonderful hyperbole whose very extremity sometimes captures the truth of the feelings. Incidentally, in the fiction of the canonized lovers these two realize physical immortality together, a state which the other Mutual Lovers only wish for.

The other poem of mutual love in which the speaker opens the lovers' intimacy to an outsider is "The Exstasie." Religious images intrude in this poem, but without the heavy sexual overtones of "The Canonization." Nevertheless, as the immense critical controversy about "The Exstasie" evidences, religious justification for sexual passion fills the lines and creates much of the difficulty in interpretation.[39] In addition the totally narrative rendering of "The Exstasie," even with its dramatic overlay in the latter half, departs radically from Donne's usual face-to-face exchanges in the poems of Mutual Lovers. In fact, the only other solely narrative poems in the *Songs and Sonnets* belong to speakers espousing extreme views of love, as I discussed in Chapter 3. The presence of an outside listener in this poem of mutual love, then, coincides with several other unusual factors and suggests the signal importance of both the listener and the narrative form to the poem's interpretation.

We begin with a puzzle: To whom is the lover speaking? Where? When? What is his relationship with the listener? And we stumble into another puzzle: Why is the man telling the story of his ecstasy at all? Initially, the last question offers a more obvious answer: the lover tells his story to teach someone else about the miraculous union of soul and body he shares with his lady and perhaps to reform that someone else as well. This same man invents the hypothetical lover, who is

> so by love refin'd,
> That he soules language understood (ll. 21–22),

in order to confirm the purifying effect of "this dialogue of one" (l. 74). We can with some justification assume that he repeats the story verbatim, complete with the souls' dialogue, for the same purpose. With some explanation of why this man relates his experience, then, the question of listener returns.

The absence of such devices as rhetorical questions and *sententiae* and the presence of a meandering narrative suggest a certain intimacy between the speaker and his listener. The details of the personal story and the lyrical ballad-measure in which it lies reinforce this closeness. Perhaps one or two good friends attend the speaker. Maybe his mistress is there. We do not know. He never addresses her and refers to her once in the third person (l. 16), as if she were not present. With some sense of a listener, the "where" and "when" of the narration become unimportant, for the speaker, with all of his concern with the location of the ecstasy, never establishes either a present time or an actual place in which he relates his story.

What is paramount to the lover is the setting of the ecstasy itself. He opens his narration with it, and he returns to it in his analogies.

> Where, like a pillow on a bed,
>   A Pregnant banke swel'd up, to rest
> The violets reclining head,
>   Sat we two, one anothers best. (ll. 1–4)

In a few words he sketches a secluded outdoor scene: a hill, a flower, and, depending on how we read *banke*, a stream somewhere. The sexual undercurrents make the passage strangely reminiscent of an erotic pastoral landscape. And although the lovers do not for the moment conduct amatory adventures there, they do take on natural characteristics that illustrate their fitness for this erotic pastoral place. A "fast balme" springs from their hands (l. 6), which in turn are "entergraft[ed]" (l. 9). Moreover, their virtue and goodness qualify them as arcadian sojourners: they are "one anothers best."[40] That is, the narrator establishes immediately that the lovers are nature figures together in a pastoral scene. And from this fact he arouses the pastoral expectations that they will consummate their passion and that their love, however physical, will be innocent.[41]

He continues shaping his introduction to the souls' discourse with witty versions of pastoral commonplaces. As befits sojourners in arcadia, the lovers enjoy their ease, their *otium*—almost to a fault:

> Wee like sepulchrall statues lay;
> All day, the same our postures were,
>   And wee said nothing, all the day. (ll. 18–20)

Meanwhile their souls carry on the business from which the bodies are diurnally free for once, the *negotium*: "our soules negotiate there" (l. 17). The translingual pun on *negotium* calls attention to the narrator's witty juggling of pastoral conventions, which he handles deftly throughout the description of the bargaining souls. They, intent on advancing their state (l. 15) and perhaps hot from a passionate battle with one another ("two equal Armies," l. 13), have no place in this pastoral landscape, nor, for that matter, within the pastoral lovers. And the narrator gives them none.

> Our soules, (which to advance their state,
>   Were gone out), hung 'twixt her, and mee. (ll. 15–16)

Instead they discourse suspended in the air, becoming fully infused in the pastoral scene only when they reenter the lovers' bodies, which have enjoyed their free time in the place all along, even "making babies" with their eyes (ll. 11–12) in a parody of lovers' usual procreative activities.[42] In other words, these lovers take their *negotium* into their *otium*: they carry the results of their bargaining into the leisure of their lovemaking—a neat reversal of the practice in many Renaissance pastorals, such as Marvell's "The Garden," where the person carries the mental and spiritual regeneration of his *otium* back into the world of *negotium*.[43] Donne's lovers, in fact, make full use of their *otium* only when they act on the conclusion the "abler soule" (l. 43) has drawn from the *negotium*: "to 'our bodies turne wee then" (l. 69). The narrator, in short, sketches a mock pastoral and creates a comic tone which runs under much of his discourse. The pastoral setting of "The Exstasie" gives the narrator a frame of reference on which he can build a parody, the exact subject of which for the moment remains elusive.

One measure of that parody is the hypothetical bystander who could attest to the purifying effect of the souls' "dialogue of one." Even before his spiritual purging this onlooker is

>   so by love refin'd,
> That he soules language understood,
> And by good love . . . grown all minde. (ll. 21–23)

And yet from the souls' discourse even he

> Might thence a new concoction take,
>   And part farre purer then he came. (ll. 27–28)

This man's initial virtue surpasses even that of the abstemious lovers, who at least hold hands and sweat a bit in the process.[44] Yet if he is to follow both the teachings and the practice of the "abler soule," the onlooker will depart no longer "all minde," but, like the souls, ready to enjoy the body—a "farre purer" state because of the spiritual exchange that precedes it. That is, even before the listeners hear the souls' explanation of their love, they meet an almost perfect ear-witness who has been purified and saved by the discourse of the souls. But contrary to our (and surely their) expectations, this bystander found his salvation in sexual intercourse. The slightest hint of a debate between reason and passion, or soul and body, with the bystander as the judge, thus emerges even before the "dialogue" gets underway.

The souls' explanation of the basis for their love affirms both its goodness and its permanence:

> Th'Atomies of which we grow,
> Are soules, whom no change can invade. (ll. 47–48)

Such a deep love, they agree, "defects of lonelinesse controules" (l. 44). Yet the souls' duet opens with strangely comic terms, given the scholastic tone of the explanations that follow and considering the spiritual and intellectual nature of the souls.[45]

> This Exstasie doth unperplex
>   (We said) and tell us what we love,
> Wee see by this, it was not sexe,
>   Wee see, we saw not what did move. (ll. 29–32)

The souls' choice of "unperplex" itself perplexes. Its Latin root *plexus*, p.p. of *plecto*, "to plait," intensified by *per*, "thoroughly," expresses the tight intertwining and confusion of an issue with which we associate *perplex*. Yet lightly the souls dismiss this entangling with the prefix *un*, as if their separation from the bodies had simplified all the complexities of "what we love." Moreover, the literal braid or twist of "unperplexed" glances back at the lovers' "eye-beames twisted" (l. 7), as if the souls were commenting on the bodies' rapt and entangled eye contact and at the same time noting their own clear vision: "wee see." Moreover, the souls' playing with sound and tense in "(we said)," "wee see," "we saw" belittles the human dilemma that sexual attraction sometimes seems like love.[46]

Once the souls assure each other of the spirituality of the love that fills them and once they have enacted their parody of a marriage and sealed that with love's "interinanimat[ions]" (l. 42), they decide to reincarnate themselves so that their bodies too may consummate their love.[47] But first they evince a bit of hesitation about their return and split some scholastic hairs to affirm the rightness of that retreat. Insisting on their distinction from and superiority to the bodies, they agree:

> They'are ours, though they'are not wee, Wee are
>   Th'intelligences, they the spheare. (ll. 51–52)

Like two philosophers they agree with Aquinas, who separates body and soul but comments extensively on the soul's natural tendency to embodiment, even if it has in some way been displaced.[48] Yet they hunt for some virtue in their physical beings and hence for a rationalization for reentering them.

> We owe them thankes, because they thus,
>   Did us, to us, at first convay,
> Yeelded their forces, sense, to us,
>   Nor are drosse to us, but allay. (ll. 53–56)

Their press for separation from the body echoes through their tattoos of "us" and "to us," even as their images suggest a more homogenous relationship between soul and body, "allay." And they speak of the bodies as the vanquished, recently defeated in the battle fought presumably about the nature of love: "Yeelded their forces, sense, to us." Hence like victors the souls can possess their conquests. That is, these souls rationalize their reentry into their bodies, yet insist on their distinction from the bodies.

The souls' continued discriminations about the bodies whom they have defeated intellectually—they call themselves "th'intelligences"—suggests the debates between soul and body which fill both medieval and Renaissance literature: the dialogues, as they were and are routinely called.[49] The souls in "The Exstasie" label their discourse likewise, "this dialogue of one" (l. 74), thus noting the concord in their conversation. But these souls are so alike that they are able to blend into one. Finally they offer a religious reason for sexual intercourse,

>   that so
> Weake men on love reveal'd may looke. (ll. 69–70)

Like evangelicals, they believe they have a social responsibility to manifest their love for the benefit of others.[50] Even the onlooker they invent watches the physical consummation in order to note the "small change, when we'are to bodies gone" (l. 76). Both of these justifications expose the souls' continuing difficulty with the bodies, their insensitivity to the bodies' viewpoint, and the intransigence of their arguments—all qualities so antithetical to one's normal expectations for a soul that the "dialogue" stands revealed as a parody of numerous similar debates about the nature of love, many of which, like "The Exstasie," occur in a pastoral world.

Once the note of parody enters these arguments, the souls' mutual leap to the dramatic present tense as they contemplate reincarnation seems wryly comic:

> But O alas, so long, so farre
> Our bodies why doe wee forbeare? (ll. 49–50)

They offer convincing arguments about the perfection of spiritual and physical entangling in "that subtile knot, which makes us man" (l. 64). Yet the disparity between the souls' distinctions from the bodies and the souls' words of praise for a blend of spiritual and physical love creates a subtle, ironic edge. They begin with the analogy of the blood begetting spirits of a middle nature between body and soul in order that the corporal and spiritual parts of man might entwine, "knit that subtile knot." Then the souls compare this joining to the union of the soul and such physical faculties "which sense may reach and apprehend" (l. 67).[51] The equality implicit in the knitting metaphor gives way to a superiority, however, as the souls apply the analogy.

> So must pure lovers soules descend
> T'affections, and to faculties,
> Which sense may reach and apprehend,
> Else a great Prince in prison lies. (ll. 65–68)

They resign themselves to incarnation in order to manifest their spiritual nature ("a great Prince") and to produce an offspring, that same prince, containing both body and soul.[52] Immediately they explain sexual intercourse as religious necessity and validate their interpretation with an eyewitness's account of the small change in them. Hence, in spite of the fact that the souls reenter the bodies and assent to sexual relations, thereby allowing the bodies' importance in love, they win their "argument" by construing intercourse as a religious necessity, a spiritual act over which they, as souls, have full control.

By the end of the souls' ironic dialogue of one, which is to say, by the end of the poem, the narrator has virtually disappeared behind the voice of the "abler soule." In some sense his verbatim repetition of the souls' words as part of his own autobiography suggests his concurrence with their view and therefore the rightness of his disappearance. Most interpretations of "The Exstasie" as a straightforward poem make this assumption; most interpretations of it as a seduction do not. The issue is paramount, for it touches the central questions about the poem: How consciously does the narrator create his autobiography? And to what end?[53] The element of parody in both the introduction and the dialogue strongly suggests that the narrator shapes the souls' words as deliberately as he fashions his own, so that the souls will reveal their own limitations. (Donne uses the same technique in presenting all the autobiographical narrators in the *Songs and Sonnets.*) By setting their dialogue in an erotic pastoral landscape, moreover, the narrator introduces a measure of incongruity about the souls that would otherwise be elusive. Logically, therefore, insofar as the narrator identifies with the souls and their viewpoint, he must also regard himself and his ideas somewhat ironically. His narrative, in addition, is structured on a network of correspondences between the bodies and the soul and between the speaker and the speaking souls; the one parodies the other. First, the union of the souls imitates physical consummation and even produces an offspring, the "abler soule." The proposed sexual union, in turn, will generate a new creature as well, this one composed of body and soul, the "great Prince." In another parallel both the souls and the narrator validate their arguments for the purity of their love with hypothetical eyewitnesses. These and other parallels underscore the artistry of the whole narration and by extension the deliberateness and subtle irony with which the speaker shapes his tale.

Once more the questions of listener and purpose obtrude. The closeness between the speaker and his listener becomes signally important in assessing the parody and irony in the poem. Unless the listener catches the literary parody of the dialogue, the witty reversal of *otium* and *negotium*, the burlesque of the souls' language, the assumption of innocence in an erotic pastoral landscape, the puns on propagation, a good portion of the narrator's invention evaporates, and the speaker is left with the somewhat less satisfying endeavor of convincing his friend (or perhaps his mistress) of the purity and sanctity of his love. The sheer amount of literary parody in "The Exstasie" argues for at least one listener who appreciates it. Hence "The Exstasie" is, if nothing else, a parody of the numerous dialogues on love. The extent to which the speaker also tries to convince another of the sanctity of his love—in a Christian sense and hence unlike the mock saintliness of love in "The Canonization"—offers more difficult problems. Some clues, however, do exist. Simply because the parodies and ironies in the poem are subtle and the strong intellectual defense of Neoplatonic love draws on such diverse teachings as medical science and Aquinas's definition of the soul, the poem presents a mountain of persuasive evidence and implies a listener to be induced. Whether that listener is male or female, however, remains a mystery.

To consider "The Exstasie" and "The Canonization" with Donne's more straightforward lyrics of mutual love is to notice the extent to which the speakers in these two poems exaggerate their love in order to justify it. That exaggeration in "The Canonization" not only provides the comedy of the lover's argument and therefore his best defense against ridicule, it also paradoxically expresses his feelings, in that wonderous way that hyperbole, by inflating the facts, can sometimes touch the truth of the sentiment. In "The Exstasie" the exaggeration is part of a more sophisticated and literary game that ends in persuasion. But whether the persuasion itself is only rhetorical the poem never quite reveals.

The hyperbolic defense of love in these lyrics coincides with the presence of a listener other than the speaker's beloved, hence with a breakdown of the insular sufficiency of the lovers' microcosm. And perhaps that fact accounts for some of the need for justification, particularly in "The Canonization." Simply because the Mutual Lovers do create a world for each other that no outsider can grasp, the lover has to resort to exaggeration, even in a comic context, if he is to come close to expressing his feelings to anyone outside that world. And incidentally the hyperbole may make him feel more comfortable in an encounter with such a stranger.

Most of the Mutual Lovers, alone with their ladies and hence free from the need to defend themselves, celebrate their love as an experience far beyond their comprehension.

> A love, so much refin'd,
> That our selves know not what it is (ll. 17–18),

concedes the man in "A Valediction: forbidding Mourning" and sees his inability to understand his love as proof that it can endure separation. The man in "Loves Growth" concludes his careful examination of his ever-deepening love with an illogical, metaphorical explanation: "No winter shall abate the springs encrease" (l. 28). And the lover in "The Anniversarie" backs away from contemplating the increase of his love in heaven to enjoy love "here upon earth" (l. 23) as long and as fully as possible. Even in "Aire and Angels," that poem of mutual love that pursues definition almost exclusively, the man seeks not to understand his love but to find a proper object for it. He accepts without boasting or analysis the spiritual parentage of his love; "my soule, whose child love is" (l. 7), he notes in passing. Yet he seeks the proper object for a love that would also "doe" (l. 8), one of Donne's favorite terms for sexual intercourse. Indeed, with a bit of self-mockery, the man tells his lady that he almost drowned his love by concentrating too much on her physical beauty, which doubtless aroused his desire to "doe":

> Whilst thus to ballast love, I thought,
> And so more steddily to have gone,

With wares which would sinke admiration,
I saw, I had loves pinnace overfraught. (ll. 15–18)

The autobiographical thrust of "Aire and Angels" suggests that the
lover has come to understand the nature of his affections by loving, not
by intellectualizing.

Yet in the best-known celebration of mutual love in the *Songs and
Sonnets*, "A Valediction: forbidding Mourning," the speaker seems to
intellectualize his love and to sanctify it. To acknowledge as much and
yet to insist on the magnificent affirmation of earthly love in the poem
requires an exacting examination of its definitions and elevations of
love, as well as of its dramatic structure.

Although the title implies a poignant scene of parting, the opening
analogy and the series of analogies that follow detract from the illusion
of a dramatic encounter in the poem.[54] Untypically for Donne, the poem
might be written rather than spoken. The speaker seems remote both
from his mistress and from any anxiety over his imminent departure.
His control and reasoned argument seem to refute his words of consolation. Yet the title mollifies such reasoning, demanding that the farewell
contain something of the impersonality of a decree, something austere
and distant enough to justify the authoritarian *forbidding*. This impersonality in turn creates an ambiguity about the listener or listeners. Just
who is forbidden to mourn at this leave-taking? Whose absence will
seem like death to which lover? As befits Mutual Lovers, the questions
apply to both. So does the prohibition in the poem. And the speaker's
reliance on literary comparisons to ease the pain of parting indicates that
he follows his own advice.

This phenomenon of the self as both counselor and counselled, as
both speaker and listener, rhetorically removes the man from some of
the emotional turmoil of a farewell. Like thousands of literary lovers, he
voices his distress at leaving by means of the Petrarchan commonplace
'the lover dies in parting.' Yet his witty refashioning of that conceit
distinguishes these lovers from those whose "teare-floods" and "sigh-
tempests" (l. 6) fill lyric poetry so that he can press his prohibition
against mourning.

As virtuous men passe mildly'away,
    And whisper to their soules, to goe,
Whilst some of their sad friends doe say,
    The breath goes now, and some say, no:

So let us melt, and make no noise. (ll. 1–5)

He almost subsumes the destruction of the separation in his plea for
dignity and quiet resolve. Yet the comparison gets away from him.

Unexpectedly the analogy for serenity at the moment of departure reveals a stark contrast between the lovers and the dying men who urge their souls to heavenly bliss. Perfect happiness for the lovers depends upon being together; paradoxically the pair resembles the "sad friends" who wait upon the dying men, both anxious and bereaved at the moment of death. The speaker's gratuitous inclusion of the friends seems to project that aspect of the separation he wants to dismiss, but cannot; for the sense of physical loss overpowers him as he figures forth his departure in terms of death.

Subtly his very complex analogy discloses yet another dimension of the physical separation he cannot dispel, his sexual yearning for his beloved. Perhaps the death scene in his analogy brings into mental play the sexual "death" he would prefer. In any case, his word choices for both his departure and the quiet dissolution of the lovers contain sexual connotations. The lovers, like the virtuous men, send their souls (that is, each other) into bliss by encouraging them "to goe," a phrase that can mean "to experience a sexual climax." Further, the man describes the couple's disintegration at parting with the word *melt*, a common term for "to experience orgasm": "So let us melt, and make no noise." And his explanation of why the lovers should part quietly emphasizes the near-sacredness of their intimate relations, their "joyes":

> 'Twere prophanation of our joyes
>   To tell the layetie our love. (ll. 7–8)[55]

This undercurrent confirms the man's physical yearning for his lady at the very moment when he intellectually minimizes it, thus helping to establish the dramatic situation of the poem.

In the final lines of his first analogy the speaker introduces a mild version of the religious metaphors in "The Canonization" and "The Exstasie." He and his mistress keep their sacred knowledge secret, becoming priests of love, more knowledgeable and devoted than the "layetie." The comparison suggests superiority, but not arrogance; for the speaker ignores the implications of his metaphor, as if he had grasped it hurriedly. Indeed, it so complicates his original analogy of the lovers and the virtuous men that the priestly trope has only superficial application as another means of "forbidding Mourning." Most strikingly it contrasts with the evangelical prerogatives which the religious metaphors in "The Canonization" and "The Exstasie" (as well as "The Relique" and "Twicknam Garden") press. This pair, having discovered the intellectual and spiritual strength of their love, will maintain quiet dignity during their separation because of their faith in one another. They neither need nor want followers.

The religious metaphor, then, initiates no well-designed Neoplatonic argument or no religious fiction. But it does provide one of the lover's increasingly abstract and ethereal terms for the couple. They move from priests of love to spheres (an idealized version of 'the lovers are the world to each other' without that conceit's earthly connotations or its liability to change), to souls united, creatures without any shape or body whatsoever (an antithesis of the movement to bodies in "The Exstasie"). That is, the metaphor of the priests of love works not to define the sacred nature of the couple's affection, but to focus on the nonphysical aspects of their love—the very elements the speaker must stress if either he or his lady is to live through their separation without mourning. By the force of his argument he seems to isolate them from other human couples by setting up straw "sublunary lovers" whose "dull" (l. 13) sensual attraction cannot withstand absence at all, then assuring his lady that they are no such thing. Only obliquely does he acknowledge that they too will miss "eyes, lips, and hands" (l. 20). Paradoxically, his pauses in that elongated line suggest that he ponders those features as he lists them, perhaps storing up mental pictures to carry him through the separation.

With a virtual non sequitur he returns from "eyes, lips, and hands" to his central focus in this valediction, the lovers' spiritual and intellectual ties. The formal like and as of analogy recur; the formal therefore (l. 21) signals a conclusion. In other words, the man's firmest assurances to his lady have something studied about them, as if he had previously rehearsed an argument and sought out images to comfort both of them during their final moments together. Indeed, his increasingly solid and stable images for their souls—from airy gold to stiff compasses—adumbrate the certainty of their continuing love. But for all their aptness as figures of unity in disparity, these tropes, like the opening one, reverberate with intimations of fear and doubt. Straightaway the man affirms the oneness of the lovers' souls during his absence:

> Our two soules therefore, which are one,
>   Though I must goe, endure not yet
> A breach, but an expansion. (ll. 21–23)

His word expansion seems to indicate that the lovers' souls will increase during his absence, and its ambiguity almost pushes the man into concluding that the separation will prove beneficial to the lovers. But persuasive oratory has no place in an intimate and sad farewell. And more devoted to the truth of his feelings than to rhetoric, the lover qualifies his conclusion and defines his terms with an image, "like gold to ayery thinnesse beate" (l. 24). Here is expansion without increase: absence does not enlarge the soul, it just stretches it. The comparison, though beautiful and pure, remains fragile; the union so imaged likewise is insubstantial, as it must be without a physical being on which to center the affection.[56] And in the man's ambiguous "not yet a breach," his fears surface through his certitude.

This splintering between words and meaning, particularly in the analogies, reflects the persona's own fragmentation. As the confident man consoling his lady, the stalwart and self-assured lover about to embark on a journey, in other words, as the speaker acting out a role he has created for this occasion, he affirms the continuation of their love. But the role he assumes does not quite fit with his feelings during that parting, and his emotions bubble the smooth surface of his consolation. This split between the man and his role perhaps accounts for the frequent observation that even though "A Valediction: forbidding Mourning" is very literary, it still evokes a dramatic situation.

This splintering within the speaker intensifies in the compass image, as he attempts to modify his studied consolation to suit the emotional demands of his situation. First he introduces the compass figure to refine his avowal of the oneness of their souls in the gold image.[57]

> If they be two, they are two so
>   As stiffe twin compasses are two,
> Thy soule the fixt foot, makes no show
>   To move, but doth, if the'other doe. (ll. 25–28)

The tangential union of the compasses at the vertex qualifies his affirmation of the integral union of their souls, a sentiment at odds with the reality of his departure. Instead, appropriately he figures forth sympathetic rather than intrinsic oneness. Then he shifts the meaning of his simile altogether. Face to face with his mistress, he feels the distinction between body and soul to be irrelevant to his experience, and he responds perhaps subconsciously by expanding the tenor of the image to include both body and soul:

> Such wilt thou be to mee, who must
>   Like th'other foot, obliquely runne. (ll. 33–34)

This change in meaning corresponds with a complication in the rhetorical relationship between the man and his beloved. Ostensibly he has been solacing her grief at their imminent separation. Once he identifies fully with the running foot of the compass, however, he no longer simply consoles her but asks, almost commands, her to follow the steadfastness of the compass emblem: "Such wilt thou be to mee." His ambiguous imperative/declarative verb simultaneously assures her and pleads for an assurance from her. The man thus subconsciously accommodates his imagined role as a confident lover to his immediate need for some certainty from her about their relationship.

His modification of the compass emblem, traditionally a figure for constancy of purpose, illustrates this splintering most emphatically of all. The lover's compass draws both a circle and a radius; and all the suggestions of God and man, soul and body, which those figures hold in the Renaissance, reverberate through the emblem, depicting the lovers' own spiritual and physical bonds.[58] Primarily, however, through the figure of the compass the lover sketches a reassuring diagram of the couple's continuing relationship: together, apart but in spiritual sympathy, then together again.

> Thy soule the fixt foot, makes no show
>   To move, but doth, if the'other doe.

> And though it in the center sit,
>   Yet when the other far doth rome,
> It leanes, and harkens after it,
>   And growes erect, as it comes home. (ll. 27–32)

The man's clear identification of the souls with the feet of the compass insists upon such continuity. But the initial correspondence dissipates as the lover progresses through his conceit, as if his feelings unhinge his original comparison and in effect illuminate the limitations of any purely spiritual consolation. As soon as he begins tracing the path of the compasses, he envisions his mistress sitting at home while he "doth rome." That is, his imagination focuses on their whole beings, not just their souls. And he pictures his beloved inclining toward him as he completes the round of his journey, keeping him in line and ascertaining that he does not break the circle of their love. In his mind, then, her physical posture reflects her spiritual constancy.

His mental overlay reveals even more strands of his feelings as he sees the compass drawing its radius, coming home. He describes his return as the closing of the compass, where the foot "growes erect." The ambiguity of reference here and the fact that both feet do straighten as a compass draws together expose an underlying phallic suggestion. Thus even as the lover argues for the sufficient unity of their souls, his imagination sparks his physical desire. Almost as soon as this sexual intimation arises, the speaker begins to fear his lady's constancy and once again modifies his emphasis in his application of the compass image.

> Thy firmnes makes my circle just,
>   And makes me end, where I begunne. (ll. 35–36)

In other compass emblems the perfection of the circle depends either on both feet equally or on the steadiness of the hand that turns the instrument.[59] Donne's speaker, however, insists that the central foot control the precision of the figure and, by extension, that his beloved's faithfulness insure his return to her. His witty geometry lesson thus teaches the woman how she must manage her life if she wants her lover back. And the man's consolation yields a half-threat, half-entreaty as his fears of losing her surface. His plea for her constancy opens up yet another of the speaker's worries, his fear that he may perish on the journey. And in appealing for her "firmnes," he asks as well for help in keeping him alive, in making him "end" where he "begunne." Like the lover in "Song: 'Sweetest love, I do not goe,' " he attributes sympathetic powers to her and puts his fate in her hand. This thread of the lover's feelings hearkens back to the opening of his farewell. The deathbed scene, too, intimates his fears of dying on the journey—fears he wants to quell by forbidding either of them to mourn his departure, but fears that neither his prohibition nor his consolation can put down.

Like the Mutual Lover in "The Anniversarie," the man in "A Valediction: forbidding Mourning" seeks consolation for his fears of death and separation by defining the spiritual and mental dimensions of his love: "we by . . . love . . . refined" (l. 17), "inter-assured of the mind" (l. 19), "our two soules . . . are one." But these explanations neither quell his disquiet nor ease the pain of parting, as similar intellection fails to soothe the emotional needs of the man in "The Anniversarie." The imminent departure of the lover in "A Valediction," however, requires that to some extent he rely on such solaces, and he does. But through them runs the undercurrent of his wish to live fully all the moments of his life with his beloved.

In "A Valediction: forbidding Mourning," then, Donne weaves a complex strand of lyric and dramatic elements. The speaker seems at least partially to have prepared his valediction in advance and created for himself the role of a consoling lover who will keep his lady from weeping by explaining the enduring nature of their love to her and by assuring her of his faithfulness. But under the emotional strain of parting, the speaker pulls his own disquiet into his valediction. His fears about death and about losing his beloved as well as his physical yearning for her surface as seeming irrelevancies in his conceits, or as puns and ambiguities. Yet he continues his consolation, as his concern for his lady determines he must. Nevertheless he adjusts the culminating image of his farewell to conform a bit more closely to his true feelings. The dramatic situation in this poem, then, does not so much "develop" between the speaker and the listener as exert pressure on the speaker, which he, perhaps unwittingly, disperses into his farewell utterance. Yet he never really tells his lady all his fears, never destroys his prepared role altogether. For he has a responsibility to her to be—or seem—the stalwart lover and the confident traveler. One measure of his love is that he keeps such a responsibility.

In all the poems of mutual love either metaphoric or philosophical reminders of death pierce the speakers' celebrations. In three of them the speakers face the death of women who have meant the world and all to them. Like Petrarch's lover after the death of Laura, these men find that their little worlds have turned rank without their ladies to give meaning and purpose to their existence. And the metaphor 'the lovers are the world to each other,' which enunciates their self-sufficiency, turns in these poems to a cry of despair over the emptiness and barrenness of a world without their women.

These three poems—"A Feaver," "The Dissolution," and "A Nocturnall upon S. Lucies Day: being the shortest day"—share not only situations in which the speaker confronts the death of his beloved; they also depict the lovers crying out to virtual strangers, people who cannot possibly understand the emotional import of their utterances, as if, isolated and alienated from the world at large, these men grasp at anyone who will listen or with whom they can register their essentially lyric outpourings of grief and despair. In "A Feaver," for example, the lover summons long-dead philosophers to validate what purports to be his scientific discovery but what is in fact his hopeless outburst against his lady's death. The stranger-listeners in these poems serve either as sounding boards or as externalizations of the speakers themselves so that in confronting their listeners the lovers ultimately confront themselves. These men must find their resolutions within themselves, and at the close of the poems the speakers do turn inward for whatever fortitude they can muster to continue life alone.

The penchant exhibited by Donne's Mutual Lovers for arguing away problems takes a bitter twist in these poems as the speakers weave fallacious webs to cover, somehow, the fact of death or to hide themselves from the realities of existing without their loved ones. Indeed, in "A Feaver" especially, the speaker's wrangling at the bedside of his dying lady sounds callous and self-centered, until he exposes his disputations as his only defense against the inevitable and unacceptable fact of her death. These poems, then, illustrate the dangers of self-deception latent in the facile tongue and the ready wit—the very tools that create the high comedy of "The Sunne Rising" and "The Canonization."

Like the lover in "A Valediction: forbidding Mourning," the lover in "A Feaver" adopts stylized roles for facing the unacceptable and unendurable circumstance of his lady's approaching death. But because his stances are more callow and his situation far worse than that of a lover bidding farewell, he appears at first grossly immature and self-centered. And he never exhibits the generosity and love that self-control expresses.

At the bedside of his dying lady, he jests about her illness as he takes on one pose and then another. First, in the guise of a love poet he threatens her with the poetic justice of anonymity if she frustrates him by dying:

> Oh doe not die, for I shall hate
>   All women so, when thou art gone,
> That thee I shall not celebrate,
>   When I remember, thou wast one. (ll. 1–4).

Treating her illness as an infidelity, he plays the injured poet-lover to the hilt, vowing to deny her immortality through verse if she "dies." His hyperbolic threats, however, sit uneasily in a sickroom. Almost immediately he drops that pose and assumes the posture of a logician, first arguing away his beloved's death and then, in a grand Petrarchan manner, arguing away the world should she die: "But yet thou canst not die, I know" (l. 5), and

> Or if, when thou, the worlds soule, goest,
>   It stay . . . (ll. 9–10)

That he debates both positions equally well indicates both his lack of conviction and his great rhetorical skill. He even caps his oratory with a chiasmus, a figure used exclusively to please the ear.

> The fairest woman, but thy ghost,
>   But corrupt wormes, the worthyest men. (ll. 11–12)

Although this figure depicts the desolation of a world without its soul and hence of the lover without his beloved, its hyperbole and oratorical neatness suggest the speaker's concentration on his creative ingenuity. Indeed, he seems to be donning these various guises as bedside entertainment for his lady, but with the hollow humor of any banter about a serious question. As if to amuse her even more, then, he tries on a third role, this time that of a genius. He transports himself through time and space to engage with the "wrangling schooles" (l. 13) of philosophers who once argued about which fire would burn the earth. Matching his "wit" (l. 14) against theirs, he concludes that "her feaver" (l. 16) will consume the world. The telling third-person reference to his beloved implies a mock drama enacted at her bedstead, as does the vocative "o wrangling schooles." Yet witty as he is, he has not calculated all of the scholastic questions involved with his answer and retracts:

> And yet she cannot wast by this,
>   Nor long beare this torturing wrong,

> For much corruption needfull is
>   To fuell such a feaver long. (ll. 17–20)

His witty dialectic not only pulls him up short on his Petrarchan definition of his lady's perfection; it also trips him into the realization of her
suffering, her "torturing wrong." And for the first time the lover's roles
collapse and he confronts his dying mistress face to face.

Turning to her, perhaps really looking at her for the first time, the
lover then celebrates her beauty, her perfection, and her immortality:

> Thy beauty, 'and all parts, which are thee,
>   Are unchangeable firmament. (ll. 23–24)

He reminds her that the fever has not damaged her looks. He tells her
what she probably wants to hear most and in the affirmation frees her
from the ravages of time and disease. For all of its assertion of the lady's
immortality, however, the lover's statement has something tentative
about it. Perhaps because it is a consolation to a very ill woman, the
statement implies the qualifying "to me," which the lover's final assertion makes explicit.

Momentarily, making light of a serious subject, the speaker resumes
his role of the injured lover. Once more he makes the fever his sexual
rival for possession of the lady. This time, however, his joke is witty; for
he says of the fever:

> Yet 'twas of my minde, seising thee,
>   Though it in thee cannot persever. (ll. 25–26)

The brief fiction of a fever-wooer who cannot remain constant relieves
the tension of this deathbed encounter, even as it introduces the lover as
a superior suitor. The man bends his wit to make his lady laugh here,
not to protect himself as he does earlier. His generosity thus silently
underscores the fact that he has dropped his self-consciousness and
self-centeredness. Then, breaking from all the fictions and postures and
tropes that he has adopted throughout the meeting, he declares his love
for her:

> For I had rather owner bee
>   Of thee one houre, then all else ever. (ll. 27–28)

The speaker, like the fever, desires her more than anything else in the
world, now and for all eternity. He protests as much, and except for his
reference to time he might be reiterating one of man's most outworn
hyperboles. But because he sits at his lady's sickbed and because both of
them are haunted by the possibility of her death, his reference to time

holds a peculiar poignancy and his declaration a terrible urgency. His "one houre" sharply defines how little time the lovers have together; yet even those short moments with her are more precious to him than eternity without her. Thus, as he places his beloved in time, as he discredits his hyperbolic oaths and protestations by admitting her mortality, he paradoxically elevates her above immortals and values life, even short life, with her more than eternal life without her. He conquers time, in other words, and death, by living and loving fully, even if for only an hour.

The woman's presence in "A Feaver" pulls the speaker away from his fictions, postures, and ingenious scientific conclusions so that he can appraise his love and his circumstances fairly. In "The Dissolution," however, the speaker's beloved is dead. And left with vacancy and void, he exercises his ingenuity to argue away his loneliness and despair. Whether, in accordance with the standard lyric fiction, he is alone as he utters his thoughts and feelings aloud or whether he directs his argument to a listener is unclear—and ultimately unimportant. His careful progress through axioms, analogies, and conclusions suggests a listener. Yet if one reads the poem as a straightforward albeit self-deluded utterance, the fact that speaker's specious arguments go unchallenged indicates an unresponsive listener and a speaker unconcerned with his hearer. No matter who is in the room with him, then, the lover is psychologically alone, convincing himself of his impending death because to live without his lady is anathema—is, as he says, to "live long wretched so" (l. 14).

This isolation gives rise to self-delusion after his lady's death, as the speaker develops his argument for his own death through the fallacy of speech respective. He equates the symbolic and sexual oneness he and his beloved shared with the literal unity of an organism. From this premise he reasons that at her death he received her share of their mutual physical elements, and can therefore thrive on such an abundant supply. His consolation stems from the same fallacious premise, when he considers that since her death his "fire of Passion" (l. 9) has grown steadily and continues to increase because of increased bodily elements. He concludes, therefore, that not only will he die soon, but that his soul will overtake the lady's, since it leaves his body more ardently and willingly than hers did.

Running through this clever consolation, the image of the sexually frustrated Petrarchan lover seeking fulfillment suggests that the speaker appraises his feelings inaccurately. His rationale for his imminent demise covers sexual fantasies he does not recognize. And he sublimates his desire into a yearning for physical death and spiritual release. But the presence of such sexually associated words as *die* (l. 1) and *death* (ll.

13, 20), together with the comparisons to kings who "spend more, and soonest breake" (l. 18) and to "bullets" (l. 23)—often used in a slang sense for testicles and sometimes for semen—reveals his longing for a far different kind of death.[60]

Because the speaker's elaborate analysis of 'the lovers are the world to each other' accrues about it an interest of its own, moreover, it detracts from his viability as a grief-stricken lover. He seems so bent on creating a clever solace or even a clever enlargement of the microcosm conceit that he offers little indication of mourning. His only mention of the woman other than as a part of himself or as a competitor with him occurs in the bare, factual opening: "Shee'is dead" (l. 1). Immediately he launches into logical proofs for his imminent demise. The sexual undercurrent in his utterance further corroborates the preponderant selfishness in his wish to be reunited with his lady. Yet, unlike poems such as "The Broken Heart" or "The Expiration," in which the speaker's creation ultimately reveals him to be a clever poet writing for the benefit of a witty reader, "The Dissolution" never yields to such pressure. Unlike the epigrammatic closures of many of Donne's comic and satiric manipulations, moreover, the final lines and analogies of "The Dissolution" spring no joke, mock no idea. If anything, the preposterous competitiveness in the last comparison offers insight about the speaker—a man unwilling to be outdone even in death, yet still an ardent lover.

> And so my soule more earnestly releas'd,
> Will outstrip hers; As bullets flown before
> A latter bullet may o'rtake, the pouder being more. (ll. 22–24)

The speaker's fiction and analogies, then, do cast doubt on his grief but not on his situation. The man's hyperactive imagination contributes to his self-delusion in that it keeps him from assessing and understanding himself and his circumstances. But his imagination generates fictions in response to his lady's death, the only fact in the poem.

In "A Nocturnall upon S. Lucies Day, being the shortest day," as in "The Dissolution," the speaker's beloved is dead; and he, like that other Mutual Lover, cries out in despair. At least ostensibly, however, he directs his comments to some young lovers who neither know him nor know the pain of loss in love. In other words, they are people emotionally unequipped to understand his desolation. Yet for all their remoteness, the listeners ultimately help the speaker break out of his obsessive despair.

He approaches the young lovers with what seems like an observation on the time and the season: " 'Tis the yeares midnight, and it is the dayes" (l. 1), and he continues by noting the paradox that this day of light, St. Lucy's Day, lasts for only seven hours:

> *Lucies*, who scarce seaven houres herself unmaskes,
>   The Sunne is spent, and now his flasks
>   Send forth light squibs, no constant rayes. (ll. 2–4)

His observations, however, reverberate with an emotional urgency inappropriate to a weather report and gather about them a metaphorical dimension no doubt inexplicable to the stranger-listeners:

> The world's whole sap is sunke:
> The generall blame th'hydroptique earth hath drunk,
> Whither, as to the beds-feet, life is shrunke,
> Dead and enterr'd. (ll. 5–8)

His personification of this bleak winter day as a flirtatious woman who "herself unmaskes" to arouse and frustrate an impotent sun disturbs the seeming casualness of his remarks, as does his comparison of the swollen earth to an insatiable drunkard who has consumed all the vital fluids.[61] In fact, the speaker has changed his subject (or clarified it) from the time and the weather to his feelings, which find a pale approximation in the desolate day:

> Yet all these seeme to laugh,
> Compar'd with mee, who am their Epitaph. (ll. 8–9)

This shift in subject (or perspective) would normally suggest a change in or a clarification of the relationship between the speaker and his listeners from that of chance acquaintances to that of intimates. But that development does not occur. Instead the speaker buttonholes total strangers to tell them his story under the pretense of commenting on the surroundings.

Into the tight metaphorical texture of his comments he weaves snatches of his melancholy love tale. Like Saint Lucy, whose name and legend promise both light and restored vision and yet who seems to renege on those promises in her alter ego as a bleak winter's day, so the speaker's love, once bright, vital, and life-sustaining, brings only desolation since his lady's death. The sexual overtones of flirtation and impotence redound upon the speaker who, like the traditionally masculine sun, is "spent." The fluid connections between love and death run through his metaphors, puns, and analogies, suggesting not only his impotence since the death of his mistress but the impossibility of regeneration within him. "Whither," a pun on "wither," links with "as to the beds-feet" in an image of impotence. "The world's whole sap is sunke" suggests, however fleetingly, universal and perhaps permanent infertility, then compounds that suggestion with the image of a bloated earth that has already drained the "generall balme."

This last image catches snatches of the complex splintering and inter-weaving of feeling and idea within the speaker. At once the balm is the man's dead and buried lady, his impotency since her death, and the universal sterility of which the frozen winter's day is an image—love and death all. Moreover, since *balme* is used in the Renaissance for both an aromatic healing substance (hence figuratively the cure for lovesick-ness) and for embalming fluid, the word crystallizes the intimations of love and death that flow throughout the passage.[62]

This compression and fragmentation of association in the speaker's description, while capturing his despair, nonetheless makes his outcry incoherent and incomprehensible to anyone unfamiliar with his story. The speaker thus uses the young lovers as an excuse to pour forth his woe and relate his tale. Their presence affords him the opportunity to retrace his love story out loud and to present himself as love's victim, in other words, to cry out in psychological if not physical isolation, as lyric personae are wont to do.

As the title of the poem indicates, this cry comprises the man's song, his "Nocturnall upon S. Lucies Day." The nocturnal or nocturne, a section of the Roman Catholic matins sung during the Renaissance be-tween midnight and four o'clock in the morning, traditionally consists of praises with which to welcome the new day, in the form of scriptural readings, psalms, hymns, and prayers. The structure of Donne's poem—five stanzas of nine lines each—reflects both the five-fold pattern of matins and its trinal instructure of nine psalms, nine lessons, and nine responses.[63] With diabolical irony this speaker parodies the reli-gious forms of welcome and their suggestion of renewal by celebrating the desolation and despair in both his surroundings on this winter sol-stice and in himself. More subtly and more profoundly, moreover, he disavows the communion of religious commemoration that a nocturnal implies by singing *of* himself in the guise of glorifying the bleak day and *to* himself in the guise of speaking to young lovers, people he does not even address until the second stanza, and then only with the order, "study me" (l. 10).

The speaker's command to the young lovers at first seems to define a didactic purpose in his autobiography and to make the beginning of some communication:

> Study me then, you who shall lovers bee
> At the next world, that is, at the next Spring:
>   For I am every dead thing,
>   In whom love wrought new Alchimie. (ll. 10–13)

He does establish an identification between himself and them, under-scoring it by the repetition of *lovers* and *love*. The man, however, loses cognizance of his listeners once he launches into his tale. The import of his autobiography is that through the death of his lady, love trans- formed him from an ordinary nothing ("dull privations, and leane emptinesse," l. 16, a rather traditional version of self-denigration among lovers) to the "quintessence" (l. 15) of nothingness: "absence, dark- nesse, death" (l. 18) and "of the first nothing, the Elixer" (l. 29). His extreme claims point not only to his despair but to his isolation. Only people for whom, like the speaker, love was all (as he says, "the whole world, us two," l. 24) could understand his hyperbole as apt rather than outrageous. The extremity of his desolation is surely lost on youngsters "who shall lovers bee . . . at the next Spring." They are unequipped to "study" him, unable to comprehend him as a *memento mori* of the dev- astation possible when love ends. Moreover, his command notwith- standing, the speaker drifts into self-definition and reverie, as if he were trying to understand his own emotional circumstances rather than to instruct novices on the dangers of love. Indeed, he never offers advice on that point.

Launched on his solitary emotional journey through his life with his beloved, the speaker nostalgically commemorates their lovers' quarrels and separations:

> Oft a flood
>   Have wee two wept, and so
> Drownd the whole world, us two; oft did we grow
> To be two Chaosses, when we did show
> Care to ought else; and often absences
> Withdrew our soules, and made us carcasses. (ll. 22–27)

The great devastations the couple felt after an argument or during a separation—and the speaker's microcosm-macrocosm metaphor insists on the immensity of their despair—pale beside the man's feelings of utter negation since her death. With that he lost not only his sense of being but all kinship with the earth and its creatures, a kinship he once stressed by identifying himself as a little world. With bitter glee he disclaims identity with everything from men to stones on the great chain, whose essential quality, he says, is the ability to feel. He even denies the existence of his body, the sensible vessel, since his light, his "Lucy," is gone:

> If I an ordinary nothing were,
> As shadow, 'a light, and body must be here. (ll. 35–36)

And he concludes with a terse self-delineation and a calm acceptance of death in life: "But I am None; nor will my Sunne renew" (l. 37). By

plunging again into the emotional abysses of his past love life and returning to the emotional numbness of his present solitude, the speaker
is able to define his current situation and to plan for his future. His lyric
journey brings him self-knowledge and resignation.

The pun of "None" and "nun" has something of the solemnity of a
vow about it, a renunciation of further sexual love, a promise to break all
contact with generation and regeneration.[64] Even without the pun, the
demise of his "Sunne" assures him that he can no longer participate in
the normal cycles of growth and generation, as can the young lovers
under the influence of the "lesser Sunne" (l. 38), which is just moving
into the zone of Capricorn. But in dissolving his ties with the life and
world of the young lovers, the speaker chooses to participate in spiritual
communion with his deceased lady: "Let mee prepare towards her" (l.
43), he says, not only in the sense of walking toward her monument but
the sense of bringing himself to a state of mental and spiritual readiness
(OED) for communion with her as well. He underscores the solemnity of
his decision by speaking of his mourning in religious terms:

> Since shee enjoyes her long nights festivall,
> Let mee prepare towards her, and let mee call
> This houre her Vigill, and her Eve. (ll. 42–44)

His lament and the retracing of their lives together make up the "Vigill,"
his nocturnal service in her honor (OED) as well as his devotional watching. And the lover acknowledges the appropriateness of the bleak hour
and season for this high solemnization:

> Let mee call
> This houre her Vigill, and her Eve, since this
> Both the yeares, and the dayes deep midnight is. (ll. 43–45)

Paradoxically, however, only after the lover has renounced the world
and come to terms with himself and his future does he really respond to
the young lovers, offering them advice about life and love from his own
experience:

> You lovers, for whose sake, the lesser Sunne
>   At this time to the Goat is runne
>   To fetch new lust, and give it you,
>   Enjoy your summer all. (ll. 38–41)

He urges them to love and live as long as possible. His final word, *all*,
enunciates both the intensity and the tenacity of his entreaty. His lesson
virtually contradicts the message of devastation and frustration in his
autobiography, as if he has passed through anger and can once more

appreciate his love. For all that, his advice is tempered by experience. As if to counter and discourage the illusion of love's permanence, he speaks in terms of time, sets limits to romantic happiness: "Enjoy your summer." Yet even with this restriction he advises them to love. Then he prepares towards his lady on "the yeares and dayes deep midnight."

The lover has come full circle in returning to the winter bleakness with which he began his nocturnal. But on the interior voyage from which he emerges to greet the young lovers, that is, on his journey from lyric isolation to dramatic community, he has gained the vision of insight that Saint Lucy promises. The calmness with which he finally remarks the deadness of the year, by contrasting sharply with his bitter opening outcry on the same subject, implies his inner change. So does his choice of the nocturnal as the form of commemorating his lady's death rather than, say, the *epitaphium recens* (immediate epitaph). For the trinal form of the nocturnal signifies the movement from a dead world to a renewal through grace.[65] The lover's decision to redirect his life from despair to solemn commemoration of his lost love mirrors that movement and intimates the possibility that in time he may even turn to a new life and a new love, despite his protest to the contrary.[66]

*   *   *

The poems depicting mutual love in the *Songs and Sonnets* for the most part spring from particularly important moments in these men's lives. ("Aire and Angels" and "Loves Infinitenesse" have looser ties to a pinpointed minute than the others, although both take their impetus from a man's reflection about love and time.) These lyrics run the emotional gamut from the dawning joy of new love to the loneliness and despair after the death of the beloved: the happiness of commemorating an anniversary, the delighted shock of discovering that love improves as it endures, the intimate playfulness of a mock-angry *aubade*, the half-comic, half-serious defense of one's love to a friend who advises against it, the scarcely controlled sorrow at a parting, the anger and despondency as a lover travels through the bleak inner journey to an acceptance of death. By traversing a lifetime of love, these poems, taken together, validate the possibility of love's endurance. Time and its contingent vicissitudes eat at but never devour mutual affection. Among the *Songs and Sonnets* only these poems treat a lover's response to the death of his lady; into only these has Donne drawn the all too frequent occurrence in the Renaissance of a woman's dying very young, as Donne's wife did. For finally only lovers whom death alone can part put their affection to the test of ultimate separation.

To put all of this in a larger perspective, in lyrics such as "A Nocturnall upon S. Lucies Day" Donne shows love conquering mutability in some sense. And the wrestling with mutability is, perhaps, the central issue in the poems of mutual love. The terms of the issue are modified as lovers define more narrowly and more realistically what kind of immortality will satisfy their need to be lifted out of time. The speakers in "The Good-morrow" and "The Sunne Rising" want nothing less than to remain as they are forever. Their realizations of that impossibility only slightly dampen their ebullient sense of permanence since their transformation through love. In "Loves Growth" and "Loves Infinitenesse" the question of immortality shifts to the lesser but cognate problem of growth amid permanence. The speaker's bewilderment in these poems springs from the shock of change, even for the better, in what seemed a constant relationship. Rather than exploring the question of love's immortality, both men transmute it through metaphor. In the valedictions the problem of permanence amid flux arises again, this time in very earthbound terms. To these speakers a separation with its ominous resemblance to death becomes the gulf which their love must span. And they equate constancy throughout the severance with permanence, thereby subtly placing lovers' immutability in the ebb and flow of time. These men are too emotionally consumed by their impending journeys to contemplate death consciously. Insofar as they do confront death, they envision their own demise and as if by magic—or rhetoric—endow their ladies with the power to sustain life. This modified definition of permanence in time gets precise treatment in "The Anniversarie," where the lover's definition of immortality is that the couple "love nobly, 'and live": "Yeares and yeares unto yeares, till we attaine / To write threescore." In "A Feaver," where the woman is dying, the value rather than the length of time the lovers have together constitutes something akin to, or something as precious as, immortality. The lover cries out to his ailing lady, "I had rather owner bee / Of thee one houre, then all else ever." Thus intensity of experience here substitutes for longevity, even permanence, as the speaker revalues his life and imagines existence without his beloved. The reality of living without one's love arises only in "The Dissolution" and "A Nocturnall upon S. Lucies Day." The question of conquering death, that is, of love's immortality, adjusts to an even narrower definition in these poems. In "The Dissolution" the man, believing he cannot endure without his lady, invents a witty fiction whereby her death will kill him so speedily that his soul will arrive in heaven before hers. Presumably the pair will continue through eternity as they have throughout their lives. The man in "A Nocturnall upon S. Lucies Day" finds no such solace. He endures the pain of loving after the death of his lady and relieves that pain only by a commitment to continue the same constancy to her in death as he practiced when she was alive. By envisioning her enjoying "her long nights festivall," he lifts her out of time and makes himself worthy of a reunion with her, thus making his devotion a bulwark against death. Most of the Mutual Lovers, then, search for a source of permanence within the flux of time so that their lives attain some meaning in spite of accidents, the vicissitudes of time, and mutability.[67] Thus many of these poems endow a moment in the onrush of love and life with the immortality that the present tense of lyric poetry affirms and with the completeness that makes the frantic pleasure-seeking of much *carpe diem* poetry unnecessary. When the man in "The Good-morrow" declares the lovers' "one little roome, an every where" and the man in "The Sunne Rising" announces, "All here in one bed lay," they are affirming the sufficiency of their love, even in the face of death.

Conclusion

The varieties of love in the *Songs and Sonnets* continue to receive critical attention. Theodore Redpath notes that the poems "convey a very wide range of feeling from flippant cynicism to the most tender and even idealistic love."[1] Clay Hunt suggests that in the poems Donne explores the many facets of romance: "From the kaleidoscopic succession of different attitudes toward love which one encounters in the 'Songs and Sonets,' one suspects, in fact, that an important intellectual purpose behind Donne's verse was to demonstrate how rich and strange love could be."[2] And Louis Martz compares the many kinds of love in the *Songs and Sonnets* with the varied portraits of John Donne.[3] Donne's interest in love's variety is not particularly philosophical, although he includes many major beliefs about love in his poems. He focuses rather on people in love, on their dramatic, emotional, and imaginative responses to their passions. Hence his personae are lovers of almost every stripe save the homosexual and the narcissist. A few of his speakers, of course, only pretend to be lovers, but they soon enough give themselves away.

The seven types of lovers discussed in the preceding pages provide the major focus of this analysis, as Donne details these men wrangling with themselves, their ladies, or their friends; justifying their viewpoints; confronting their fears; and sometimes, overcome with joy, singing the oldest and loveliest praises to their mistresses. A few additional poems present lovers who differ, sometimes quite slightly, from the dominant characterizations in the *Songs and Sonnets* and a few other speakers who play with the words of love.

The man in "Loves Exchange," for example, seems cut from much the same cloth as the comic Cavalier Petrarchists and the humorous Dreaming Cynics—a patched fellow, he, with the Cynics' penchant for revenge and the gamesomeness and posturing of the Cavalier Petrarchists. Like these latter he pretends to be Love's victim, "rack't" (l. 42) by the torture of an unrequited affection. Like the Cynics he seeks revenge through insult. But because his rebuke is directed at the implacable god of love, the speaker's *argutia* stings no one, resounding instead as an ineffectual taunt from a hapless lover:

> Kill, and dissect me, Love; for this
> Torture against thine owne end is,
> Rack't carcasses make ill Anatomies. (ll. 40–42)

This somewhat unsatisfactory mixture of comic posturing and cynicism stems from the particular manipulation of speaker and listeners in the poem. "Loves Exchange" opens with a direct address to Love and thus promises to be that special blend of complaint and tirade at which Donne excels:

> *Love,* any devill else but you,
> Would for a given Soule give something too.
>
> Give mee thy weaknesse, make mee blinde,
> Both ways, as thou and thine, in eies and minde. (ll. 1–2, 14–15)

With delicious affrontery and sparkling wit, this man plays with such commonplaces as love's blindness and divinity. He also mocks that labyrinth of lovers' guessing games: they know that she knows that he knows that I know.

> Let me not know that others know
> That she knowes my paine. (ll. 19–20)

Under the guise of a dejected lover engaged in a face-to-face confrontation with Love, then, this witty man demonstrates his comic creativity and reveals himself to be a parodist of great skill, even to the burlesquing of his hapless situation.

Slightly more than halfway through the poem, however, the speaker turns from Love to his mistress, as if to enlist her support or agreement against the amorous god:

> Such in loves warfare is my case,
> I may not article for grace
> Having put Love at last to shew this face. (ll. 26–28)

That is, he carries his mask of a dejected lover from a purely fictional encounter into a potentially realistic one, but to little purpose. He changes his comic rebuke of Love to hyperbolic flattery of his mistress, who is Cupid's ultimate weapon in the arsenal of amorous war, as if that outrageous hyperbole would lead to a stinging deflation, as it does in such poems as "The Apparition" or "Song: 'Goe, and catche a falling starre.'" It does not. Instead the man retreats once more behind his mask of a dejected lover, returns to his original listener, and notes wryly that his emaciated body will not quite serve Love's purposes as a warning against rebellion.

Donne here seems to be experimenting with dual listeners, a technique he uses in "The Will" and perfects in "The Funerall" and "The Sunne Rising." In these other poems, one listener plays foil to the other. A dramatic relationship exists among the speaker, his lady, and the sun in "The Sunne Rising," for example, which the speaker exploits in order to compliment and entertain his lady. For he knows, first, the purpose of his utterance and, second, his particular relationship with his listener. The man in "Loves Exchange" seems to have clarified neither.

Three of the poems in the *Song and Sonnets* that take their impetus from objects seem more like witty games than affirmations of love, witty games that arise because the men and women are in love. The speakers of "A Lecture upon the Shadow," "The Flea," and "The Primrose" all invent a creation in order to expound upon an object, as if they set themselves such a task. Hence all three poems have a studied cleverness about them that turns their dramatic situation into a background for their poetic performance. All three poems create something like emblems in that they describe an object and then make a philosophical application of it to life and love.

In "A Lecture upon the Shadow" the lover purports to be stopping his mistress at noon, in the midst of their long walk; his observations and cogitations about their shadows have led him to some conclusions in "loves philosophy" (l. 2). He describes to her the change of their shadows during the walk, compares that change to their love, and pronounces a *sententia* about love in general from his observations:

> That love hath not attain'd the high'st degree,
> Which is still diligent lest others see. (ll. 12–13)

The observation, although not terribly profound, illustrates the lover's adroitness at creating an emblem poem from the image of shadows and suggests a carefree playfulness between the lovers.

His second conclusion derives not from his immediate observation but from his imagination as he comments on the shadows of the afternoon and their application to love:

> Love is a growing, or full constant light;
> And his first minute, after noone, is night. (ll. 25–26)

Unlike his earlier *sententia*, this one by ignoring empirical evidence moves away from occasional, emblematic wit. Its hyperbole seems calculated to frighten the lady—or playfully frighten her—into constancy and truthfulness. Thus he turns his creativity to practical use in his confrontation, as the lyric and dramatic elements of the poems coalesce. In "A Lecture upon the Shadow," then, the man displays his extemporaneous creativity: he can write an emblem to suit the occasion, offer "learned" pronouncements on the nature of love, and perhaps in the process teasingly alarm his lady into constancy.

Like "A Lecture upon the Shadow," "The Primrose" explores the emblematic possibilities of an object, the five-petaled primrose that symbolizes the feminine number five. The speaker in this poem ponders, sometimes wryly, his ideal woman, his "true love" (l. 8), as he wanders up and down a "Primrose hill" (l. 1). Toying with the idea of his dream lady, he occasionally drifts into a bit of bawdy innuendo; but his interest is so much more mathematical than sensual that even his risqué remarks come from multiplication and division:

> If halfe ten
> Belonge unto each woman, then
> Each woman may take halfe us men;
> Or if this will not serve their turne, Since all
> Numbers are odde, or even, and they fall
> First into this, five, women may take us all. (l. 25–30)

That is, finally the poem has nothing to do with love in general or a lover in particular; it is a scholastic and numerological game, "curiously frigid," as Gardner remarks.[4]

Almost opposite to "The Primrose" in its illusion of passion, "The Flea" develops its subject as an emblem also. That tiny bug which sucks the lovers' blood becomes in the poem their sexual union, their marriage temple, their marriage bed, their home—almost every place and aspect of their intimate relationship, and, of course, the stratagem for the man's seduction speech.

The pretense of a seduction, indeed of an encounter between lovers, however, merely heightens the outrageousness and delight of the speaker's invention. The woman listener plays straight-man, as she does in such poems as "The Broken Heart" and "The Legacie," swatting the flea as the cue for the man's mock tirade on murder or sacrilege:

> Cruell and sodaine, has thou since
> Purpled thy naile, in blood of innocence? (ll. 19–20)

In this respect "The Flea" resembles some of the comic poems of the Cavalier Petrarchists. But unlike them, this speaker never develops a view of love, even one couched in a comic fiction. The fiction itself dominates and provides the vehicle for his invention, where, by construing a flea bite as an emblem of sexual union, he argues that his mistress can keep her honor and still lose her virtue.

"The Primrose," "A Lecture upon the Shadow," and "The Flea," then, for all their differences, develop as word games for which every scene and dramatic encounter becomes a backdrop. "The Flea," with its well-defined listener who swats the bug on cue, remains as essentially lyric as "The Primrose," in which the speaker muses aloud to himself. In both the man's invention, his product as a creator, renders all other elements in the poem secondary. In none of these poems does the persona offer a viewpoint on love to compete with his word games.

Finally a second woman speaks in the *Songs and Sonnets*, in "Breake of Day," where she reproves her lover for caring more about his business than about her. Her witty variation of the *aubade* dismisses the convention by seriously questioning the validity of assigning a time to love. Rather than lament the coming of dawn with its implied parting of lovers (which, as she notes, also intimates that in loving at night one is following the dictates of the hour), one should simply love, oblivious to both time and outside activities.

> Love which in spight of darknesse brought us hether,
> Should in despight of light keepe us together. (ll. 5–6)

She removes love from the schedules of an ordered life and thus in some sense lifts it out of time, as do the speakers in Donne's other two *aubades*, "The Sunne Rising" and "The Good-morrow." But she never confuses irresponsibility and immortality as they do. She is content with time (or oblivious to it); she is distressed at her lover's practical use of it.

To urge him to reconsider staying in bed, she pretends to call in the foremost authority on time, that masculine order bringer, the sun. Under the fiction of providing a tongue for light, she speaks for herself, as her pun makes clear—"Light . . . is all eye" (l. 7)—and advises her lover to stay with his lady.

> That being well, I faine would stay
> And that I lov'd my heart and honor so,
> That I would not from him, that had them, goe. (ll. 10–12)

With coy impudence she not only has the sun split its bond with the active world of business, she also has it define honor as constancy to that which one loves, thus severing all connection between honor and duty. Through her make-believe, then, complete with the sun as a mock witness in her defense, this woman tries to cajole her lover into remaining with her. Perhaps she even intimidates him a bit by mentioning "honor." But all to no avail.

Finally she upbraids him with a maxim that calls their whole relationship into question:

> He which hath businesse, and makes love, doth doe
> Such wrong, as when a maryed man doth wooe. (ll. 17–18)

But even here her tact prevails. Although her reproach lets him know she sees several possibilities in his departure, it does not undercut her love for him and thus does not reveal her as a cynical woman on the defensive (a poem such as "Womans Constancy" comes to mind by way of contrast). She chides him with something of the good humor she exhibits in her imaginative playlet. Her epigrammatic *argutia* has very little sting.

As he does in "The Sunne Rising," Donne here sets up a triangle of two lovers and the sun. In both poems the speaker engages the sun in a make-believe encounter partly to entertain his lover/listener. Given this striking similarity in two of Donne's three *aubades*, one is tempted to see the distinctions as reflections of sexual differences. The man in "The Sunne Rising" defies his masculine counterpart, engaging old Sol in a face-to-beam confrontation that illustrates not so much the man's equality as his superiority to the sun. After all, he has the sun find proof for the supremacy of the lovers' world; he taunts and ridicules the sun; and finally out of compassion he invites the sun to share the small perfection of the lovers' realm. The woman in "Breake of Day," on the other hand, brings in the sun to provide authority—vital, masculine authority—for her point of view, as if she cannot persuade her lover on her own. Moreover, by attributing her words to the sun, the woman turns a potential argument into a game and plays on her lover's good humor to get her way. Unrequited masculine lovers in the *Songs and Sonnets* seek their satisfaction through flattery and insult.

Donne's single woman in love (one cannot use that word for the woman in "Confined Love") postures less than do the men in unrequited relationships. Even when she reminds her lover of his words and promises to her, she has both the generosity and security (or tact) not to deflate his ego by sardonically mocking their love. Moreover, she views love as an immediate, human, temporal experience, one not defined by poetic traditions, not subject to custom, and not entwined with eternal concerns. Although her ideas sound somewhat simplistic, her delicate wit and the precision with which she verbalizes the fundamental wish of lovers to be alone together transform that simplicity into an essential verity.

Taken together, the *Songs and Sonnets* present a rather full picture of the many faces of love, as if Donne had long pondered the nature of love

and sought his answers in its various guises. Unlike many of his contemporary philosophers and poets, Donne lets the term *love* cover all
shades of amorous relationships between the sexes; *lust* appears only
twice in the *Songs and Sonnets*, in neither place as a description of the
speaker's passion.[5] Hence the *Songs and Sonnets* do not point toward a
single, totally satisfying vision of love like, say, Petrarch's *Rime sparse* or
Spenser's "Amoretti" and "Epithalamion." Donne's lovers are also
rather reticent about defining their feelings or applying philosophical
labels to them. The only figures who routinely analyze their passions
and drop philosophical catchwords are the Hedonists. They also work
hardest at self-justification. Moreover, the Hedonists never engage a
woman face to face in the *Songs and Sonnets*. Even these few facts suggest
that to Donne love inheres in the interchanges between two people.
Men resort to textbook labels and philosophical justifications for self-
aggrandizement and for relief from guilt. That most of Donne's lovers
participate in some entanglement with their ladies reemphasizes the
sense that love in the *Songs and Sonnets* emerges through living and
loving. It is not a passion from the pages of a book. The spoofing of the
Petrarchan language of love reiterates just this point. By treating fanciful
conceits as literal truths, some of Donne's wits expose the folly of literary language, and more profoundly, the insubstantial nature of the
affections and assumptions that language conveys. Nor does love in the
Songs and Sonnets have immortal ties. Some of the men yearn for permanence with their mistresses; they settle for living so deeply that fixed
moments in their love provide them with a bulwark against change.
Perhaps calling Donne's poetry realistic has become a critical commonplace because of the poems' insistence on living rather than talking
about love.

From all of this living several essential aspects of love emerge in the
Songs and Sonnets. First, love on earth is tied to physical consummation.
The only speakers who deny themselves intercourse are the Negative
Lover and the Platonic Lovers. The first denigrates all love because he is
worried about the lateness of his physical maturity. The Platonic speakers settle rather uneasily for a nonphysical relationship by projecting
future rewards for their virtue. And in "The Relique," at least, the
possibility of sexual union arises. If we accept the term *love* as appropriate to all relationships in the *Songs and Sonnets*, however, it is immediately apparent that neither friendship nor spiritual kinship is a necessary
ingredient to love, although the happiest lovers in the book do possess
these qualities.

A second aspect of love is self-deception. Each man in the poems
pushes his wishes beyond the facts of his experience. The Dreaming
Cynics go farthest, perhaps, inventing imaginary wills, spectral encoun-

ters, conversations with their undertakers, or personal metamorphoses to avenge themselves on their mistresses. They seem terribly confused between love and hate. The Platonic Lovers are oblivious to their need for reward; the Hedonists cannot examine their assumptions about love. Even the Mutual Lovers try to immortalize their happy union. Self-deception, then, seems endemic to man or at least to man in love. Perhaps the spoofing poems illuminate self-deception most brightly of all, for in exposing the folly of the fanciful language of love, the poems also reveal the sometimes absurd postures that lovers adopt.

Ultimately, in the *Songs and Sonnets* no love satisfies completely. In the happiest poem, "The Anniversarie," the lover's joy overwhelms him only after he has resolved to "love nobly, and live" (l. 28), no matter what happens to his love after death. Before he can immerse himself in his love and perform that miracle of losing track of time, he has to banish his wishes for immortality. Even in this most joyous poem, then, happiness depends upon hard acceptances. My negative note, however, should not minimize the wide disparity between the satisfaction the various speakers find with their love. The Mutual Lovers, for all their immortal longing, delight in their bliss. Indeed their wish for permanence grows out of the depth of that delight. What else could command the playful abandon of "The Sunne Rising" or the still joy of acceptance in "A Nocturnall upon S. Lucies Day"? At the other end of the pleasure scale lies the hateful siege between sexual disgust and sexual desire in the Hedonists. As the speaker of "Loves Alchymie" says:

> So, lovers dreame a rich and long delight,
> But get a winter-seeming summers night. (ll. 11–12)

At both extremes in the range of happiness, interestingly, the men find the obstacle to their fulfillment within themselves. The Hedonists apparently do not lack for sexual partners.

> I have lov'd, and got, and told,
> But should I love, get, tell, till I were old . . . (ll. 3–4),

complains the man in "Loves Alchymie," contemplating the elusiveness of love. Yet for all his amours, he is constantly disillusioned and disappointed with love.

> Ah cannot wee,
> As well as Cocks and Lyons jocund be,
> After such pleasures? (ll. 21–23),

asks the man in "Farewell to Love," wishing to be free of moral responsibility for his actions. The profound dissatisfaction these men feel with love has nothing to do with outside circumstances; it reflects their self-hatred, although they refuse to acknowledge such a connection. Likewise the discontent the Mutual Lovers feel arises from their deep immortal longings, not from a fault or limitation within their ladies. The men deceive themselves by imagining that their bliss will continue forever, even though they know it cannot, and their yearning for immortality interrupts their loving. To be happy they must abandon their illusions and live. For most of the other men and women in the *Songs and Sonnets*, however, dissatisfaction with love stems from outside problems. The man in "[Image and Dream]" is tormented because his ideal lady remains chaste; the Cynic in "Twicknam Garden" cries out because his mistress has left him and he has no means to avenge himself; and the lover in "A Valediction: of Weeping" mourns because he must leave his beloved. In general the Dreaming Cynics believe they would be happy if they could wreak revenge on women. All attribute their discontent to an outside cause and thus keep their discontent at a distance. Those few lovers who find an additional reason for their misfortune in love within themselves suffer very intensely. The man in "Twicknam Garden," for example, acknowledges his destructive power by comparing himself to the serpent. And to some extent the speaker in "The Funerall" realizes his complicity in his antagonistic love relationship. Both of these men despair because they know their misfortune is in part of their own making. A similar despair overcomes the Mutual Lovers whose ladies die, when they acknowledge that their belief in love's immortality contributes to their depression. As the man in "A Nocturnall" says:

> I am by her death, (which word wrongs her)
> Of the first nothing, the Elixer grown. (ll. 28–29)

One measure for happiness in the *Songs and Sonnets*, then, is the speaker's capacity to attribute his difficulties to outside causes.

It remains yet to ponder again the tone of these love poems. Donne wrote comic and straightforward versions of all the kinds of lovers in the *Songs and Sonnets* except the Mutual Lovers. For them he devised playful, joyous, and ceremonious lyrics; "The Sunne Rising," "The Anniversarie," and "A Nocturnall upon S. Lucies Day" mark these different shades of joy. This departure from his division of comic and straightforward lyrics suggests that to some extent all the other kinds of lovers in the *Songs and Sonnets* contain the stuff of romantic jokes or the ridiculous traits of a prose Character: the vengeful, unrequited lover, the Platonic Lover who redirects his sexual energies, the playboy, and the phony man-about-town. These kinds of men, of course, exist in life too, where their aberrations disturb them; hence they are found in straightforward poems like "The Relique," "The Funerall," or "[Image and Dream]." The Mutual Lovers, however, contain no comic germ; they are not subject to satire (even when, as in "The Canonization," they satirize themselves), only to celebration.

The paucity of general observations about love that emerges from the *Songs and Sonnets* points back to Donne's method in the poems, perhaps even to a vague plan underlying the series of poems. The generic modifications Donne wrought on the lyric emphasize the truths of an encounter, the possibilities in a tone of voice, the distractions and disturbances of a passing thought rather than the considerations and conclusions of philosophy or meditation. These smaller realities weave the fabric of love's ways and lovers' ways, not the whole cloth of philosophy or morality. Conclusions about love, therefore, are too varied to be authoritative. By imposing a dramatic overlay on the lyric, Donne not only creates lovers separate from himself but also emphasizes that love is a living experience, not the distilled analysis of a book. In the *Songs and Sonnets* love defines itself in process, just as the lover does. To sound the whole chorus of love's voices, Donne has not only lovers but all who profess or pretend to be lovers sing their songs, go through their acts, show their stuff—whatever it is.

One is tempted to see the *Songs and Sonnets* as the kind of book on love that the speaker imagines in "A Valediction: of the Booke," where he advises his mistress to write a compendium of love made from the letters that have passed between the two of them, in which will be

> To all whom loves subliming fire invades,
>   Rule and example found. (ll. 13–14)

Of course the speaker exaggerates the comprehensiveness of his love affair and thus flatters both his lady and himself. Indeed he wants her to write the compendium primarily to keep her mind on him while he is away. As a description of the *Songs and Sonnets*, however, this passage seems appropriate. A bit later the speaker returns to the subject, this time commenting on the readers of his book:

> Here Loves Divines . . .
>   . . . may finde all they seeke,
> Whether abstract spirituall love they like,
> Their Soules exhal'd with what they do not see,
>   Or, loth so to amuze
>   Faiths infirmitie, they chuse
> Something which they may see and use. (ll. 28–34)

Once again the passage seems to apply to the *Songs and Sonnets*. We in the twentieth century have seen best those poems of Mutual Love that we "like," as any survey of Donne criticism shows. Other readers, like the speaker, will find whatever—or almost whatever—they call love here. This fanciful superimposing of the *Songs and Sonnets* onto "A Valediction: of the Booke," however, is just that: fanciful. For like the other *Songs and Sonnets*, this poem is controlled by a speaker with a very definite purpose. He wants to keep his mistress faithful while he is away, even if he must resort to flattery to do so.

Notes

Chapter 1: Coming to Terms

1. For various discussions of *dramatic* as it applies to Donne's poems, see: H. J. C. Grierson, ed., *The Poems of John Donne*, 2 vols. (1912; rpt. London: Oxford University Press, 1963), 2:xlii; Pierre Legouis, *Donne the Craftsman: An Essay upon the Structure of the Songs and Sonnets* (1928; rpt. New York: Russell and Russell, 1952), p. 50 ff.; J. B. Leishman, *The Monarch of Wit: An Analytical and Comparative Study of the Poetry of John Donne*, 6th ed. (1951; rpt. New York: Harper Torchbooks, 1966), pp. 61, 75, 88, 159–60; A. J. Smith, *John Donne: "The Songs and Sonets"* (London: Edward Arnold, 1965), pp. 7–8, 16; Helen Gardner, ed, *The Elegies and the Songs and Sonnets* (Oxford: At the Clarendon Press, 1965), pp. xix–xxii; Donald Guss, *John Donne, Petrarchist: Italianate Conceits and Love Theory in the Songs and Sonets* (Detroit: Wayne State University Press, 1966), pp. 67, 91–92; Earl Roy Miner, *The Metaphysical Mode from Donne to Cowley* (Princeton: Princeton University Press, 1969), pp. 15–23, 54–90; Lowry Nelson, Jr., *Baroque Lyric Poetry* (New Haven: Yale University Press, 1961), pp. 87–90; and Judah Stampfer, *John Donne and the Metaphysical Gesture* (New York: Funk and Wagnalls, 1971), pp. ix–xx and 23–32.

2. All of Donne's poems, unless otherwise indicated, follow the text of *The Elegies and the Songs and Sonnets*, ed. Helen Gardner. "The Canonization," l. 1; "Womans Constancy," ll. 1–2; "The Good-morrow," ll. 1–2. I am deeply indebted to the commentary of Gardner, Grierson, Hayward, and Redpath.

3. Miner, *Metaphysical Mode*, p. x.

4. For a differing analysis of the rhetorical members of a poem, see Nelson, *Baroque Lyric Poetry*, pp. 87–89 et passim; and Alan Armstrong, "The Apprenticeship of John Donne: Ovid and the Elegies," *ELH* 44 (1977): 419–42.

5. Northrop Frye, *Anatomy of Criticism: Four Essays* (1957; rpt. New York: Atheneum Books, 1966), pp. 246–50, 274.

6. Cf. ibid., pp. 249–50.

7. For the view that all literature is dramatic, see Nelson, *Baroque Lyric Poetry*, pp. 87–98; and Kenneth Burke, "Rhetoric and Poetics," *Language as Symbolic Action: Essays on Life, Literature, and Method* (Berkeley and Los Angeles: University of California Press, 1968), pp. 295–307.

8. See, for example, Richard Ohmann, "Speech Acts and the Definition of Literature," *Philosophy and Rhetoric* 4 (1971): 1–19.

9. Grierson, *The Poems of John Donne*, 2:xl–xliii; Leishman, *The Monarch of Wit*, pp. 145–239; Stampfer, *John Donne and the Metaphysical Gesture*, pp. 37–61; and obliquely John Carey, *John Donne: Life, Mind, and Art* (New York: Oxford University Press, 1981), pp. 37–59, 94–130 et passim.

10. George T. Wright, *The Poet in the Poem: The Personae of Eliot, Yeats, and Pound* (Berkeley and Los Angeles: University of California Press, 1962), pp. 1–59. I am deeply indebted to Wright's discussion for my own analysis of Donne's generic hybrid.

11. Catherine Ing, *Elizabethan Lyrics: A Study in the Development of English Meters and Their Relation to Poet Effect* (London: Barnes and Noble, 1951), p. 15. For a careful distinction between the public and private modes in seventeenth-century literature, see Miner, *Metaphysical Mode*, pp. 3–47; and idem, *The Cavalier Mode from Jonson to Cotton* (Princeton: Princeton University Press, 1971), pp. 3–15.

12. Robert Langbaum, *The Poetry of Experience: The Dramatic Monologue in Modern Literary Tradition* (1957; rpt. New York: W. W. Norton and Co., 1963), pp. 9–37; and Wright, *Poet in the Poem*, pp. 30–50.

13. Legouis, *Donne the Craftsman*, p. 38; and Robert Ellrodt, *L'Inspiration personnelle et l'espirit du temps chez les poetes metaphysiques anglais* (Paris: Librarie José Corti, 1960).

14. For a discussion of the identification of the lyric speaker with the poet, see Frye, *Anatomy of Criticism*, p. 249; Susanne Langer, *Feeling and Form* (New York: Charles Scribner's Sons, 1953), p. 259; and Armstrong, "Apprenticeship of John Donne," pp. 419–42.

15. "The Canonization," "The Triple Foole," "The Relique," and "Loves Deitie." In *All in War with Time* (Cambridge: Harvard University Press, 1975), Anne Ferry builds much of her discussion of Donne's treatment of mutability on the fact that his speakers are not poets.

16. Frye, *Anatomy of Criticism*, p. 249.

17. Nelson, *Baroque Lyric Poetry*, pp. 99 ff.; and Miner, *Metaphysical Mode*, pp. 48–59.

18. Langer, *Feeling and Form*, p. 306.

19. "A Feaver," ll. 1–2; "Loves Alchymie," ll. 15–18; "The Dreame," ll. 1–2; and "The Good-morrow," ll. 10–11. See also George T. Wright, "The Lyric Present: Simple Present Verbs in English Poems," *PMLA* 89 (1974): 575–76.

20. Langer, *Feeling and Form*, p. 268. See also Wright, "The Lyric Present," pp. 563–73.

21. Cf. Langer, *Feeling and Form*, p. 267.

22. Ibid., p. 261.

23. Philip Sidney, "An Apology for Poetry," in *Elizabethan Critical Essays*, ed. G. Gregory Smith (Oxford: At the Clarendon Press, 1904), 1:201.

24. Ibid., p. 203.

25. See, for example, H. M. Richmond, "Donne's Master: The Young Shakespeare," *Criticism* 15 (1973): 126–44.

26. Paul Oskar Kristeller, *Renaissance Thought II: Papers on Humanism and the Arts* (New York: Harper and Row, 1965), p. 65.

27. *The Riverside Shakespeare*, ed. G. Blakemore Evans et al. (Boston: Houghton Mifflin, 1974), pp. 168 and 411.

28. *The Characters of Theophrastus,* ed. and trans. J. M. Edmonds, Loeb Classical Library (New York: G. P. Putnam's Sons, 1929), p. 105.

29. Thomas Overbury, *The Overburian Characters, to Which is Added A Wife,* ed. W. J. Paylor (Oxford: Basil Blackwell, 1936), pp. 10–11.

30. *Ben Jonson,* ed. C. H. Hereford, Percy Simpson, and Evelyn Simpson (Oxford: At the Clarendon Press, 1947), 8:76.

31. George Puttenham, *The Arte of English Poesie,* ed. Edward Arber (1906; rpt. Kent, Ohio: Kent State University Press, 1970), p. 96.

32. Ibid., pp. 93–94.

33. Ibid., p. 261.

34. George Gascoigne, "Certayne Notes of Instruction in English Verse," in *English Reprints,* ed. Edward Arber (London: A. Constable, 1869), 3:32.

35. Puttenham, *The Arte of English Poesie,* pp. 260–61.

36. Ibid., pp. 124–25.

37. Letter to Sir Henry Wotton in John Donne, *Selected Prose,* chosen by Evelyn Simpson, ed. Helen Gardner and Timothy Healy (Oxford: At the Clarendon Press, 1967), p. 111.

38. Letter to Sir Henry Goodyer in ibid., p. 126.

39. Letter to Sir Henry Goodyer in ibid., p. 145.

Chapter 2: The Petrarchists

1. For a summary of Petrarchan sentiment in the *Songs and Sonnets,* see Donald L. Guss, *John Donne, Petrarchist: Italianate Conceits and Love Theory in the Songs and Sonets* (Detroit: Wayne State University Press, 1966), pp. 137–38; and R. W. Hamilton, "John Donne's Petrarchist Poems," *Renaissance and Modern Studies* 23 (1979): 45–62. See also Silvia Ruffo-Fiore, "Donne's 'Parody' of the Petrarchan Lady," *Comparative Literature Studies* 9 (1972): 392–406.

2. Guss, *John Donne, Petrarchist,* pp. 66–67. For a concise analysis of the conceit and its parodies, see K. K. Ruthven, *The Conceit.* The Critical Idiom, No. 4, ed. John D. Jump (London: Methuen and Co., 1969).

3. All quotations of Petrarch's poetry and the English translations are from Petrarch, *Sonnets and Songs,* trans. Anna Maria Armi (1946; rpt. New York: Grosset and Dunlap, 1969). The sestet of Sonnet 15 follows:

Talor m'assale in mezzo a' tristi pianti
Un dubbio: come posson queste membra
Da lo spirito lor viver lontane?

Ma rispondemi Amor: —Non
ti rimembra
Che questo è privilegio de gli amanti,
Sciolti da tutte qualitati umane?—

Sonnet 39:
Io temo sí dé begli occhi l'assalto,
Ne' quali Amore e la mia morte alberga,
Chi'i' fuggo lor come fanciul la verga;

E gran tempo è ch'i' presi il primier salto.
Da ora inanzi faticoso od alto
Loco non fia dove 'l voler non s'erga,
Per no scontrar chi miei sensi disperga,
Lassando, come suol, me freddo smalto.

Dunque, s'a veder vio tardo mi volsi,
Per non ravvicinarmi a chi mi strugge,
Fallir forse non fu di scusa indegno.

Piu dico, che'l tornare a quel ch'uom fugge,
E 'l cor che di paura tanta sciolsi,
Fur de la fede mia non leggier pegno.

4. The poems are: George Puttenham, "Cruel you be," and William Percy, "Sonnet," from *Elizabethan Lyrics from the Original Texts,* ed. Norman Ault (1949; rpt. New York: Capricorn Books, 1960), pp. 136–37, p. 192, and "Dreames and Imaginations" in *An Elizabethan Song Book,* ed. Noah Greenberg, W. H. Auden, and Chester Kallman (Garden City, N.Y.: Doubleday, 1955), p. 166.

5. George Puttenham, *The Arte of English Poesie,* ed. Edward Arber (1906; rpt. Kent, Ohio: Kent State University Press, 1970), p. 149.

6. Ibid., p. 150.

7. I discuss the following poems under the heading "The Witty Lovers": "A Valediction: of Weeping," "Song: 'Sweetest love, I do not goe,' " and "A Valediction: of my Name in the Window."

8. This particular image and the apparent mutuality of the love expressed in these poems associate them with those of the Mutual Lovers in Chap. 5. However, none of these poems defines or describes the nature of love, as those in Chap. 5 do.

9. Helen Gardner, ed., *The Elegies and the Songs and Sonnets* (Oxford: At the Clarendon Press, 1965), p. 196.

10. I discuss the following poems under the heading "The Cavalier Petrarchists": "The Broken Heart," "The Dreame," "[Image and Dream]," "The Baite," "Loves Deitie," "The Triple Foole," and "The Dampe."

11. Erving Goffman, *The Presentation of Self in Everyday Life* (Garden City, N.Y.: Doubleday Anchor Books, 1959), pp. 186–87.

12. Arnold Stein, *John Donne's Lyrics: The Eloquence of Action* (Minneapolis: University of Minnesota Press, 1962), pp. 136–37, analyzes the importance of what he calls the "ternary form" in Donne's poetry, the exploration of two extremes of a question, then the fusion of those extremes into a satisfactory conclusion.

13. Leone Ebreo, *The Philosophy of Love (Dialoghi D'Amore),* trans. F. Friedberg-Seeley and Jean H. Barnes (London: Soncino Press, 1937), p. 57, states that perfect and true love is born of reason and begets desire. Gardner, *The Elegies and the Songs and Sonnets,* p. 182, comments on Donne's debt to Ebreo's philosophy of love.

14. Northrop Frye, *Anatomy of Criticism: Four Essays* (1957; rpt. New York:

Atheneum, 1965), p. 301, relates this kind of double vision to the poem of expanded consciousness.

15. Manfred Weidhorn, *Dreams in Seventeenth-Century English Poetry* (The Hague: Mouton, 1970), p. 99.

16. Cf. Petrarch, Canzone 30 and Sonnet 298.

17. Cf. G. M. Matthews, "Sex and the Sonnet," *Essays in Criticism* 2 (1952): 128–30, where he analyzes stylized language as a practical means of seduction.

18. Rosemond Tuve, *Elizabethan and Metaphysical Imagery: Renaissance Poetic and Twentieth-Century Critics* (1947; rpt. Chicago: Phoenix, 1961), pp. 145–79.

19. H. J. C. Greirson, ed. *The Poems of John Donne,* 2 vols. (1912; rpt. London: Oxford University Press, 1963), 2:76, comments on the illusion of an encounter in this poem.

20. Pierre Legouis, *Donne the Craftsman: An Essay upon the Structure of the Songs and Sonnets* (1928; rpt. New York: Harper Torchbooks, 1966), pp. 45–46, comments that "Loves Deitie" never quite lives up to the promise of its dramatic opening. Cf. "Loves Deitie" with the anonymous "Cupid" in Ault, ed., *Elizabethan Lyrics,* p. 329: "Loves god is a boy, / None but cowherds regard him; / His dart is a toy, / Great opinion hath marred him" (ll. 1–4) and with the anonymous "Cupid thou Art A sluggish boye" in *Seventeenth Century Songs and Lyrics,* ed. John P. Cutts (Columbia: University of Missouri Press, 1959), p. 80: "Cupid thou Art A sluggish boye / & doost neglect thy callinge / thy bow and arrowes are a Toye, / thy Monarchye is fallinge." (ll. 1–4).

21. Mario Praz and Pierre Legouis, as recounted in *Donne the Craftsman,* pp. 45–46, both see the refrain as one of Donne's most brilliant ways of creating the contrast between the traditionally poetic and normally prosaic aspects of his lyrics.

Chapter 3: The Extremists

1. Earl Roy Miner, *The Metaphysical Mode from Donne to Cowley* (Princeton: Princeton University Press), pp. 169–74, discusses themes that imply distance between the speaker and his listener. My distinctions are narrower.

2. The exceptions are "The Apparition," "The Exstasie," and "The Canonization."

3. Robert Scholes and Robert Kellogg, *The Nature of Narrative* (New York: Oxford University Press, 1966), p. 73. See also Northrop Frye, *Anatomy of Criticism: Four Essays* (1957; rpt. New York: Atheneum, 1965), p. 307.

4. Frye, *Anatomy of Criticism,* pp. 272–76.

5. The poems discussed under "The Hedonists" are: "Loves Usury," "Loves Diet," "Communitie," "Confined Love," "Loves Alchymie," and "Farewell to Love."

6. See Eric Partridge, *Shakespeare's Bawdy: A Literary and Psychological Essay and a Glossary,* rev. ed. (New York: E. P. Dutton and Co., 1969), pp. 98 and 147, entries under "eat" and "meat."

7. Since the *it* in *'tis* has no grammatical antecedent, by context it refers to the sexual act. For other interpretations that wrestle with grammatical syntax, see

Theodore Redpath, ed. *The Songs and Sonets of John Donne* (London: Methuen and Co., 1956), p. 131; and Katherine Emerson, "Two Problems in Donne's 'Farewell to Love,' " *MLN* 72 (1957): 95. Helen Gardner, ed., *The Elegies and the Songs and Sonnets* (Oxford: At the Clarendon Press, 1965), p. 214, glosses "worme-seed" as an anaphrodisiac. The entry for "wormseed" in the *OED* with reference to Gerard's *Herbal*, 1594, 2.xxii.213, suggests its possibilities as a metaphor for the vagina. Marvin Morillo, "Donne's 'Farewell to Love': The Force of the Shutting Up," *Tulane Studies in English* 13 (1963): 33–40, equates sexual intercourse with "worm-seed."

8. See, for example, Judah Stampfer, *John Donne and the Metaphysical Gesture* (New York: Funk and Wagnalls, 1971), p. 78; and N. J. C. Andreasen, *John Donne: Conservative Revolutionary* (Princeton: Princeton University Press, 1967), pp. 86 and 90.

9. *The Complete Poetical Works of Spenser*, ed. R. E. Neil Dodge (Cambridge: Houghton Mifflin, 1936), p. 719.

10. Gardner, *The Elegies and the Songs and Sonnets*, p. 167 and Robert Gleckner and Gerald Smith, "Donne's 'Love's Usury,' " *Explicator* 8 (1950), item 43.

11. Socrates' description of the charioteer controlling the winged horses of both his passions and his spiritedness in Plato's *Phaedrus* provides one significant image of man's reasonable domination over love.

12. See Erving Goffman, *The Presentation of Self in Everyday Life* (Garden City, N.Y.: Doubleday Anchor Books, 1959), p. 67.

13. Frye, *Anatomy of Criticism*, p. 275.

14. Cf. Andreasen, *Conservative Revolutionary*, pp. 19, 98, and 114.

15. Clay Hunt, *Donne's Poetry: Essays in Literary Analysis* (New Haven: Yale University Press, 1954), pp. 34–39, demonstrates Donne's ingenious twisting of many Platonic ideas and metaphors in this poem. Andreasen, *Conservative Revolutionary*, pp. 121–24, discusses the speaker's impudent opposition to Platonic love theory. Redpath, ed., *The Songs and Sonets*, p. 63, comments on the ambiguity of the philosophical terms in this poem. Cf. Marsilio Ficino, *Commentary on the "Symposium" of Plato on the Subject of Love*, trans. Sears Jayne, University of Missouri Studies, 19 (Columbia: University of Missouri Press, 1944), p. 140.

16. Cf. Wilbur Sanders, *John Donne's Poetry* (Cambridge: Cambridge University Press, 1971), p. 49.

17. Redpath, ed., *Songs and Sonets*, p. 63. See also *The Apologie and Treatise of Ambriose Paré, Containing the Voyages Made into Divers Places with Many of His Writings upon Surgery*, ed. Geoffrey Keynes (1952; rpt. New York: Dover Publications, 1968), pp. 143–46. For a contrasting view to mine, see Gardner, *The Elegies and the Songs and Sonnets*, p. 212.

18. For extended discussion of this idea in the poem, see Gardner, *The Elegies and the Songs and Sonnets*, pp. 213–14; John Hayward, ed. *John Donne Dean of St. Paul's Complete Poetry and Selected Prose* (1929; rpt. New York: Random House, 1941), pp. 766–67; and Redpath, ed., *The Songs and Sonets*, pp. 145–49.

19. Emerson, "Two Problems in Donne's 'Farewell to Love,' " pp. 93–95, first discusses the possibility of Donne's speaker justifying his position through the use of euphemism.

20. The poems discussed in this section are "The Undertaking" and "The Relique."

21. The seven-syllable opening line not only accents *I*, but creates a pause after it. The 1633 edition, used by Grierson, adds an *and* at the beginning of line 3, further differentiating line 1 from the rest of the text and throwing additional stress on *I*.

22. Paul Oskar Kristeller, *Renaissance Thought II: Papers on Humanism and the Arts* (New York: Harper and Row, 1965), p. 53. See also his discussion of the degradation of Ficino's concept of Platonic love, p. 96. Compare the speaker's deprecation of physical beauty with Baldesar Castiglione, *The Book of the Courtier*, trans. George Bull (Baltimore: Penguin Books, 1967), p. 326, and with Ficino, *Commentary on the "Symposium" of Plato*, p. 130.

23. Andreasen, *Conservative Revolutionary*, pp. 207–8, dismisses the contradictions as poetic compliment.

24. Sanders, *John Donne's Poetry*, p. 107.

25. For a different, although not conflicting interpretation, see Marvin Morillo, "Donne's 'The Relique' as Satire," *Tulane Studies in English* 21 (1974):52.

26. Leone Ebreo, *The Philosophy of Love (Dialoghi D'Amore)*, trans. F. Friedberg-Seeley and Jean H. Barnes (London: Soncino Press, 1937), pp. 56–57.

27. This reference to *thou* is the only occasion in the narrated (as opposed to the read) section of the poem where the woman's identity is separated from the speaker's.

28. H. M. Richmond, "The Intangible Mistress," *Modern Philology* 56 (1959): 212–13, sees the speaker as an ironic figure primarily interested in defining his thoughts about love.

29. Gardner, ed., *The Elegies and the Songs and Sonnets*, p. 178. She cites the *Summa theologica* Ia, 2.111.

30. Partridge, *Shakespeare's Bawdy*, pp. 186–87.

Chapter 4: The Dreaming Cynics

1. I have classified the following poems under this heading: "Song: 'Goe, and catche a falling starre,' " "The Will," "Womans Constancy," "The Indifferent," "The Apparition," "The Legacie," "The Funerall," "Twicknam Garden," "The Message," "The Blossome," and "A Jeat Ring Sent."

2. This brief survey of some major interpretations of the poems suggests the difficulty of assessing them. H. J. C. Grierson, ed. *The Poems of John Donne*, 2 vols. (1912; rpt. London: Oxford University Press, 1963), 2:9, calls most of these poems "evaporations"; and J. B. Leishman, *The Monarch of Wit: An Analytical and Comparative Study of the Poems of John Donne*, 6th ed. (1951; rpt. New York: Harper Torchbooks, 1966), p. 178, agrees with him. In "Donne in Our Time," *A Garland for John Donne*, ed. Theodore Spencer (1931; rpt. Gloucester, Mass.: Peter Smith, 1958), p. 10, T. S. Eliot states: "The courtly cynicism was a poetic convention of the time; Donne's sometimes scoffing attitude towards the fickleness of women may be hardly more than immature bravado." On the other hand, Joan Bennett

in *Five Metaphysical Poets* (1934; rpt. Cambridge: Cambridge University Press, 1964), p. 17, treats "The Apparition," one of these poems, as a bitter outcry. Donald Guss, *John Donne, Petrarchist: Italianate Conceits and Love Theory in the Songs and Sonets* (Detroit: Wayne State University Press, 1966), p. 54, advances a similar interpretation of that poem.

3. Arnold Stein, *John Donne's Lyrics: The Eloquence of Action* (Minneapolis: University of Minnesota Press, 1962), pp. 130–35, and Hanford Henderson, "Donne's 'The Will,' "*Explicator* 7 (1949), item 57.

4. D. C. Allen, "Donne on the Mandrake," *MLN* 74 (1959): 394–96.

5. J. P. Kirby and J. E. Whitesell, "Donne's Song, 'Go and Catch a Falling Star,' " *Explicator* 1 (1943), item 29.

6. For further discussion of this topos, see Helen Gardner, ed., *The Elegies and the Songs and Sonnets* (Oxford: At the Clarendon Press, 1965), p. 152, and Ernst Robert Curtius, *European Literature and the Latin Middle Ages*, trans. Willard Trask (1953; rpt. New York: Harper Torchbooks, 1963), p. 96.

7. Grierson, *The Poems of John Donne*, 2:49–50: " 'Thou' is the pronoun of feeling and intimacy, 'you' of respect."

8. Northrop Frye, *Anatomy of Criticism: Four Essays* (1957; rpt. New York: Atheneum, 1965), p. 186. See also Stein, *John Donne's Lyrics*, p. 191.

9. George Puttenham, *The Arte of English Poesie*, ed. Edward Arber (1906; rpt. Kent, Ohio: Kent State University Press, 1970), p. 202, and Quintilian, *Institutiones oratoriae*, VIII.vi.74.

10. Guss, *John Donne, Petrarchist*, p. 114; Stein, *John Donne's Lyrics*, p. 102; and Wilbur Sanders, *John Donne's Poetry* (Cambridge: Cambridge University Press, 1971), pp. 46–47.

11. My italics. Stein, *John Donne's Lyrics*, p. 103, also finds the stress on *just*.

12. For a thorough discussion of epigrammatic theory in the Renaissance, see Rosalie Colie, *Shakespeare's Living Art* (Princeton: Princeton University Press, 1974), pp. 68–96. See also, for example, Ben Jonson, "On Cashierd Capt. Surly," and Martial, *Epigrams*, III.li.

13. For a contrasting but not contradictory explanation, see Stein, *John Donne's Lyrics*, p. 103.

14. Cf. Clay Hunt, *Donne's Poetry: Essays in Literary Analysis* (New Haven: Yale University Press, 1954), p. 10: "Though the intent of these poems [such as "Womans Constancy" and "The Indifferent"] is clearly comic . . . they have an energy and dramatic force which shoves them toward the borderline between merely entertaining light verse and serious poetry."

15. For a discussion of the motivation for "sour grapes," see Kenneth Burke, *Terms for Order*, ed. Stanley Edgar Hyman (Bloomington: Indiana University Press, 1964), pp. 70–71. Puttenham, *The Arte of English Poesie*, pp. 29–30, using less contemporary jargon, also explains a misogynistic Latin epigram as "sour grapes."

16. Earl Roy Miner, *The Metaphysical Mode from Donne to Cowley* (Princeton: Princeton University Press, 1969), p. 16 ff., and Hunt, *Donne's Poetry*, p. 6.

17. Lorenzo daPonte, libretto to Mozart's *Don Giovanni*, trans. Peggie Cochrane (London: Decca Record Co., 1960).

18. Hunt, *Donne's Poetry*, pp. 6–8, analyzes the relationship of "The Indifferent" to Petrarchan love conventions.

19. Robert Langbaum, *The Poetry of Experience: The Dramatic Monologue in Modern Literary Tradition* (1957; rpt. New York: W. W. Norton and Co., 1963), p. 182, describes the gratuitous nature of the utterances in Browning's dialogues: "To appreciate the victory of character over action in the dramatic monologue we have only to consider the motive for which the speakers undertake to speak. Although the utterance is dramatic because it is entirely strategic, we find that the motive for speaking is inadequate to the utterance, that the utterance is in other words largely gratuitous—it need never have occurred. The result is that the dramatic situation, incomplete in itself, serves an ultimately self-expressive or lyrical purpose which gives it its resolution."

20. A comparison with Ovid's *Amores* 2.4 indicates how extensively Donne penetrates the psychological complexities of the speaker in "The Indifferent." Ovid's lover, after a brief pretense of repentence, details the attributes of the many women who arouse his appetite and concludes: "All-embracing, I think is the proper term for my passion: / There's not a sweetheart in town I'd be reluctant to love" (*The Art of Love*, trans. Rolfe Humphries [Bloomington: Indiana University Press, 1957], p. 45). Or see Ovid, *The Heroides and Amores*, Loeb Classical Library (New York: William Heinemann, 1921), p. 392.

21. Both Hunt and Stein share this position.

22. Bennett, *Five Metaphysical Poets*, pp. 17–18.

23. Sir Thomas Wyatt, *Collected Poems*, ed. Joost Daadler (New York: Oxford University Press, 1975), p. 37.

24. Guss, *John Donne, Petrarchist*, pp. 53–60, offers examples of Italian Petrarchist poems in which the unrequited lover promises supernatural revenge to his aloof mistress. A. J. Smith, *John Donne: "The Songs and Sonets"* (London: Edward Arnold, 1965), p. 66, analyzes the poem's repudiation of Petrarchan commitments.

25. C. William Miller and Daniel S. Norton, "Donne's 'The Apparition,' " *Explicator* 4 (1946), item 24. For an opposing view see Allan H. Gilbert, "Donne's 'The Apparition,' " *Explicator* 4 (1946), item 56.

26. Guss, *John Donne, Petrarchist*, pp. 53–54.

27. Colie, *Shakespeare's Living Art*, pp. 76 and 86.

28. Puttenham, *The Arte of English Poesie*, p. 68.

29. Quintilian, *Institutiones oratoriae*, trans. and ed. H. E. Butler, 4 vols., Loeb Classical Library (Cambridge: Harvard University Press, 1920), VI.ii. 29 and 32.

30. Ibid., III.viii.39–41.

31. Guss, *John Donne, Petrarchist*, p. 62.

32. Puttenham, *The Arte of English Poesie*, p. 202. See also Brian Vickers, "The 'Songs and Sonnets' and the Rhetoric of Hyperbole," in *John Donne: Essays in Celebration*, ed. A. J. Smith (London: Methuen and Co., 1972), p. 139.

33. N.J.C. Andreasen, *John Donne: Conservative Revolutionary* (Princeton: Princeton University Press), p. 142, also argues for a sexual reading here, but for a far different overall interpretation.

34. Perhaps Donne subtly makes use of the Paracelsian theory that like cures

like in his love complaints. Puttenham, *The Arte of English Poesie*, p. 63, believes that laments and love complaints do operate in a Paracelsian manner.

35. Lowry Nelson, Jr., *Baroque Lyric Poetry* (New Haven: Yale University Press, 1961), pp. 132–36, discusses the shifting audiences in the poem and the speaker's consequent movement to more general and public resolutions for lovesickness. But, as Miner indicates in *Metaphysical Mode*, pp. 16–23, metaphysical poetry creates the illusion that a speaker is really engaged with his listener.

36. Nelson, *Baroque Lyric Poetry*, p. 133.

37. For the Arachne story, see Ovid, *Metamorphoses*, VI.i. and Edward Topsell, *The History of Four-Footed Beasts and Serpents and Insects*, 3 vols. (1658; rpt. New York: DeCapo Press, 1967), 2:777. Volume 2 is a facsimile of Topsell's second edition of *The History of Four-Footed Beasts* (London, 1608). All three volumes are translations of older Latin works, which would have been available to Donne.

38. I cite Grierson's *The Poems of John Donne*, 1:29, for this reading. His editorial choice of *groane* over *grow*, which Gardner uses in l. 17, is more in keeping with the parallelism between the mandrake and the fountain. Both choices have manuscript support. For a discussion of the two, see Grierson, 2:26, and Gardner, ed., *The Elegies and the Songs and Sonnets*, p. 216.

39. These lines return to the Gardner text.

40. D. C. Allen, "Donne on the Mandrake," pp. 394–96.

41. Quintilian, *Institutionis oratoriae*, VIII.v.2–11.

42. Leonard Unger, *Donne's Poetry and Modern Criticism* (Chicago: Regency, 1950), p. 33, treats the man's emotion as the subject of the poem.

Chapter 5: The Mutual Lovers

1. In this chapter I discuss the following poems: "The Good-morrow," "The Sunne Rising," "Song: 'Sweetest love, I do not goe,' " "The Extasie," "Aire and Angels," "A Valediction: forbidding Mourning," "A Feaver," "The Dissolution," and "A Nocturnall upon S. Lucies Day, being the shortest day."

2. Joan Bennett, *Five Metaphysical Poets* (1934; rpt. Cambridge: Cambridge University Press, 1964), p. 18; Helen Gardner, ed., *The Elegies and the Songs and Sonnets* (Oxford: At the Clarendon Press, 1965), p. xvii; H. J. C. Grierson, ed., *The Poems of John Donne*, 2 vols. (1912; rpt. London: Oxford University Press, 1963), 2:xlii.

3. For a discussion of the relationship between formality and the sublime, see Kenneth Burke, *The Philosophy of Literary Form: Studies in Symbolic Action* (New York: Vintage Books, 1957), p. 52. Dennis Quinn, "Donne and the Wane of Wonder," *ELH* 36 (1969):626–47, concludes that in Donne's most serious poems he presents persons wondering at the great mysteries, including nature, and attempting to commune with them.

4. Earl Roy Miner, *The Metaphysical Mode from Donne to Cowley* (Princeton: Princeton University Press, 1969), p. 160. See especially Miner's perceptive distinctions between satire as genre and satire as a general outlash.

5. "The Sunne Rising," l. 10; "The Anniversarie," l. 29; and "A Nocturnall upon S. Lucies Day, being the shortest day," l. 18.

6. Thomas Browne, *Religio Medici and Other Works*, ed. L. C. Martin (London: Oxford University Press, 1964), p. 123.

7. John Donne, *Letters to Severall Persons of Honour* (1651; rpt. Delmar, N.Y.: Scholars Facsimiles and Reprints, 1977), p. 23.

8. Leone Ebreo, *The Philosophy of Love (Dialoghi D'Amore)*, trans. F. Friedberg-Seeley and Jean H. Barnes (London: Soncino Press, 1937), p. 57.

9. The metaphor 'the lovers are the world to each other' connects this poem with those of the Witty Lover in Chap. 2. James Olney, *Metaphors of Self: The Meaning of Autobiography* (Princeton: Princeton University Press, 1972), explores the implications of an autobiographer's creating a world in his own image. Chap. 1 of Olney's book is extremely provocative in connection with the *Songs and Sonnets*.

10. In Poem 22, for example, Petrarch yearns for a dawn of love with his Laura. A. J. Smith, *John Donne: "The Songs and Sonets"* (London: Edward Arnold, 1965), p. 26, calls "The Good-morrow" a mundane version of Dante's *La vita nuova*.

11. For a fine discussion of the speaker's attempt to conquer time through his love, see Anne D. Ferry, *All in War with Time* (Cambridge: Harvard University Press, 1975), pp. 71–78.

12. Gardner, ed., *The Elegies and the Songs and Sonnets*, p. 198.

13. For a detailed discussion and fine synopsis of the linkage between the eyes and souls of lovers, see Clay Hunt, *Donne's Poetry: Essays in Literary Analysis* (New Haven: Yale University Press, 1954), pp. 62–63.

14. Quintilian, *Institutiones oratoriae*, VIII.v.6–8.

15. Ferry, *All in War with Time*, p. 77, makes a similar point.

16. Gardner, ed., *The Elegies and the Songs and Sonnets*, p. 199, like Grierson, ed., *The Poems of John Donne*, 2:11, glosses these lines with a passage from Aquinas. See also Ferry, *All in War with Time*, pp. 76–78.

17. Gardner, ed. *The Elegies and the Songs and Sonnets*, p. 199; and Arnold Stein, *John Donne's Lyrics: The Eloquence of Action* (Minneapolis: University of Minnesota Press, 1962), pp. 74–77.

18. See [Cicero], *Ad herennium*, IV.xv.22, and Quintilian, *Institutiones oratoriae*, VI.iii.57, for a discussion of pointing up resemblances in disparate things as a means for generating laughter.

19. Quintilian, *Institutiones oratoriae*, VI.iii.8.

20. Lowry Nelson, Jr., *Baroque Lyric Poetry* (New Haven: Yale University Press, 1961), p. 93, discusses the implications of imperatives and questions in metaphysical poetry. Burke, *The Philosophy of Literary Form*, p. 52, analyzes man's penchant for assertion in the face of something sublime or vastly powerful.

21. Cf. Quintilian, *Institutiones oratoriae*, IV.ii.38–39.

22. Wilbur Sanders, *John Donne's Poetry* (Cambridge: Cambridge University Press, 1971), p. 71, makes a similar witticism.

23. Stein, *John Donne's Lyrics*, p. 148, comments on the sonnetlike structure of the stanzas.

24. Eric Partridge, *Shakespeare's Bawdy: A Literary and Psychological Essay and a Glossary*, rev. ed. (New York: Dutton, 1969), p. 176, says that *root* is a common term for *penis*. For the possibility that the poem refers to a woman's pregnancy, see *John Donne's Poetry: Authoritative Texts and Criticism*, ed. A. L. Clements (New York: W. W. Norton and Co., 1966), p. 19.

25. Stephen D. Ring, "Donne's 'Love's Growth' 25–28," *Explicator* 29 (1971), item 58, points out the intensification from literal to literal and metaphoric meaning in the word *spring*.

26. For a discussion of the tension between infinite love and finite lovers in this poem, see Stein, *John Donne's Lyrics*, pp. 154–61.

27. Frank Manley in a lecture commemorating the quatrocentenary of John Donne's birth, Agnes Scott College, Decatur, Ga., Feb. 25, 1972, pointed out the link with the death anniversary in this poem. His lecture is reprinted in *That Subtile Wreath*, ed. M. W. Pepperdene (Decatur, Ga.: Agnes Scott College, 1974), pp. 5–27. Two recent studies which discuss the speaker's commitment to life are Sanders, *John Donne's Poetry*, pp. 74–82, and Ferry, *All in War with Time*, pp. 101–6.

28. Much criticism glosses "threescore" as the biblical length of a man's life. Not so. That is "threescore and ten" (*Ps.* 90:10). The particular grammatical construction in "till we attaine / To write threescore" is the intransitive form of "attain" used with an infinitive in a construction of purpose (*OED*).

29. Among many commentators on the problem of the poem, Sanders, *John Donne's Poetry*, pp. 20–25, 50–56, finds "The Canonization" unsatisfying—magnificent, but ultimately unsuccessful. Hunt, *Donne's Poetry*, pp. 72–93 and p. 174, says that the poem does not achieve the final artistic order of a serious lyric and finds an ugliness in the speaker's self-righteousness. Ferry, *All in War with Time*, pp. 113–25, sees the poem as a parody of eternizing, Petrarchan conceits. William Rooney, " 'The Canonization': The Language of Paradox Reconsidered," *ELH* 23 (1956): 36–47, sees the poem as pure artifice.

30. Puttenham, *The Arte of English Poesie*, p. 174.

31. Quintilian, *Institutiones oratoriae*, IX.iii.74.

32. Rooney, " 'The Canonization'—The Language of Paradox Reconsidered," p. 40, and Sanders, *John Donne's Poetry*, p. 51, discuss Donne's parody of Petrarchan conceits.

33. Cf. Quintilian, *Instituiones oratoriae*, VI.iii.72–78, and Brian Vickers, "The 'Songs and Sonnets' and the Rhetoric of Hyperbole," in *John Donne: Essays in Celebration*, ed. A. J. Smith (London: Methuen and Co., 1972), p. 139.

34. Quintilian, *Institutiones oratoriae*, VI.iii.1.

35. Both flies and butterflies were supposed to have copulated for inordinately long periods of time. The fly is more salacious, however, and to my thinking a fitter reading here. For contrast, see Gardner, ed., *The Elegies and the Songs and Sonnets*, pp. 203–4.

36. Cf. *The Bestiary, A Book of Beasts: Being a Translation from a Latin Bestiary of the Twelfth Century*, trans. T. H. White (New York: Capricorn Books, 1960), p. 126. See Ferry, *All in War with Time*, pp. 116–17, for the sexual meaning of *phoenix*. For further evidence of the Christian import of Donne's imagery, see

Albert Labriola, "Donne's 'The Canonization': Its Theological Context and Religious Imagery," *Huntington Library Quarterly*, 36 (1972–73):327–39.

37. John A. Clair, "Donne's 'The Canonization,' " *PMLA* 80 (1965): 300–302.

38. Vickers, "The 'Songs and Sonnets' and the Rhetoric of Hyperbole," pp. 167–68, sees the ultimate hyperbole as the lovers' transformation into saints, cult figures.

39. Sanders, *John Donne's Poetry*, pp. 96–104, is among the latest commentators to take exception to the poem. Pierre Legouis, *Donne the Craftsman: An Essay upon the Structure of the Songs and Sonnets* (1928; rpt. New York: Russell and Russell, 1952), pp. 61–71, started the controversy in 1928, when he labeled the poem a cleverly concealed piece of seduction. For a summary of the argument, see Gardner, ed., *The Elegies and the Songs and Sonnets*, pp. 259–65.

40. For a similar use of *best*, see George Wither, "Faire Virtue, the Mistresse of Phil'Arete," Sonnet 4.

41. George Williamson, "The Convention of 'The Exstasie,' " in *Seventeenth-Century Contexts* (London: Faber and Faber, 1960), pp. 63–77, discusses the sexual expectations of the pastoral poem.

42. Gardner, ed., *The Elegies and the Songs and Sonnets*, p. 184.

43. See Thomas Rosenmeyer's discussion of *otium* in *The Green Cabinet: Theocritus and the European Pastoral Lyric* (Berkeley and Los Angeles: University of California Press, 1969), pp. 65–97, and Peter Marinelli, *Pastoral*, The Critical Idiom, ed. John D. Jump (London: Methuen and Co., 1971), pp. 57–71. Miner, *Metaphysical Mode*, p. 86, mentions "The Garden" in connection with "The Exstasie."

44. Legouis, *Donne the Craftsman*, p. 62, and after him, N.J.C Andreasen, *John Donne: Conservative Revolutionary* (Princeton: Princeton University Press, 1967), p. 172, comment on the parallel with Othello's interpretation of Desdemona's moist hand. See also Gardner, ed., *The Elegies and the Songs and Sonnets*, p. 183.

45. Cf. Saint Thomas Aquinas, *Summa theologica*, Ia.Q.75 and Q.87.1, and Michael McCanles, "Distinguish in Order to Unite: Donne's 'The Exstasie,' " *Studies in English Literature, 1500–1900* 6 (1966): 59–75, who argues that the poem is about the Thomistic notion of union amidst separation in the body-soul composition.

46. Sanders, *John Donne's Poetry*, p. 101, compares the wordplay here with the nursery rhyme "See-Saw, Margery Daw."

47. Miner, *Metaphysical Mode*, p. 79.

48. Aquinas, *Summa theologica*, Ia.Q.76.1.

49. E.g., Andrew Marvell, "A Dialogue Between the Resolved Soul, and Created Pleasure" and "A Dialogue between the Soul and Body."

50. Barbara Lewalski, "A Donnean Perspective on 'The Exstasie,' " *English Language Notes* 10 (1972–73):262.

51. I cite Grierson's text, which follows both manuscripts and the 1633 edition, 1:53. Gardner amends *which* to *that* to accommodate her interpretation. See *The Elegies and the Songs and Sonnets*, p. 187; and Miner, *Metaphysical Mode*, pp. 80–81.

52. Miner, *Metaphysical Mode*, pp. 77–82.

53. For a rhetorical analysis of the poem that, like mine, focuses on the game playing, see Arthur F. Marotti, "Donne and 'The Exstasie,' " in *The Rhetoric of Renaissance Poetry from Wyatt to Milton*, ed. Thomas O. Sloan and Raymond B. Waddington (Berkeley and Los Angeles: University of California Press, 1974), pp. 140–73.

54. Ferry, *All in War with Time*, pp. 92–95, notes the similarity between the lover's analogies and common eternizing conceits in Renaissance poetry.

55. Cf. *goe* in "The Expiration," l. 7; cf. *melt* in "A Valediction: of my Name in the Window," ll. 49–51; and Partridge, *Shakespeare's Bawdy*, p. 148. For *joy* see Partridge, p. 128.

56. If, as some critics argue, the thinly beaten gold alludes to the stage in alchemy where the gold acts to ferment the base metals, Donne's lover resorts to a seventeenth-century equivalent of science fiction to prove that absence makes the heart grow fonder. For a contrasting view, see Urmilla Khanna, "Donne's 'A Valediction: Forbidding Mourning'—Some Alchemical Allusions," *Notes and Queries* (1970): 404–5.

57. Cf., for example, Carol Sicherman, "Donne's Discoveries," *Studies in English Literature, 1500–1900* 11 (1971): 80.

58. Marvin Morillo, "Donne's Compasses: Circles and Right Lines," *English Language Notes* 3 (1965–66): 173–76, and Sicherman, "Donne's Discoveries."

59. The poem attached to George Wither's compass emblem stresses the mutual responsibility of the feet. See Rosemary Freeman, *English Emblem Books* (London: Chatto and Windus, 1948), p. 146.

60. Partridge, *Shakespeare's Bawdy*, p. 73. Cf. Donne's "Loves Warre," l. 38. For different interpretations, see Jay Arnold Levine, " 'The Dissolution': Donne's Twofold Elegy," *ELH* 28 (1961): 301–15, and Judah Stampfer, *John Donne and the Metaphysical Gesture* (New York: Funk and Wagnalls, 1971), p. 190.

61. Stampfer, *John Donne and the Metaphysical Gesture*, pp. 192–93, discusses the sexual overtones in this passage.

62. Partridge, *Shakespeare's Bawdy*, p. 178, and the *OED*.

63. Clarence H. Miller, "Donne's 'A Nocturnall upon S. Lucies Day' and the Nocturne of Matins," *Studies in English Literature, 1500–1900* 6 (1966): 80–81.

64. Stampfer, *John Donne and the Metaphysical Gesture*, p. 195.

65. Miller, "Donne's 'A Nocturnall upon S. Lucies Day,' " p. 81.

66. Richard Sleight, "John Donne: 'A Nocturnall upon S. Lucies Day, Being the Shortest Day,' " in *Interpretations*, ed. John Wain (London: Routledge and Kegan Paul, 1955), p. 39.

67. G. F. Waller, "John Donne's Changing Attitudes to Time," *Studies in English Literature, 1500–1900* 14 (1974):81–82.

Conclusion

1. Theodore Redpath, ed., *The Songs and Sonets of John Donne* (London: Methuen, 1956), p. xvi.

2. Clay Hunt, *Donnne's Poetry: Essays in Literary Analysis* (New Haven, Yale University Press, 1954), p. 120.

3. *The Wit of Love,* University of Notre Dame Ward-Phillips Lecture in English Language and Literature, vol. 3 (South Bend, Ind.: University of Notre Dame Press, 1969).

4. Helen Gardner, ed., *The Elegies and the Songs and Sonnets* (Oxford: At the Clarendon Press, 1965), p. 256.

5. "To fetch new lust, and give it you" ("A Nocturnall upon S. Lucies Day, being the shortest day," l. 40) and "to rage, to lust, to write to, to commend" ("Loves Deitie," l. 17).

Bibliography

Primary Sources

Ad Herennium. Translated by Harry Caplan. Loeb Classical Library. 1954. Reprint. Cambridge: Harvard University Press, 1977.

Aquinas, Thomas. *Summa theologicae: Latin Text and English Translation.* Vols. 1–5. New York: McGraw Hill, 1964.

The Bestiary, a Book of Beasts: Being a Translation from a Latin Bestiary of the Twelfth Century. Translated by T. H. White. New York: Capricorn Books, 1960.

Browne, Thomas. *Religio Medici and Other Works.* Edited by L. C. Martin. London: Oxford University Press, 1964.

Castiglione, Baldesar. *The Book of the Courtier.* Translated by George Bull. Baltimore: Penguin Books, 1967.

Donne, John. *The Elegies and the Songs and Sonnets.* Edited by Helen Gardner. Oxford: At the Clarendon Press, 1965.

———. *John Donne Dean of St. Paul's Complete Poetry and Selected Prose.* Edited by John Hayward. 1929. Reprint. New York: Random House, 1941.

———. *John Donne's Poetry: Authoritative Texts and Criticism.* Edited by A. L. Clements. New York: W. W. Norton and Co., 1966.

———. *Juvenilia.* 1633. Reprint. New York: DeCapo Press, 1970.

———. *Letters to Severall Persons of Honour.* 1651. Reprint. Delmar, N.Y.: Scholars Facsimiles and Reprints, 1977.

———. *The Poems of John Donne.* Edited by H. J. C. Grierson, 2 vols. 1912. Reprint. London: Oxford University Press, 1963.

———. *Selected Prose.* Chosen by Evelyn Simpson. Edited by Helen Gardner and Timothy Healy. Oxford: At the Clarendon Press, 1967.

———. *The Songs and Sonets of John Donne.* Edited by Theodore Redpath. London: Methuen and Co., 1956.

Ebreo, Leone. *The Philosophy of Love (Dialoghi D'Amore).* Translated by F. Friedberg-Seeley and Jean H. Barnes. London: Soncino Press, 1937.

Elizabethan Lyrics from the Original Texts. Edited by Norman Ault. 1949. Reprint. New York: Capricorn Books, 1960.

An Elizabethan Song Book. Edited by Noah Greenberg, W. H. Auden, and Chester Kallman. Garden City, N.Y.: Doubleday, 1955.

Evans, Blakemore, et al., eds. *The Riverside Shakespeare.* Boston: Houghton Mifflin, 1974.

Ficino, Marsilio. *Commentary on the "Symposium" of Plato on the Subject of Love.*

Translated by Sears Jayne. University of Missouri Studies, 19. Columbia: University of Missouri Press, 1944.

Gascoigne, George. "Certayne Notes of Instruction in English Verse." In *English Reprints*. Vol. 3. Edited by Edward Arber. London: A. Constable, 1896.

Jonson, Ben. *Ben Jonson*. Vol. 8. Edited by C. H. Herford, Percy Simpson, and Evelyn Simpson. Oxford: At the Clarendon Press, 1947.

Martial. *Epigrams*. 2 vols. Translated by Walter C. A. Ker. Loeb Classical Library. Revised 1919. Reprint. Cambridge: Harvard University Press, 1968.

Overbury, Thomas. *The Overburian Characters, to Which is Added a Wife*. Ed. W. J. Paylor. Oxford: Basil Blackwell, 1936.

Ovid. *The Art of Love*. Translated by Rolfe Humphries. Bloomington: Indiana University Press, 1957.

———. *The Heroides and Amores*. Loeb Classical Library. New York: William Heinemann, 1921.

———. *The Metamorphoses*. Translated by Horace Gregory. 1958. Reprint. New York: Mentor Books, 1960.

Paré, Ambriose. *The Apologie and Treatise of Ambriose Paré, Containing the Voyages Made into Divers Places with Many of His Writings upon Surgery*. Edited by Geoffrey Keynes. 1952. Reprint. New York: Dover Publications, 1968.

Petrarch, Francesco. *Sonnets and Songs*. Translated by Anna Maria Armi. 1946. Reprint. New York: Grosset and Dunlap. 1968.

Plato. *The Works of Plato*. Edited by Irwin Edman. Translated by Benjamin Jowett. New York: Modern Library, 1928.

daPonte, Lorenzo. Libretto. *Don Giovanni*. By W. A. Mozart. Translated by Peggie Cochrane. London: Decca Record Co., 1960.

Puttenham, George. *The Arte of English Poesie*. Edited by Edward Arber. 1906. Reprint. Kent, Ohio: Kent State University Press, 1970.

Quintilian. *Institutiones oratoriae*. 4 vols. Translated and edited by H. E. Butler. Loeb Classical Library. Cambridge: Harvard University Press, 1920.

Seventeenth Century Songs and Lyrics. Edited by John P. Cutts. Columbia: University of Missouri Press, 1959.

Sidney, Philip. "An Apology for Poetry." In *Elizabethan Critical Essays*. Edited by G. Gregory Smith. Vol. 1. Oxford: At the Clarendon Press, 1904.

Spenser, Edmund. *The Complete Poetical Works of Spenser*. Edited by R. E. Neil Dodge. Cambridge: Houghton Mifflin, 1936.

Theophrastus. *The Characters of Theophrastus*. Edited and translated by J. M. Edmonds. Loeb Classical Library. New York: G. P. Putnam's Sons, 1929.

Topsell, Edward. *The History of Four-Footed Beasts*. 3 vols. 1658. Reprint. New York: DeCapo Press, 1967.

Wyatt, Thomas. *Collected Poems*. Edited by Joost Daalder. New York: Oxford University Press, 1975.

Secondary Sources

Allen, D. C. "Donne on the Mandrake." *MLN* 74 (1959):393–97.

Andreasen, N. J. C. *John Donne: Conservative Revolutionary*. Princeton: Princeton University Press, 1967.

Armstrong, Alan. "The Apprenticeship of John Donne: Ovid and the *Elegies*." *ELH* 44 (1977): 419–42.

Bennett, Joan. *Five Metaphysical Poets*. 1934. Reprinted with new title. Cambridge: Cambridge University Press, 1964.

Burke, Kenneth. *Language as Symbolic Action: Essays on Life, Literature, and Method*. Berkeley and Los Angeles: University of California Press, 1968.

———. *The Philosophy of Literary Form: Studies in Symbolic Action*. New York: Vintage Books, 1957.

———. *Terms for Order*. Edited by Stanley Edgar Hyman. Bloomington: Indiana University Press, 1964.

Carey, John. *John Donne: Life, Mind, and Art*. New York: Oxford University Press, 1981.

Clair, John A. "Donne's 'The Canonization,' " *PMLA* 80 (1965): 300–302.

Colie, Rosalie. *Shakespeare's Living Art*. Princeton: Princeton University Press, 1974.

Combs, Homer and Zay Sullens. *A Concordance to the English Poems of John Donne*. Chicago: Packard and Co., 1940.

Curtius, Ernst Robert. *European Literature and the Latin Middle Ages*. Translated by Willard R. Trask. 1953. Reprint. New York: Harper Torchbooks, 1963.

Ellrodt, Robert. *L'Inspiration personnelle et l'espirit du temps chez les poetes metaphysiques anglais*. Paris: Librarie José Corti, 1960.

Eliot, Thomas Stearns. "Donne in Our Time." In *A Garland for John Donne*. Edited by Theodore Spencer. 1931. Reprint. Gloucester, Mass.: Peter Smith, 1958.

Emerson, Katherine. "Two Problems in Donne's 'Farewell to Love.' " *MLN* 72 (1957): 93–95.

Ferry, Anne D. *All in War with Time*. Cambridge: Harvard University Press, 1975.

Freeman, Rosemary. *English Emblem Books*. London: Chatto and Windus, 1948.

Frye, Northrop. *Anatomy of Criticism: Four Essays*. 1957. Reprint. New York: Atheneum, 1965.

Gilbert, Allan H. "Donne's 'The Apparition.' " *Explicator* 4 (1946), item 56.

Gleckner, Robert, and Gerald Smith. "Donne's 'Love's Usury.' " *Explicator* 8 (1950), item 43.

Goffman, Erving. *The Presentation of Self in Everyday Life*. Garden City, N.Y.: Doubleday Anchor Books, 1959.

Guss, Donald L. *John Donne, Petrarchist: Italianate Conceits and Love Theory in the Songs and Sonets*. Detroit: Wayne State University Press, 1966.

Hamilton, R. W. "John Donne's Petrarchist Poems." *Renaissance and Modern Studies* 23 (1979): 45–62.

Henderson, Hanford. "Donne's 'The Will.' " *Explicator* 7 (1949), item 57.

Hunt, Clay. *Donne's Poetry: Essays in Literary Analysis*. New Haven: Yale University Press, 1954.

Ing, Catherine. *Elizabethan Lyrics: A Study in the Development of English Meters and Their Relation to Poetic Effect*. London: Barnes and Noble, 1951.

Joseph, Sister Miriam. *Rhetoric in Shakespeare's Time: Literary Theory of Renaissance Europe*. 1947. Reprint. New York: Harcourt, Brace, and World, 1962.

Khanna, Urmilla. "Donne's 'A Valediction: Forbidding Mourning'—Some Alchemical Allusions." *Notes and Queries* (1970): 404–5.

Kirby, J. P., and J. E. Whitesell. "Donne's Song 'Go and Catch a Falling Star.' " *Explicator* 1 (1943), item 29.

Kristeller, Paul Oskar. *Renaissance Thought II: Papers on Humanism and the Arts.* New York: Harper and Row, 1965.

Labriola, Albert. "Donne's 'The Canonization': Its Theological Context and Religious Imagery." *Huntington Library Quarterly* 36 (1972–73): 327–39.

Langbaum, Robert. *The Poetry of Experience: The Dramatic Monologue in Modern Literary Tradition.* 1957. Reprint. New York: W. W. Norton and Co., 1963.

Langer, Susanne K. *Feeling and Form.* New York: Charles Scribner's Sons, 1953.

Legouis, Pierre. *Donne the Craftsman: An Essay upon the Structure of the Songs and Sonnets.* 1928. Reprint. New York: Russell and Russell, 1952.

Leishman, J. B. *The Monarch of Wit: An Analytical and Comparative Study of the Poetry of John Donne.* 6th ed. 1951. Reprint. New York: Harper Torchbooks, 1966.

Levine, Jay Arnold. " 'The Dissolution': Donne's Twofold Elegy." *ELH* 28 (1961): 301–15.

Lewalski, Barbara. "A Donnean Perspective on 'The Exstasie.' " *English Language Notes* 10 (1972–73): 258–62.

McCanles, Michael. "Distinguish in Order to Unite: Donne's 'The Exstasie.' " *Studies in English Literature, 1500–1900* 6 (1966): 59–75.

Manley, Frank. "Formal Wit in the 'Songs and Sonnets.' " In *That Subtile Wreath.* Edited by M. W. Pepperdene. Decatur, Ga.: Agnes Scott College, 1974.

Marinelli, Peter. *Pastoral.* The Critical Idiom. Edited by John D. Jump. London: Methuen and Co., 1971.

Marotti, Arthur F. "Donne and 'The Exstasie.' " In *The Rhetoric of Renaissance Poetry from Wyatt to Milton.* Edited by Thomas O. Sloan and Raymond B. Waddington. Berkeley and Los Angeles: University of California Press, 1974.

Martz, Louis. *The Wit of Love.* University of Notre Dame Ward-Phillips Lectures in English Language and Literature, 3. South Bend, Ind.: University of Notre Dame Press, 1969.

Matthews, G. M. "Sex and the Sonnet." *Essays in Criticism* 2 (1952): 119–37.

Miller, C. William and Daniel S. Norton. "Donne's 'The Apparition.' " *Explicator* 6 (1946), item 24.

Miller, Clarence H. "Donne's 'A Nocturnall upon S. Lucies Day' and the Nocturne of Matins." *Studies in English Literature, 1500–1900* 6 (1966): 77–86.

Miner, Earl Roy. *The Cavalier Mode from Jonson to Cotton.* Princeton: Princeton University Press, 1971.

———. *The Metaphysical Mode from Donne to Cowley.* Princeton: Princeton University Press, 1969.

Morillo, Marvin. "Donne's Compasses: Circles and Right Lines." *English Language Notes* 3 (1965–66): 173–76.

———. "Donne's 'Farewell to Love': The Force of the Shutting Up." *Tulane Studies in English* 13 (1963): 33–40.

———. "Donne's 'The Relique' as Satire." *Tulane Studies in English* 21 (1974): 47–55.

Nelson, Lowry, Jr. *Baroque Lyric Poetry.* New Haven: Yale University Press, 1961.

Ohmann, Richard. "Speech Acts and the Definition of Literature." *Philosophy and Rhetoric* 4 (1971): 1–19.

Olney, James. *Metaphors of Self: The Meaning of Autobiography*. Princeton: Princeton University Press, 1972.

Partridge, Eric. *Shakespeare's Bawdy: A Literary and Psychological Essay and a Glossary*. Revised 1948. Reprint. New York: E. P. Dutton and Co., 1969.

Quinn, Dennis. "Donne and the Wane of Wonder." *ELH* 36 (1969): 626–47.

Richmond, H. M. "Donne's Master: The Young Shakespeare." *Criticism* 15 (1973): 126–44.

———. "The Intangible Mistress." *Modern Philology* 56 (1959): 217–23.

Ring, Stephen D. "Donne's 'Love's Growth' 25–28." *Explicator* 29 (1971), item 58.

Rooney, William J. " 'The Canonization': The Language of Paradox Reconsidered." *ELH* 23 (1956): 36–47.

Rosenmeyer, Thomas. *The Green Cabinet: Theocritus and the European Pastoral Lyric*. Berkeley and Los Angeles: University of California Press, 1969.

Ruffo-Fiore, Silvia. "Donne's 'Parody' of the Petrarchan Lady." *Comparative Literature Studies* 9 (1972): 392–406.

Ruthven, K. K. *The Conceit*. The Critical Idiom. Edited by John D. Jump. London: Methuen and Co., 1969.

Sanders, Wilbur. *John Donne's Poetry*. Cambridge: Cambridge University Press, 1971.

Scholes, Robert, and Robert Kellogg. *The Nature of Narrative*. New York: Oxford University Press, 1966.

Sicherman, Carol Marks. "Donne's Discoveries." *Studies in English Literature, 1500–1900* 11 (1971): 69–88.

Sleight, Richard. "John Donne: 'A Nocturnall upon S. Lucies Day, Being the Shortest Day.' " In *Interpretations*. Edited by John Wain. London: Routledge and Kegan Paul, 1955, pp. 31–58.

Smith, A. J. *John Donne: "The Songs and Sonets."* London: Edward Arnold, 1965.

Stampfer, Judah. *John Donne and the Metaphysical Gesture*. New York: Funk and Wagnalls, 1971.

Stein, Arnold. *John Donne's Lyrics: The Eloquence of Action*. Minneapolis: University of Minnesota Press, 1962.

Tuve, Rosemond. *Elizabethan and Metaphysical Imagery: Renaissance Poetic and Twentieth-Century Critics*. 1947. Reprint. Chicago: Phoenix Books, 1961.

Unger, Leonard. *Donne's Poetry and Modern Criticism*. Chicago: University of Chicago Press, 1950.

Vickers, Brian. "The 'Songs and Sonnets' and the Rhetoric of Hyperbole." In *John Donne: Essay in Celebration*. Edited by A. J. Smith. London: Methuen and Co., 1972.

Waller, G. F. "John Donne's Changing Attitudes to Time." *Studies in English Literature, 1500–1900* 14 (1974):79–89.

Weidhorn, Manfred. *Dreams in Seventeenth-Century English Poetry*. The Hague, Mouton, 1970.

Williamson, George. "The Convention of 'The Extasie.' " In *Seventeenth-Century Contexts*. London: Faber and Faber, 1960.

Wright, George T. "The Lyric Present: Simple Present Tense Verbs in English Poems." *PMLA* 89 (1974): 563–79.

———. *The Poet in the Poem: The Personae of Eliot, Yeats, and Pound.* Berkeley and Los Angeles: University of California Press, 1962.

Index

Adynaton, 76, 78

Antithesis, 128

Aphorism, 101, 102, 110, 163. *See also Sententia*

Aquinas, Saint Thomas, 73, 136, 138

Arachne, 99–100

Argutia, 83, 90, 98, 163. *See also* Epigram

Aubade, 108, 112, 113, 116, 118, 155, 162, 163. *See also Aube*

Aube, 108

Autobiography, 50, 51

Bedford, Lucy, Countess of, 106

Browne, Sir Thomas, 106

Browning, Robert, 85, 174 (n. 19)

Canonization: Roman Catholic Procedures for, 130–31

Carpe diem, 157

Casaubon, Isaac, 12

Cavalier Petrarchist, 15, 27, 38–49, 158, 161; affirmation of Petrarchan sentiment, 15, 39; mocks Petrarchan language, 15, 38, 39, 40, 43; self-parody of, 16, 39, 40, 41, 42; different audiences of, 39; fiction of, 39, 43; guise as long-suffering lover, 39; as creator, 39, 42, 43, 44, 45, 46, 47; as lover, 39, 44; stance of, 43; humor of, 48

Character essays, 11, 12; as single trait, 12; individualizing details of, 12; as social type, 12, 13; moral purpose of, 13; moral judgment of, 14; objectivity of, 14

Character types, 11, 15, 26, 54. *See also* Stock characters

Chiasmus, 128, 147

Cicero, Marcus Tullius, 92, 128

Colie, Rosalie, 90

Comic tone: speaker's self-consciousness as

creator, 7, 18, 22, 24, 76–77; destruction of dramatic encounter, 17, 18, 19; impulse to joy in words, 18; game quality of, 19; energy of, 20; fiction of, 22; bawdy puns, 22–23, 60; manipulation of oratorical conventions, 23; playing with sound, 59

Complaint, 7, 27, 39, 46, 47, 58, 76, 77, 84, 86, 87, 103, 159; ironic, 54, 55, 57, 88, 89; pastoral, 98

Cupid, 22, 46, 47, 48, 52, 53, 54, 55, 56, 57, 59, 100, 101, 158, 159, 160, 173 (n. 20)

Dialogue, 133, 134, 135, 136, 137, 138

Donne, John, 25, 155; Poetry, *The Anniversaries*, ix; "Farewell to Love," x, 13, 20–21, 22, 52, 53, 60, 64, 165; "Loves Alchymie," x, 12, 60–64, 165; "Loves Diet," x, 20–21, 22, 57–60; "The funerall," x, 7, 93, 94–98, 160, 166, 167; "Womans Constancy," x, 19, 81–84, 88, 102, 103, 163; "Communitie," 5, 12, 50, 52, 53, 64; "The Expiration," 5, 7, 27, 32–33, 74, 132, 150; *Elegies*, 6; "The Undertaking," 6, 66–67; "[Image and Dream]," 7, 44–45, 48, 49, 166, 167; "The Anniversarie," 7, 8, 18–19, 106, 117, 121–26, 139, 145, 156, 165, 166; "The Broken Heart," 7, 43, 45, 48, 150; "The Sunne Rising," 7, 23, 108, 113–17, 126–27, 146, 156, 157, 160, 162, 163, 165, 166; "Loves Exchange," 13, 14, 158–60; "Platonic Love," 14; "The Legacie," 14, 18, 77, 95, 103, 132; "The Nothing," 14; "Twicknam Garden," 14, 93, 98–103, 141, 166; "Song: 'Goe, and catche a falling starre,' " 19, 78–81, 93, 103, 160; "The Apparition," 19, 52, 83, 88–93, 94, 95, 160; "The

Canonization," 19, 23, 106, 126–32, 138, 139, 141, 146, 167; "The Will," 19, 77, 82, 93, 94, 160; "The Computation," 27, 30–32; "The Paradox," 27, 32; "Witchcraft by a Picture," 27, 32; "A Valediction: of Weeping," 34–37, 84, 166; "A Valediction: of my Name in the Window," 37–38; "Song: 'Sweetest love, I do not goe' " 37, 117–18, 145; "The Dreame," 39–42, 43, 45, 48, 49, 84; "The Baite," 42–43; "The Dampe," 42, 44; "Loves Deitie," 45–47, 48; "The Triple Foole," 45, 47–48, 89; "Confined Love," 50, 52, 64, 65, 163; "Loves Usury," 52, 53, 54–57; "The Extasie," 52, 106, 126, 132–39, 141, 142; "The Relique," 67–72, 141, 164, 167; "Negative Love," 72–75; "The Bracelet," 74; "The Message," 77, 93; "The Indifferent," 81, 84–88, 89, 93, 103; "A Jeat Ring Sent," 93; "The Blossome," 93; "A Feaver," 106, 146–49, 156; "A Nocturnall upon S. Lucies Day, being the shortest day," 107, 126, 146, 150–55, 165, 166; "A Valediction: forbidding Mourning," 107, 139, 140–45, 146; "The Good-morrow," 107, 108–13, 156, 157, 162; "Loves Infiniteness," 117, 120–21, 156; "Loves Growth," 117, 118–20, 121, 156; "Aire and Angels," 139–40; "The Dissolution," 146, 149–50, 156; "A Lecture upon the Shadow," 160–61, 162; "The Flea," 160, 161–62; "The Primrose," 160, 161, 162; "Breake of Day," 162–63; "A Valediction: of the Booke," 167–68; Prose, letters, 25, 106–07; paradoxes, 25; problems, 25–26; *Juvenilia*, 52; "A Defence of Womens Constancy," 83; *Paradoxes and Problems*, 53

Double entendre, 41, 42, 61

Drama, x–xi, 1, 3, 4, 26; play within a play, 7, 113, 147, 163; psychodrama, 7, 44, 45, 49, 86, 87, 88, 89

"Dreames and Imaginations," 29

Dreaming Cynic, x, 15, 76–104, 158, 164, 166; love-hate ambivalence toward women, 17, 88, 93, 94; yearning for love, 17, 76; revenge of, 17, 76, 83, 88; as creator of fictional realm, 17, 77, 79; as savior, 77, 93, 101, 102; rhetorical relationship of, 79, 80; heroic bravado of, 94, 97; self-deception of, 94

Ebreo, Leone, 69
Eden, 98, 100
Eliot, T. S., 1
Emblem, 160, 161, 162
Epigram, 21, 82, 89, 90, 91; epigrammatic closure, 13, 81, 82, 83, 85, 92, 93, 98, 150, 163
Epitaphium recens, 155

Fallacious reasoning, 5, 59, 64, 65, 146; fallacy of speech respective, 121, 129, 149
Ficino, Marsilio, 16, 67
Frye, Northrop, 2, 3, 9, 59

Games of wit, 19, 28, 30, 32, 53, 160, 161, 162
Gardner, Helen, 6, 41, 73, 161
Gascoigne, George, 22
Goffman, Erving, 39, 41, 45
Goodyer, Sir Henry, 25
Grierson, H. J. C., 41

Hagiography, 67, 68, 69, 70, 72, 130–31. *See also* Sanctity of love
Hedonist, x, 15, 20–21, 50, 52–66, 72, 73, 126, 164, 165; definition of love, 16, 52; disillusionment with love and women, 20; as autobiographer, 16, 20, 52, 56, 57–58, 59, 60, 61, 64; as victim, 16, 52, 53; rejection of the present, 16, 57; as creator of the world in his image, 52, 56, 64; identification with his listener, 52, 61, 62, 63; gamelike quality of, 53; guilt of, 57, 59, 61, 64; distance from listener, 58; graphic metaphors of, 62
Hermeticism, 61
Homoeoteleuton, 128
Hunt, Clay, 158
Hyperbole, 79, 95, 96, 127, 132, 139, 153, 159, 160

Inns of Court, 6
Invention, 22, 46, 161, 152

Jonson, Ben, 5, 82; "An Epistle to Master John Selden," 6; *Epigrammes*, 13; "On GVT," 14

Keats, John, 4
Kellogg, Robert, 51

Langer, Susanne, 8, 9

Listener: as carbon copy of speaker, 6; as cardboard figure, 7, 18, 132, 161; in fictional drama, 7; as sounding board for speaker, 9; as Character type, 14. *See also* Rhetorical relationship

Litotes, 29

Love: Renaissance theories of, 5; as living experience, 164, 167; necessity of physical consummation of, 164; necessity of self-deception in, 164–65; mortality of, 164; imperfection of, 165

Lyric, x–xi, 2, 5, 26; present tense of action in, 7, 8; timelessness of present tense in, 8. *See also* Time, Timelessness

Marlowe, Christopher: "The Passionate Shepherd to his Love," 42

Martial, 82

Martz, Louis, 158

Marvell, Andrew: "The Garden," 134

Memento mori, 37, 153

Milton, John, 98

Miner, Earl, 105

Mozart, W. A.: *Don Giovanni*, 84–86

Mummy, 63, 64

Mutual Lover, 15, 16, 105–57, 165, 166, 167; yearning for immortality of, 16, 105–06, 111–12, 113, 117, 121, 122, 132, 148, 155–56; happiness with love, 17, 105, 109–10, 124; haunted by death, 17, 105, 106, 122, 146, 147; timelessness of celebration, 17, 107, 149; time and place in the poems of, 106, 124–25, 133, 148–49, 155; reciprocity of love, 107–08, 109, 125; microcosm of, 107, 112, 115, 120, 126, 132, 139, 142, 146, 150, 153; mistress as incarnation of union, 107, 109, 115, 132; as autobiographer, 130, 137–38, 152, 153; outsider as listener, 130, 139, 146, 150–51, 154; as speaker and listener, 140, 146, 152; rhetorical relationship of, 143; endurance of love of, 155

Narrative, x–xi, 9, 26, 50, 51, 68; time in, 9, 51, 54; ironic potential of, 51; lyrical elements of, 51

Natural law, 65

Negative Lover, 15, 50, 72–75, 164; rejection of love, 72; sarcastic wit of, 72–73; defensiveness of, 73; audience of, 74

Negotium, 134, 138

Neoplatonism, 16, 60, 61, 62, 63, 64, 69, 106, 125, 138, 141

Nocturne, 152, 154–55

Oration, classical, 90, 113; *argumentatio* of, 23, 115; *peroratio* of, 23, 91, 116; *exordium* of, 113, 115, 127; *narratio* of, 114–15; parody of, 114; *refutatio* of, 116

Otium, 133–34, 138. *See also* Pastoral

Overbury, Thomas, 14; *Characters*, 12, 14; "An Amorist," 13

Ovid, 1, 6, 99, 114; *Amores* 2.7 and 8, 55; *Amores* 2.4, 84, 177 (n. 20)

Paracelcus, 177 (n. 34)

Paré, Dr. Ambriose, 63

Parodist, 15, 27–33, 49; as mock Petrarchist, 15; as lyric singer, 15, 30–31; self-consciousness as a creator, 28, 30; as unrequited lover, 30, 32; as Character type, 31; game quality of, 31

Partridge, Eric, 74

Pastoral, 98, 133, 134, 137, 138; parody of, 134, 137, 138

Percy, William: "It Shall be said I died for Coelia!" 29

Personae, ix–xi, 2, 4, 5, 6, 10–17; as poets, 6; as exploiters of their listeners, 6–7; as autobiographers, 9, 16

Petrarch, Francesco, 1, 28, 39, 105, 107, 108, 146, 164; ironic self-perception of, 29; Sonnet 15, 29; Sonnet 39, 29

Petrarchan conceits, 27; parody of, 5, 15, 27, 164; "lover dies at parting," 15, 27, 29, 30–31, 34, 37, 38, 77, 117, 123, 140; literal truth of, 27, 30, 32–33, 36, 37; "the lady kills with scorn," 28, 29, 76, 90, 94; the lover's sighs and tears, 30, 121, 128; "the lover is worthless," 34; "the lady comprises the lover's world," 34, 35; "the lover dies of love," 43; hot and cold flashes of desire, 43; creation as a cure for heartache, 47, 48

Petrarchan stance, 27, 94; affirmation of, 15; undermining of, 15, 27, 30–31, 32–33; self-denigration of, 34

Petrarchist poets, 29

Petrarchists, the, 27–49

Plato, 1, 174 (n. 11)

Platonic Lover, 15, 50, 66–72, 73, 164, 165; happiness of, 16; superiority of, 16, 66; abstinence from sexual relations of, 16,

66; need for reward of, 16, 66, 67, 68, 72; as autobiographer, 16, 66, 67, 68, 70, 71, 72; definition of love, 66, 72; relationship with listener, 66

Poet: as creator, 4, 5, 6; as man, 5

Psychomachia, 44, 45, 80

Puritanism, 64

Puttenham, George, 22, 23, 25, 60; Tautologia, 21; excessive rhyme, 21; meter, 21; puns, 23; humane purposes of comic poetry, 24–25; "Cruel you be," 29; delighting the ear, 30–31; moderation, 33; epigram, 91; hyperbole, 96; grammatical and auricular figures, 128

Quintilian, 23, 24, 91–92, 114, 128, 129

Raleigh, Sir Walter: "The Nymph's Reply to the Shepherd," 42

Redpath, Theodore, 158

Rhetorical questions, 52, 58, 61, 62, 63, 111, 112, 124, 128, 133

Rhetorical relationship, x–xi, 1, 2, 3, 4, 6, 7, 50. See also Listener

Sanctity of love, 67, 68, 69, 97, 126, 127, 130–31, 138, 140

Scaliger, Julius Caesar, 90, 91

Scholes, Robert, 51

Sententia, 63, 102, 110, 111, 112, 114, 133, 160. See also Aphorism

Shakespeare, William, 14, 90; Sir Thurio, 11; Two Gentlemen of Verona, 11; Sir Andrew Aguecheek, 11–12; Sir Toby Belch, 11–12; Twelfth Night, 11–12; "The Passionate Pilgrim," 74

Shelley, Percy B., 4

Sidney, Sir Philip, 10, 18, 19, 105

Spenser, Edmund, ix, 105, 164; Sonnet 10, 54–55

Stock characters, x, 6, 11, 12, 13, 26. See also Character types

Stoicism, 50, 53, 64

Theocritus: Idyll 11, 98

Theophrastus, 13, 14; Characters, 12

Time, xi, 7, 26, 162. See also Lyric, Narrative

Timelessness, xi, 18, 107, 162

Tone, x, 17–26, 166–67; fine line between comic and straightforward poetry, 19, 23, 76, 83. See also Comic tone

Topsell, Edward, 99–100

Tour de force, 85, 88

Tuve, Rosemond, 43

Valediction, 33–38, 118, 140, 145, 156

Varieties of love, xi, 158, 163, 164, 167

Venus, 84, 88

Wife of Bath, 83

Witty Lover, 15, 27, 33–38, 49, 117; revitalization of Petrarchan conceits by, 16, 33, 36, 37; self-examination of, 34; mutual love of, 35

Woman speaker, 52, 162–63

Wotton, Sir Henry, 25

Wright, George T., 4

Wyatt, Thomas, 89

Zeugma, 128